# THE GOSPEL
# ACCORDING TO CHRIST

# THE GOSPEL ACCORDING TO CHRIST

## M.W. SPHERO

JD, MBA, CPL

HERMS PRESS

NEW YORK   NEW ORLEANS   SYDNEY   OXFORD   TOKYO

To all who are drawn to the Gospel of Christ
without the many enchainments of modern-day
organized religion and man-made tradition.
May you find its true simplicity and freedom
within these pages.

In addition:

* My parents – everything I have, I have because of you're love and concern. You're my inspiration, my most loyal friends, and are always in my thoughts wherever I go. I have always loved and adored you, and always will. May this work honor you both.

* My love – who saved my life, and who's wisdom is like the Book of Proverbs. Thank you for your enduring love and graciousness. You are my rock.

* My siblings – who have always stood by me and have taught me discernment with good counsel. Thank you for your sensibility.

* Joan and Rosa – true neighbors, and genuine friends.

* Migucha – you've come a long way, baby bear. Your endurance has taught me the meaning of "Faith in God – *always* forward!"

And last but certainly *never* least, Yeshua Ha'Mashiach, my First Love, who *never* left me, even when I had left you — but who always faithfully protected, unconditionally loved, and fought for me like the loyal friend who sticks closer than a brother. This work is given first and foremost to you, my dear eternal friend and *unrivaled* confidant. I love you with all my heart Yeshua.

# Contents

If any man is thirsty, let him *come* to Me and drink. He who believes in Me, as the scripture says, 'From his innermost being shall flow rivers of living water'.

JESUS CHRIST

THE GOSPEL ACCORDING TO JOHN 7:37-38

# Preface: Why Read This Book

In the turmoils and contradictions of daily life as we see it today in our "modern" 21$^{st}$ Century, there is but one man in history who's words have stood the test of time more than any other, to where the name "Jesus Christ" still holds profound meaning that cannot be ignored in this new frontier of world history. Whether one believes in who he may or may not have been, many of us would nonetheless feel very much more comfortable and protected having him *physically* by our side when times get tough than any other iconic figure – past or present – if we had the ability to choose absolutely anybody in world history who would take the role as a companion who would carry us through our darkest days.

Yes, many of us are very much aware of how organized religion has let us down time after time, and this in many rather cruel and subversive ways that can never be undone. But the name and reputation of Christ still persists nonetheless.

But when we find ourselves in this life within situations that are best described as "between a rock and a hard place", many of us would typically not choose a *religious* leader anyway to be our companion through all that life can shove at us. No. Many, if not most of us, would likely choose someone very much *like* Christ as we might imagine him... someone who would take our pain away, move those insurmountable mountains that life has thrown at us, clear up the confusions and contradictions in our heads like wind to dark clouds, and make our minds free to see the blue sky once more without having to pay, borrow, submit, convert to, or steal from an alternate source. When many think of Christ, they think of the man who is supposed to have performed miracles and healed the weakest, poorest, sickest, and at times even less than deserving of society ... and not the Christ that is now so vehemently misrepresented and limited by the politically-motivated forces of religion as we see it today.

This work gives the reader a break from religious doctrine, church-prescribed "principles", judgements on morality, and haphazard attempts at converting someone to yet *another* system of religion – and instead looks at what Christ taught *apart from* man-induced opinions on coercive theology, institutional impositions on the self, and the oft-times destructive nature of organized religion. For if in fact it is true that Christ taught the world about love for the self as well as for others *separate and apart from* religiosity, ritual, tradition, perceived 'obligation', and the expectations of others – than why do some of us keep running around in circles as we persistently try with all of our might to please just about everyone at *any* cost to ourselves just because we think it is 'expected' of us by whatever authorities or forces we might have in mind – and this without even stopping to think about *why* we're even doing so; or whether this is *really* what is expected from us in order to be considered a "good person"? Why do we so often place tradition and the opinions of others above what we can freely discern *for ourselves*?

Who are we trying to please anyway? Our parents, our church leaders, politicians, society... our so-called 'bosses'? Life's too short for that! And to attempt to *change* oneself in order to please a person, organization, or group; we only find ourselves not pleasing *anyone* ... and this often with that empty feeling that we are left with and that continually haunts us – that we have fought tooth and nail to please someone who doesn't *really* care anyway; so that we have, as a consequence, spent our precious, limited time in this life throwing our pearls at those who turn out to take our efforts, trample them under foot, to then turn and tear our emotions and self confidence to pieces in return for the good-will that we have shown with good intent. What a thankless world we live in indeed – no, not always, but enough to get to us.

But it is not *all* that bad when we stop attempting to please everyone else around us, and – to those who believe – start looking to Christ as he described himself as by authority and example – not as a man-pleaser, but rather as a pleaser of an unconditionally-loving God who has our best interests in mind and whom the world – as well as much of organized systems of religion – has forgotten about as being the ultimate personification of love.

Christ taught love for the self, love for others, and love for God. He did not teach us to be 're-ligious', "more religious", "*excessively* religious". Nor did he ever teach anyone to be submissive to others, oppressed, unhappy, confused, enchained – nor to live in perpetual frustration. No. Not even by the slightest hint! Christ taught us to be *free*. He taught us to be *independent*. He taught us to love ... and to *be* loved. Whatever the world might have to say about it. And whatever anyone might have to say about us as who we are as individuals deserving of dignity and respect – *however* the world might try to condemn us.

He taught us to *be* loved. He taught us the value of freedom. Of life. Of loving ourselves and others – and this not by sentiment, but rather through a love in *action*. He taught us to live *abundantly*. Yes – Christ taught us to be *free*.

So *why* read this book? If you are a believer in Christ, this book reminds the reader of the *basics* – the *fundamentals* if you will – of faith in Christ completely apart from and *independent of* organized religion – and this strictly as based on Christ's words alone.

If you are *not* a believer in whom Christ is purported to have been, but hold him in high esteem as an excellent example of how mankind was *meant* to interact with one another in the first place, this book shows the dear reader the very *basics* of what Christ taught and who he was purported to have been – and this apart from the modern-day and oft-times wholly inaccurate religious-based claims of what or whom Christ is presumed to represent in this day and age.

For it is Christ *alone* who was untainted by the religious of his day – whereas how he is represented in the modern age is oftentimes shadowed by subversive manipulations to *change* people into something they're not; while religious groups constantly argue and bicker about who is greatest, who is right, how followers should or should not live, and how often one should be a 'good' Christian and go to church.

But that is *not* the Christ of history, but rather a clear-cut misrepresentation of who he truly was, what he actually taught, and what he truthfully stood for as wrought about by many who turn out to be the heavy-handed and in-tensely religiously-inclined, by political groups with silent self-interests at heart – and oft-times by many other wholly oppressive and individually-controlling forces of modern times. And the world has as a result all but forgotten about what Christ *really* taught, how he lived, and what examples he set for the world to see and learn from – while many now look at modern Christianity not as a faith of hope, but rather as a group that has become weakened by internal rifts, disagreements, judgementalisms, and condemnations – both towards one another, and towards the rest of mankind. And this in itself is both ironic as well as hypocritical on the part of many (but certainly *not* all) of modern-day Christians, in that Christ himself clearly *commanded* that they love one another, when he stated:

> I give you a new commandment, that you love one another. Just as I have loved you, you also should love one another. By this *everyone* will know that you are my disciples, if you have love for one another.
>
> JOHN 13:34-35

And so it would seem as if self-righteous arrogances, dogmatic stubbornness, the *insistence* that all things to be seen only as black-and-white, and overt and controlling forms of religiosity, have both cumulatively and single-handedly taken a firm hold on *many* modern-day Christians – both in respect to how they treat one another, as well as how they represent Christ to the rest of mankind – much of which being utterly and completely *contradictory* to what Christ taught the world from the very beginning. For, as has been rightly said:

> We should feel a deep interest for the welfare of other Christians, even those whom we have *never* seen (COLOSSIANS 2:1-2). All belong to the same family, have the same enemies to contend with, are engaged in the same warfare, are traveling to the same heaven. By our prayers and sympathy, we may often do much good to those whom we shall never see until we meet them in heaven.[1]

Furthermore,

> Because of the mysterious substitution of Christ for the Christian, each encounter with a brother or sister is a real encounter with the risen Lord, an opportunity to respond creatively to the gospel and mature in the wisdom of tenderness.[2]

---

[1] As stated in Albert Barnes, *Notes on the New Testaments*. 1837.

[2] As in Brennan Manning, *Brennan Manning, The Wisdom of Tenderness: What Happens When God's Fierce Mercy Transforms Our Lives*. HarperOne, 2004.

So who *was* Christ ... really? Why is *he* so special, so relevant, for the world today? Why should we even *care*? As one well-known Christian icon, C.S. Lewis, once put it – if somewhat strongly for some, but intriguingly nonetheless:

> A man who was merely a man and said the sort of things Jesus said would not be a great moral teacher. He would either be a lunatic — on the level with the man who says he is a poached egg — or else he would be the devil of hell. You must make your choice. Either this man was, and is, the Son of God, or else a madman or something worse. You can shut him up for a fool, you can spit at him and kill him as a demon, or you can fall at his feet and call him Lord and God; but let us not come with any patronizing nonsense about his being a great human teacher. He has not left that open to us. He did not intend to.[3]

But *whatever* one might believe about Christ, once one is able to separate *who* Jesus Christ was from how we see many – but again, certainly *not* all – of his supposed 'representatives' today, one begins to see an altogether *different* Christ to how he is portrayed in modern times. Maybe he has the answers to the questions stumping kings and presidents and societies from all nations and

---

[3] See C.S. Lewis, *Mere Christianity*. Touchstone Books, 1996.

walks of life in this day and age – if only we can separate *him* – from '*them*'. Or maybe we can find clues as to the personal questions we have about our *own* personal, private, and precious lives – and of those whom we so dearly love and defend to the utmost.

Whatever the case may be, it is said that, after his resurrection, when many began to claim that they had *seen* and spoken to the physical and living Christ once more, that the apostle Thomas – one of Christ's apostles during his ministry, oftentimes now sentimentally referred to as "doubting Thomas", stated that:

> Unless I see the mark of the nails in his hands, and put my finger in the mark of the nails and my hand in his side, I will *not* believe.
>
> JOHN 20:25

It is than stated that Christ manifested himself yet again in another of many of such reputed appearances – this time when Thomas was present, to where it is said that:

> While they were talking about this, Jesus himself stood among them and said to them, 'Peace be with you.' They were startled and terrified, and thought that

they were seeing a ghost. He said to
them, 'Why are you frightened, and why
do doubts arise in your hearts? Look at
my hands and my feet; see that it is I
myself. *Touch me* and *see*; for a ghost
does *not* have flesh and bones as you see
that I have.' And when he had said this,
he showed them his hands and his feet.
While in their joy they were disbelieving
and still wondering, he said to them, 'Have
you anything here to eat?' They gave him
a piece of broiled fish, and he took it and
ate in their presence.

LUKE 24:36-43

Yes, if one reads the Gospels with a keen eye,
one might see a bit of humor coming from Christ
from time to time. Here, for instance, he makes
such an impactful appearance in the midst of the
apostles, answers Thomas' doubts with physical
evidence of his own body, and soon after asks
whether they have anything to eat. In addition,
the apostles, still bewildered at what they see
before them, can think of nothing more than to
give him a piece of broiled fish. Truly a gem.

But whatever one might believe – or even
*disbelieve* – about Christ, could he have been
speaking to those present on that occasion, as

well as to future generations such as ours, when
it is said that he added:

> Have you believed because you have *seen*
> me? Blessed [or, *happy*] are those who
> have not seen and *yet* have come to be-
> lieve.
>
> JOHN 20:29

But why would something like this be so noteworthy as for one to personally analyze and come
to one's *own* freely-arrived-at conclusions anyway
– if one so chose to, of course? Well, I would
propose to the good reader that knowledge *is*
power, and if Christ's teachings *can* somehow in
fact set us free *without* having to become 'like'
them – without having to become 'religious', that
is – without having to submit to anything other
than an honest and good heart well-intended to
live life to the full and help others along the
way in whatever manner that might manifest
itself as – than maybe Christ's teaching may
possibly deserve *at least* a cursory looking over
once more... and this time *without* any of the the
influences of organized religion. One might even
say:

> Leave me alone, and let me judge *for myself* what Christ was saying – or who he was – or what he taught – or what he did.

Whether you believe in whom Christ claimed to be or not, this book is written for everyone who seeks to have a *better life* without the enslavements of fear, anxiety, despair, obligation, hang-ups, and all things that enslave us in this world and that keep us from living life to the full in the here-and-now. Who knows *what* one might get from looking at it all from one's *personal* judgement and point of view. With that being said, I bid you a fond and warm *welcome,* dear reader, as we now delve into Good News...

*according to* Christ.

# The Fundemantal Elements to Understanding the Gospel of Christ

# Chapter One

# The Preeminent Authority of the New Testament Gospels

In regards to obtaining an adequate insight into what the historic Christ taught his followers – what works he performed, how he lived, and who he was – the Gospels in the New Testament must be looked at as preeminent authorities in regards to the person of Jesus Christ for reasons that will be elaborated on in this chapter.

The Gospels are the books of MATTHEW, MARK, LUKE, and JOHN in the New Testament Bible, and should not be considered re-interpretations or opinions of matters of faith by later heads of what to some extent became an organized institution of religion centuries after Christ's life on earth; but rather as unbiased historic *accounts* that directly quote Christ, and that likewise document what deeds this historic icon is attributed to have performed – such as his miracles; his treatment of women as equals to men; his constant defense of the poor, the outcast, and the social underdog; his acknowledgement of the homosexual;[1] and his revolt against *all* organized forms of religion as built on man's own rules and traditions – as is expounded upon throughout this work.

For instance, of women as in regards to Christ, it has rightly been said by the legendary writer and humanist Dorothy L. Sayers:

> Perhaps it is no wonder that the women were first at the Cradle and last at the Cross. They had never known a man like this Man - there has never been such another. A prophet and teacher who never nagged at them; never flattered or coaxed or patronised; who never made arch jokes about them, never treated them either as 'The women, God help us!' or 'The ladies, God bless them!'; who rebuked without querulousness and praised without condescension; who took their questions and arguments seriously; who never mapped out their sphere for them; never urged them to be feminine or jeered at them for

---

[1] See Appendix C on page 433 for a full explanation.

being female; who had no axe to grind
and no uneasy male dignity to defend;
who took them as he found them and was
completely unselfconscious. There is no
act, no sermon, no parable in the whole
Gospel that borrows its pungency from
female perversity; nobody could possibly
guess from the words and deeds of Jesus
that there was anything 'funny' [or *inferior*] about women's nature.[2]

As for the homosexual, it would seem that Christ
did in fact *allow for* homosexuality – acknowledging their existence, and stating that some
were *born* with preferences towards the same sex
when he clearly states:

> For there are *eunuchs* who were born that
> way from their mother's womb; and there
> are eunuchs who were made eunuchs by
> men; and there are also eunuchs who
> made themselves eunuchs for the sake of
> the kingdom of heaven. He who is able to
> accept this, let him accept it.
>
> MATTHEW 19:12

...the word *eunuch* also having commonly been
used during the time of Christ to refer to homo-

---

[2] As in Dorothy L. Sayers, *Are Women Human?
Penetrating, Sensible, and Witty Essays on the Role of
Women in Society*. Wm. B. Eerdmans Publishing Co., 1970.

sexuals – his listeners having been well aware of this fact without raising any issues or questions of opposition. See also Appendix C on page 433 for a fuller explanation of this, as well as how scripture never condemns homosexuality when taking contextual, historical, and linguistic considerations into account.

Of the outcasts, the rejected, and the many "black sheep" of society, Christ stated such things as the following, as he *directly* addressed the leaders of religion at the time:

> Truly I tell you, the tax collectors and the prostitutes are going into the kingdom of God ahead of you. For John came to you in the way of righteousness and you did not believe him, but the tax collectors and the prostitutes believed him; and even after you saw it, you did not change your minds and believe him.
>
> MATTHEW 21:31-32

And of the oppressed, the poor, and the broken-hearted; it was prophesied of Christ that he would set such as these captives free, as is said:

> The Spirit of the Lord God is upon me,
> because the Lord has anointed me; He
> has sent me to bring good news to the
> oppressed [*or, poor*], to bind up the bro-
> kenhearted, to proclaim liberty to the cap-
> tives, and release to the prisoners; to pro-
> claim the year of the Lord's favor, and the
> day of vengeance of our God; to comfort all
> who mourn. . .
>
> ISAIAH 61:1-2

Because Christ was very *specific* in addressing
many of life's issues, as well as touching on
many of life's gray areas; it seems that, in the
author's humble viewpoint, the Gospels – and
specifically the *teachings* of Christ themselves –
should therefore be deemed to be *the* preeminent
authorities on answering questions of conscience
for the modern-day follower of Christ; inasmuch
as these can also be the perfect building-blocks
that clarify just what Christ *himself* said, and
how he lived – so that they provide a clear
contrast as to where he might have been coming
from as in comparison to what the reader might
be curious to find out for him- or herself as completely separate and *apart from* the many voices
that are heard today from religious-based sources
that may oftentimes have their own agendas.

As such, it is from these rock-bottom foundations that the Gospels should be thought of as the *primary* books to be considered within the Christian context that clarify matters of faith and questions of what 'Christianity' was actually *meant to be* from the beginning. For is it not *much better* to hear it from the horse's mouth, so-to-speak, than from some who might fervently claim to 'represent' him in this day and age of information-overload and contradictions of opinion? For neither scripture, nor Christ *himself*, ever insinuated otherwise.

Because of this, the Gospels of MATTHEW, MARK, LUKE, and JOHN – as found within the New Testament portion of the modern Bible – may be relied upon as unbiased accounts of the life of Christ due to the investigative ability to exhaustively and accurately cross-reference each other from one book to another *without* contradiction as to meaning,[3] even though various first-

---

[3] See also Chapter 3 on page 53; which expounds on the reliability of these Gospels, as well as on the modern Bible in and of itself; and Craig L. Blomberg, *The Historical Reliability of the Gospels*. 2nd edition. IVP Academic, 2007; A. T. Robertson, *A Harmony of the Gospels*. Reprint edition edition. HarperOne, 1932; Kurt Aland et al., editors, *Synopsis of the Four Gospels: Completely Revised on the Basis of the Greek Text of the Nestle-Aland, 26th*

hand eye-witness authors wrote them at different
times within the first few decades after Christ's
death and – for the believer – resurrection.

Furthermore, as stated, the original Gospels
are first-hand eye-witness accounts of Christ's
teachings and actions. Much weight is oftentimes
given to the *Epistles*[4] of Paul on many specific
questions of faith today, while at the same time
Christ's words are routinely only glossed-over or
flat-out ignored;[5] thus causing needless confu-

---

*Edition, and Greek New Testament, 3rd Edition, English
Edition.* United Bible Societies; and NRSV; Jr. Burton H.
Throckmorton, editor, *Gospel Parallels: A Comparison
of the Synoptic Gospels, New Revised Standard Version.*
5th edition. Thomas Nelson, 1992.

[4] Epistles were letters, often also called 'books' of the
New Testament, that were written mostly by the apostles
of Christ as well as by Paul to the early Christians. On
the other hand, the Gospels are the accounts of Christ's
life, quoted teachings, and recorded deeds as written by the
apostles Matthew, Mark, Luke, and John.

[5] Which in itself is a contradiction to much of today's
modern forms of Christianity as a religion rather than as
an act of faith. For as Christ stated in reference to *his*
specific teachings as coming out of his words and actions:

> Why do you call me 'Lord, Lord,' and do not
> do what I tell you? I will show you what
> someone is like who comes to me, hears my
> words, and *acts* on them. That one is like a
> man building a house, who dug deeply and laid
> the foundation on rock; when a flood arose, the
> river burst against that house but could not

sion, which as a result propagate the division
of the original Christian faith into needless sub-
systems of 'denominations', 'sects', and theological variances when other's writings are forcefully
added to the mix of primary Gospel teachings as
established by Jesus Christ – thus resulting in
a kind of *re*-establishment of the early Gospel-
based faith into other forms of organizationally-
based 'mini-religions', so-to-speak – often established as *Paulinian* in style due to the influence of Paul's writings, and oftentimes without
deserved consideration for Christ's words themselves – the results of which ultimately serve
only to bury and cloud the teachings of Christ
through the development of man-made doctrine
and theological opinions and traditions as having
slowly developed through the last two millennia
by men from an *organizational*   rather than
from a Christ-*centric* – standpoint; and this as
often seen in stringent and draconian church

---

shake it, because it had been well built. But
the one who hears and does *not* act is like a
man who built a house on the ground without
a foundation. When the river burst against it,
immediately it fell, and great was the ruin of
that house. Luke 6:46-49.

traditions and historical blunders, traditionalist-leaning leadership and enforced hierarchy, wide doctrinal differences on simple matters of faith, and so forth.

For even Paul himself rightly stated, on emphasizing that the *individual* believer must first and foremost hold to the teachings of Christ over and above religious tradition and man-made regulatory edict:

> See to it that no one takes you captive through philosophy and empty deceit, according to human tradition, according to the rudiments of the world, and not according to Christ... God made us alive together with him, when he forgave us *all* our trespasses, *erasing* the record that stood against us with its *legal demands*. He set this aside, *nailing it to the cross*. He *disarmed* the rulers and authorities and made a public example of them, triumphing *over* them in it. Therefore do *not* let anyone condemn you in matters of food and drink or of observing festivals, new moons, or sabbaths... If with Christ you died to the *rudiments* of the world, *why* do you live as if you still *belonged* to the world? *Why* do you submit to *regulations*, 'Do not handle, Do not taste, Do not touch'? All these regulations refer to things that perish with use; they are

simply *human commands and teachings*.
These have indeed an *appearance* of wisdom in promoting self-imposed piety, humility, and severe treatment of the body,
but they are of *no value*, serving only to
indulge the lower nature.

COLOSSIANS 2:8, 13-16, 20-23

And on speaking of scripture, Paul also stated
that:

All scripture is inspired by God and is
useful for teaching, for reproof, for correc-
tion, and for training in righteousness, so
that everyone who belongs to God may be
proficient, equipped for every good work.

II TIMOTHY 3:16

For Paul, who had been one of the most knowledgeable Jewish scholars of his time, as well as
previously having been an active persecutor of
early Christians – as he himself puts it –

For you have heard of my former manner
of life in Judaism, how I used to persecute
the church of God beyond measure and
tried to destroy it; and I was advanced
in Judaism beyond many of my contemporaries among my countrymen, being more
extremely zealous for my ancestral traditions.

GALATIANS 1:13-14

... Paul, who had freely turned to Christ as the awaited and prophesied-about Jewish Messiah[6] – having previous been well-known to the early Christians as a religious radical who would seek them out in order to persecute, malign, and imprison them wherever they could be found[7] – and who as a result of his vast knowledge of Old

---

[6] The Messiah was the awaited savior or liberator of the Jews – and of mankind – as prophesied in great detail from the Old Testament. The name *Christ* – or *The Anointed One* – is a translation of the word *Messiah* – hence Jesus the Messiah, or Jesus the Christ. It is therefore more so a title than a name.

Throughout world history, there has been only *one* such expected Messiah who was ever prophesied as coming at a future time and who is described in great and meticulous detail in order to be recognizable to future generations. For specific prophetic details that were attributed to the awaited Messiah that only Jesus the Christ could have fulfilled in the entirety of world history, see Chapter 2 on page 23.

[7] As accounted in the Book of Acts:

"Saul [*later renamed Paul*] was in hearty agreement with putting him to death... but Saul began ravaging the church, entering house after house, and dragging off men and women, he would put them in prison." [Acts 8:1 & 3];
     and,

"Now Saul, still breathing threats and murder against the disciples of the Lord, went to the high priest, and asked for letters from him to the synagogues at Damascus, so that if he found any belonging to the Way, both men and women, he might bring them bound to Jerusalem." [Acts 9:1-2]

But God still chose Saul – or *Paul* – to become a vocal leader and missionary for the Gospel – the Good News – of Jesus Christ *despite* his past. For as it is written,

Testament prophecies in scripture in relation to the coming Messiah, soon realized in his rational that Jesus had *indeed* been the long-awaited and promised One who had already come decades beforehand, so that Paul now came to willingly embrace and consequently turn to Christ himself without any human or *religious* intervention of any kind – was now more than *willingly,* by his own free will, to face all forms of unimaginable persecutions that lasted for the rest of his life for the sake and name of Christ whom he now began to love above all else... as he himself states:

> If anyone else has reason to be confident in the flesh, I have more: circumcised on the eighth day, a member of the people of Israel, of the tribe of Benjamin, a Hebrew born of Hebrews; as to the law, a Pharisee; as to zeal, a persecutor of the church; as to righteousness under the law, blameless. Yet whatever gains I had, these I have come to regard as loss *because of* Christ. More than that, I regard everything as loss because of the surpassing value of *knowing* Christ Jesus my Lord. For his

---

For God does not see what man sees; for man looks at the outward appearance, but the Lord looks at the heart. [I Samuel 16:7]

> sake I have suffered the loss of *all* things,
> and I regard them as rubbish, in order
> that I may gain Christ and be found *in*
> him, not having a righteousness of my
> own that comes from the law, but one
> that comes through the *faith* of Christ, the
> righteousness from God *based* on faith.
>
> PHILIPPIANS 3:4-9

– this same Jesus, who Paul had once persecuted
by chasing and enchaining his followers was the
same who Paul now loved and valued above
even his very *own* life, religious reputation, and
legalistic tradition – to where it was this former
brute persecutor of early Christians who *himself*
became one of the persecuted,[8] and who went

---

[8] In fact, after his conversion to Christ, Paul was
persecuted from city to city as he boldly, passionately,
and faithfully preached the Good News of Christ's
unconditional love and forgiveness to all who put their
trust in Him. Paul was repeatedly and severely beaten,
arrested, jailed, harassed, and constantly pursued as a
common criminal – and never gave up – not even to
the point of extreme violence and imminent death – to
eventually be killed for the sake of Christ – as were
likewise most of the original apostles. As Paul himself
describes:

"Five times I have received from the Jews the forty
lashes minus one. Three times I was beaten with rods.
Once I received a stoning. Three times I was shipwrecked;
for a night and a day I was adrift at sea; on frequent
journeys, in danger from rivers, danger from bandits,
danger from my own people, danger from Gentiles, danger

on to write many of the Epistles of the New
Testament while excellently showing a great and
thorough understanding of whom Christ was,
what his purpose on earth had been, and how
the Christian walk fits into it all; as he now
consistently quoted from and referred to *scripture*
as being the books of the Old Testament[9] – as did
Christ's apostles[10] – and as did Christ himself.[11]

---

in the city, danger in the wilderness, danger at sea, danger
from false brothers and sisters; in toil and hardship,
through many a sleepless night, hungry and thirsty, often
without food, cold and naked. And, besides other things,
I am under daily pressure because of my anxiety for all
the churches... but he said to me, 'My grace is *sufficient*
for you, for power is made perfect in weakness.' So, I
will boast all the more gladly of my weaknesses, so that
the power of Christ may dwell *in* me. Therefore I am
content with weaknesses, insults, hardships, persecutions,
and calamities for the sake of Christ; for whenever I am
weak, then I am strong." [II Corinthians 11:24-29 & 12:9-
10]

[9] For instance, see Romans 1:2, 4:3, 9:17, 10:11, 11:2,
15:4, and 16:26; I Corinthians 15:3-4; Galatians 3:8, 3:22,
and 4:30; I Timothy 4:13 and 5:18; and the aforementioned
II Timothy 3:16.

[10] See Mark 15:28; Luke 24:27, 24:32, and 24:45; John
2:22, 7:42, 19:24, 19:28, 19:36-37, and 20:9; Acts 1:16, 8:32,
and 8:35; James 2:8, 2:23, and 4:5; I Peter 2:6; and II Peter
1:20 and 3:16.

[11] See Matthew 21:42, 22:29, 26:54, 26:56, Mark 12:10,
12:24, and 14:49; Luke 4:21; as well as John 5:39, 7:38,
10:35, 13:18, and 17:12.

For, to the believer, Christ never came to bring the world yet *another* organized religion, but rather to set the captives free through a very *simple* childlike faith; and this *without* the damaging enchainments of man-made traditions, commands, edicts – and especially without unjust, unfaithful condemnations of the innocent as coming from organized regimes of belief.

For it is *Christ* who reminds us of the Old Testament declaration given to us by God in HOSEA 6:6, when he said to the Jewish religious leaders of his day:

> But if you had known what this means,
> 'I DESIRE MERCY, AND NOT A SACRIFICE',
> you would *not* have condemned the innocent. [MATTHEW 12:7]

Furthermore, it is Christ who showed us the importance of having a relationship with God separate and *apart from* traditional organized religion, when he said to these same religious leaders:

> Isaiah prophesied rightly about you hypocrites, as it is written, 'THESE PEOPLE HONOR ME WITH THEIR LIPS, BUT THEIR HEARTS ARE FAR FROM ME; IN VAIN DO THEY WORSHIP ME, TEACHING HUMAN PRECEPTS AS DOCTRINES.' You abandon the com-

mandment of God and hold to human tradition... You have a fine way of rejecting
the commandment of God in order to keep
your tradition...   thus making void the
word of God through your tradition that
you have handed on.  And you do many
things like this.

MARK 7:6-9 & 13

And it is Christ who humbly proclaimed his
Messiahship first to a synagogue in Nazareth
on the Jewish Sabbath as he read one of the
many aforementioned prophecies about himself
from the Old Testament scroll of ISAIAH 61:1-2,
this event as having been recorded in the Gospel
of Luke:

'THE SPIRIT OF THE LORD IS UPON ME, BECAUSE
HE HAS ANOINTED ME TO BRING GOOD NEWS
TO THE POOR. HE HAS SENT ME TO PROCLAIM
RELEASE TO THE CAPTIVES AND RECOVERY OF
SIGHT TO THE BLIND, TO LET THE OPPRESSED GO
FREE, TO PROCLAIM THE YEAR OF THE LORD'S
FAVOR.' And he rolled up the scroll, gave
it back to the attendant, and sat down.
The eyes of all in the synagogue were fixed
on him.  Then he began to say to them,
'Today this scripture has been *fulfilled* in
your hearing.'

LUKE 4:18-21

Likewise, it is Christ who is called the *Living Word* of God – and God *Himself*. For as it is said in the Gospel of John:

> In the beginning was the Word, and the Word was *with* God, and the Word *was* God. He was with God in the beginning. Through him *all* things were made; without him nothing was made that has been made. In him was *life*, and that life was the *light* of all mankind. The light shines in the darkness, and the darkness has not overcome it... The true light that gives light to everyone was coming into the world. He was in the world, and though the world was made *through* him, the world did not *recognize* him. He came to that which was his own, but his own did not receive him. Yet to *all* who did receive him, to those who believed in his name, he gave the right to *become* children of God – children born *not* of natural descent, nor of human decision or a husband's will, but born *of God*. The Word *became flesh* and made his dwelling among us. We have seen his glory, the glory of the one and only Son, who came from the Father, full of grace and truth.
>
> JOHN 1:1-14

Yes, to the believer, it is Christ who *is* the living, *incarnate* Word of God – his authority and teachings being over and above what anyone else coming *after* him, and over and above what any other source – whichever it may be – might attempt to

add to, interpret on, provide commentary for, or
somehow try to modify.

As such, it is from the standpoint of the
recorded words of Christ that we *know* what the
Gospel *according to* Christ truly is. For, to the
believer, it is *he* who brings about life, and *is* life.
And yet again, Christ directly told the religious
leaders of the Jews that:

> You search the scriptures because you think
> that in them you have eternal life; and it
> is *they* that testify on *my* behalf. Yet you
> refuse to come to *me* to have life. I do
> not accept glory from human beings. But
> I know that you do not have the love of
> God in you. I have come in my Father's
> name, and you do not accept me; if another
> comes in his own name, you *will* accept
> him. How can you believe when you accept
> glory from one another and do not seek
> the glory that comes from the one who
> *alone* is God? Do not think that I will
> accuse you before the Father; your accuser
> is Moses, on whom you have set your hope.
> If you believed Moses, you would believe
> me, for he wrote *about* me. But if you do
> not believe what he wrote, *how* will you
> believe what I say?
>
> JOHN 5:39-47

And, as the Book of Proverbs states:

> For he who finds me finds life, and obtains
> favor from the Lord.
>
> PROVERBS 8:35

It is thus in the author's humble opinion that
the Gospels should be the *first* (and in some
topics, *only*) choice in studying matters of faith
for the Christian believer – especially the words
of Christ contained in these Gospels – his words
usually being found highlighted in red text in
most editions.

After all, Christ *himself* clearly stated:

> But you are not to be called 'Rabbi' [*mean-
> ing spiritual leader, teacher, or guru*], for
> you have only one Master and you are all
> brothers. And do not call anyone on earth
> 'father' [*meaning 'spiritual father'*], for you
> have one Father, and He is in heaven. Nor
> are you to be called 'teacher', for you have
> one Teacher, the Christ.
>
> Matthew 23:8-10

So therefore, to the believer, let God *Himself*
be your teacher, Father, and guide. And it is
for this very reason that it is wholeheartedly

*encouraged* that the dear reader (whether a believer or non-believer, it does not at all matter) – that the reader, at some point, conduct an *experiment* of sorts for a time, and *only* read Christ's words throughout the New Testament Gospels of MATTHEW, MARK, LUKE, and JOHN in order to get a *different perspective* on Christianity as it was *meant* to be by Jesus' own sayings, stories, and lived-out example; and this in comparison to what comes across in this day and age through much of modern forms of Christendom that might on many occasions unduly lean only on the Epistles of Paul rather than on the Gospel of Christ, or that totally divert into teachings that are very much *not* what Christ taught in order for some to get glory from man rather than approval from God, as unfortunately is sometimes the case – these the Gospels that, in combination with Old Testament scripture and with the help of the Epistles, tell us what the Good News *according to* Christ truly, clearly, and accurately is.

Chapter Two

# *The Divinity of Christ*

The question of Christ's title as the Messiah – the awaited and prophesied-about savior and liberator of both the Jewish people and all of mankind as foretold in the Old Testament of the Bible – provides a foundational basis of validity as to the authority of his words and teachings, and is therefore examined in this chapter.

The arrival of Christ amongst mankind was spoken of centuries – even millennia – before his appearance by many detailed and specific prophecies that stated such things as found in ISAIAH 9:6-7, which says:

> To us a child is born, to us a Son is given, and the government will be on his shoulders; and he will be called Wonderful Counselor, *Mighty God*,[1] Everlasting Father, Prince of Peace. Of the increase

---

[1] See also Chapter 2 on page 41.

> of his government and peace there will be
> no end. He will reign on David's throne
> and over his kingdom, establishing and
> upholding it with justice and righteous-
> ness from that time on and forever. The
> zeal of the Lord Almighty will accomplish
> this.
>
> Isaiah 9:6-7

Of the hundreds of *specific* prophecies about Jesus Christ that were all fulfilled by this *one*
particular individual when considering planet
earth's entire civilized history – prominent mathematicians have stated that the statistical probability that even a *single* human being in the
entirety of the populated history of our planet to
be able to *legitimately* fulfill even a mere 8 of the
over 300 of these *distinct* prophecies (astound-
ingly, Christ single-handedly fulfilled *each* and
every one of them) is so purely *astronomical* in
number – this being *one* chance in one-hundred-
million-billion, or $10^{17}$ ... or to put it bluntly:

     1 in 100,000,000,000,000,000

– that the odds of this occurring are trillions of
times greater than if one takes into account the
cumulative population of *all* of mankind who has
ever existed in earth's history as well as who

are likely to *ever* exist into the future of humankind into calculation. In other words, from a purely mathematical perspective, this essentially excludes *anyone else* that has ever – or who *will ever* – live on earth but Jesus of Nazareth *alone* as being able to fulfill said prophecies as the promised Messiah and liberator of mankind who was specifically written about by many different authors during a vast span of time numbering many centuries before his birth.

As is explained herein, no other person in history can make such a claim, let alone be prophesied about in such specific and non-ambiguous detail hundreds – and in some cases even *thousands* – of years before appearing on the planet... *no one*. It is essentially a mathematical *impossibility*.

One of many such mathematicians, the distinguished Dr. Peter Stoner,[2] who had 12 graduate classes consisting of 600 students work out such a calculation over several years based solely on a

---

[2] Chairman of the Departments of Mathematics and Astronomy at Pasadena City College until 1953; Chairman of the science division, Westmont College, 1953-57; Professor Emeritus of Science, Westmont College; and Professor Emeritus of Mathematics and Astronomy, Pasadena City College.

mere 8 prophecies alone (out of over 300) concerning Christ, and who submitted these same calculations and results to the American Scientific Affiliation for independent verification – who in turn verified and finally concluded after careful and lengthy examination that these calculations and results were indeed accurate and dependable – explained just how large a number $10^{17}$ is, as he stated:

> Let us try to visualize this chance. If you mark one of ten tickets, and place all of the tickets in a hat, and thoroughly stir them, and then ask a blindfolded man to draw one, his chance of getting the right ticket is one in ten. Suppose that we take $10^{17}$ silver dollars and lay them on the face of Texas. They will cover all of the state two feet deep. Now mark one of these silver dollars and stir the whole mass thoroughly, all over the state. Blindfold a man and tell him that he can travel as far as he wishes, but he must pick up one silver dollar and say that this is the right one. What chance would he have of getting the right one? Just the same chance that the prophets would have had of writing these eight prophecies and having them all come true in any one man, from their

day to the present time, providing they
wrote using their own wisdom.[3]

Surely everyone would take on any financial
investment with these odds when the possibility
of *failure* is only one in $10^{17}$. And – to the believer
– this is the kind of sure investment that God
offers those who put their trust in His Son Jesus
Christ.

Stoner's and his students' *initial* calculations
were based on a mere 8 Messianic Old Testament
prophecies as a *conservative* examination and
study – which again worked out to a result of 1 in
$10^{17}$. They then performed a similar calculation
based on only 48 of the over 300 prophecies
regarding the coming Messiah and came up with
the result of $10^{157}$. As today's statisticians know,
anything over $10^{50}$ is considered a mathematical
*impossibility*,[4] and yet Christ fulfilled *all* of the

---

[3] ...as opposed to God having revealed these very
specific and numerous prophetic details about the coming
Messiah to mankind Himself. Peter Stoner and Robert C.
Newman, *Science Speaks: Scientific Proof of the Accuracy
of Prophecy and the Bible*. Moody Press, 1969; pp. 106-7.
See also this same book for free on-line at Peter Stoner,
*Science Speaks: Online Edition*. November 2005 ⟨URL:
http://www.sciencespeaks.net⟩.
[4] See Emile Borel and Douglas Scott, *Probability
and Certainty*. Walker & Company, 1963; Nicholas

over 300 very distinct prophecies in the Old
Testament that describe in great and meticulous detail the characteristics, origin, birth, life,
death, works, and social contexts of the coming
Messiah – just as fingerprint and DNA evidence
combined to find a fit in a court case is a sure
enough thing to come to a definitive conclusion
concerning one's identity well *beyond* reasonable
doubt – in fact, enough so to send someone to his
death in a murder case in a nation that might
adopt the death penalty.

Of the hundreds of said prophetic verses that
would support these findings, the following are
but a *few*, such as ISAIAH 9:6 (as previously
quoted), which states that one *particular* human
being in the *entirety* of earth's history would
be born who would be *both* fully God and fully
man...or God *incarnate*. Who else in history
could such a claim apply to but Christ alone –
especially on considering the fact that only he

---

Georgescu-Roegen, *The Entropy Law and the Economic
Process*. iUniverse Publication, 1999; John D. Barrow,
*Impossibility: The Limits of Science and the Science of
Limits* . Oxford University Press, 1999; and Jan von Plato,
*Creating Modern Probability: Its Mathematics, Physics and
Philosophy in Historical Perspective (Cambridge Studies
in Probability, Induction and Decision Theory)*. Cambridge
University Press, 1998.

ever fulfilled *each and every one* of the Messianic prophecies in earth's entire history? Yes...

> For a child will be born to us.  A son will be given to us... and his name will be called...  Mighty God, Eternal Father, Prince of Peace...
>
> ISAIAH 9:6

MICAH 5:2 states that he would specifically be born in *no other place* but Bethlehem alone, and that he in fact existed *"from days of old"*... in other words, from the beginning of time:

> But as for you, Bethlehem Ephrathah, too little to be among the clans of Judah, from you One will go forth for me to be ruler in Israel. His appearances are from long ago, from days of old.
>
> MICAH 5:2

ISAIAH 7:14 states that he would be born of a virgin, and that *again*, he would be called God *Himself*, as per the significance of the name *Immanuel* – meaning "God with us":

> Therefore the Lord Himself will give you a sign: behold, a virgin will be with child and bear a son, and she will call his name Immanuel.
>
> ISAIAH 7:14

ISAIAH 53:3-7 describes the purpose and details of his crucifixion:

> He was despised and rejected by men, a man of sorrows, and familiar with suffering. Like one from whom men hide their faces he was despised, and we esteemed him not. Surely he took up our infirmities and carried our sorrows, yet we considered him stricken by God, smitten by Him, and afflicted. But he was pierced for our transgressions, he was crushed for our iniquities; the punishment that brought us peace was upon him, and by his wounds we are healed... he was oppressed and afflicted... yet he did not open his mouth; he was led like a lamb to the slaughter. And as a sheep before her shearers is silent, so he did not open his mouth.
>
> ISAIAH 53:3-7 NIV [5]

In addition, other ancient scriptures spanning multiple Old Testament books, authors, and wide-ranging time-spans numbering hundreds – even *thousands* – of years, prophesy about the coming Messiah in more specific detail such as:

- ISAIAH 7:14, which proclaims how he would be born of a virgin;

---

[5] NIV; Frank Charles D.D. Ph.D. Thompson, editor, *Thompson Chain-Reference Bible: New International Version*. Zondervan Bible Publishers, 1983.

- GENESIS 12:1-3 & 22:18, specifying how he would be a descendant of Abraham;

- of the tribe of Judah, as stated in GENESIS 49:10;

- and of the house of David as in II SAMUEL 7:12-16;

- and that he would be taken to Egypt as a child as in HOSEA 11:1;

- how Herod would kill male infants under two years old, hoping to kill the promised Messiah who had just been born, as in JEREMIAH 31:15;

- how he would be heralded by God's messenger (John the Baptist), as in both ISAIAH 40:3-5 as well as in MALACHI 3:1;

- how he would perform miracles such as making the blind physically see again, healing the deaf, making the lame and paralyzed walk once more; unbridling the tongue of the mute, and so on as per ISAIAH 35:5-6;

- that he would preach the good news (ISAIAH 61:1),

- as well as minister in Galilee (ISAIAH 9:1),

- and cleanse the temple from all of its rob-
  bery, self-righteousness, and religious fer-
  vor that had lost its child-like faith as in
  MALACHI 3:1;

- as well as ZECHARIAH 9:9, which explains
  how the promised Messiah would enter
  Jerusalem as a King riding on a donkey;

- while ZECHARIAH 13:7 details how everyone
  – including his own apostles – would soon
  abandon him to be crucified,

- as he was being rejected by his own people
  of faith – the Jewish nation – as per PSALM
  118:22;

- ZECHARIAH 11:12, which states he would be
  betrayed for *exactly* thirty pieces of silver;

- that this betrayal would come from a close
  friend, as in PSALM 41:9;

- ZECHARIAH 11:13, detailing how this price
  would then be given to buy a Potter's field
  after the Jews rejected the betrayer's (this

having turned out to have been Judas) return of said money; and how this blood-money would be cast back onto the floor of the temple;

- how he would furthermore be ostracized and rejected (ISAIAH 53:3), and become silent before those who falsely accused him (ISAIAH 53:7), and would consequently be mocked (PSALM 22: 7-8), beaten (ISAIAH 52:14), and spit upon (ISAIAH 50:6);

- and how he would be crucified with thieves – yet he would pray for his persecutors as per ISAIAH 53:12;

- PSALM 22:18, which details how his clothing would be divided up amongst his persecutors, and that they would cast lots for the possession of torn fragments of said clothing while he was still on the cross;

- PSALM 22:16, which details how both his hands and feet would be pierced during his crucifixion;

- PSALM 69:21, foretelling in detail how gall and vinegar would be given to him to drink while he hung on the cross;

- PSALM 34:20, stating how none of his bones would be broken through this entire ordeal;

- ZECHARIAH 12:10, explaining that his side would be pierced while he was still barely alive;

- ISAIAH 53:9, regarding his being placed in a rich man's tomb after his eventual death; and

- ISAIAH 26:19, PSALM 16:10, HOSEA 6:2, PSALM 68:18, and PSALM 110:1 – foretelling his glorious resurrection after three days; of which both the New Testament as well as secular writers affirm this having taken place as having been witnessed by over five-hundred witnesses – many of whom were later systematically persecuted and brutally killed for what they claimed to have seen with their very own eyes. I wouldn't be so willing to lay my life down for something I *knew* not to be true, would you?

...and so the list goes on – through to the rest of the three-hundred-odd specific and detailed prophecies spanning centuries and authors living historically apart from one another – all of which pointing to one single man in a future time in history who would fulfill each and every one of these and all other Old Testament prophecies concerning the coming Messiah without question or ambiguity. These, the prophecies that, in all mathematical probability, can never – nor *will* ever – be attributed to anyone else but Jesus Christ of Nazareth alone.   Jesus, the uniquely unrivaled One who, from two millennia ago, has influenced mankind more than anyone else in the entirety of human history *ever* has... to this very day. What *are* the odds?

Similarly, Dr. Will Durant, one of the most highly-regarded and probably *the* most widely-read historian in the last century himself stated, regarding the *authenticity* of the life of Christ, and the *eye-witness* testimonies recorded by those who were there, and who were likewise willing even to die for a cause they *knew* to be true – as most of them eventually did... for who in their right mind would be willing to die for a cause they *know* is a lie...

In the enthusiasm of its discoveries, the higher criticism has applied to the New Testament texts tests of authenticity so severe that by them a hundred ancient worthies, Hammurabi, David, Socrates, would fade into legend...no one reading these scenes can doubt the reality of the figure behind them ...that a few simple men should in one generation have invented so powerful and appealing a personality, so lofty an ethic and so inspiring a vision of human brotherhood, would be a miracle far more incredible than any recorded in the Gospels. After two centuries of higher criticism, the outlines of the life, character and teachings of Christ remain reasonably clear and constitute the most fascinating feature in the history of Western man.[6]

With these odds *overwhelmingly* in favor of Him, I believe that Christ deserves *at least* a cursory listening to,[7] and that he most likely *knows* what he is talking about in regards to life, love, health, homosexuality as being a characteristic

---

[6] Will Durant, *Caesar and Christ - A History of Roman Civilization and of Christianity from their Beginnings to A.D. 323 (Story of Civilization)*. Simon & Schuster, 1944.

[7] See also Lee Strobel, *The Case for Christ*. Zondervan, 1998; as well as the excellent video documentary under the same title.

from birth[8] and therefore *not* a 'sin' in and of itself, sex as a gift of God rather than as something to be abstained from or deemed as 'dirty',[9] happiness, what makes for world peace – and everything that we are, have ever been, and have the potential to *become* as distinct individuals.

But I would certainly rather consider what Jesus Christ *himself* said, and contemplate as to how he *himself* lived, rather than place my trust on the varied opinions, condemnations, and judgementalisms by *some* within organized religion when it is Christ who claims to set the captives free, that's for sure – though not all those adhering to organized religion are like this, and many *are* in fact kind-hearted, non-judgmental, and *genuine* followers of Christ ... though few others could to some be deemed as stumbling blocks to those coming to Christ in Spirit and in Truth through their perceived inability to empathize with the humble and different, and in their potential hypocrisies and stubborn zeal to judge, condemn, and spread hatred against the

---

[8] See Appendix C on page 433 for a full explanation.

[9] As many in modern forms of Christianity – as having in some circles become a regulatory system of religion – would have you believe. See also Appendix B on page 397.

poor [*humble*] in spirit;[10] while at the same time ironically tolerating systems of deceptions that Christ warned would appear on earth to deceive many (including the elect);[11] as well as global religions of hate and intolerance originating from all corners of the world from the time of Christ's appearance on this earth to this very day. But that is the author's opinion *alone*, dear reader.

Hence the importance of – to the believer – keeping one's eyes on Christ, and Christ *alone*, and not on a pulpit, preacher, religious organization, tradition, or the opinions of just anyone who comes along, speaks the loudest, writes the most scathing reviews, or threatens the strongest. For to follow Christ is to walk in *his* Spirit, in *his* love, in *his* light, and in truth ... and *not* in religion, tradition, nor politically-correct (or politically-*in*correct) opinion.

For, to the believer, it should be the Spirit of the Living Christ, and not the myriad of views coming from those who lean on the heavy-handed rule of religion and what they themselves might define to be "socially acceptable" – whether for

---

[10] As Christ stated, "Blessed are the poor [or, *humble*] in spirit, for theirs is the kingdom of heaven." Matthew 5:3.

[11] See Appendix A on page 357.

society as a whole, for a certain church denomination, or for a religious group – it is the Holy Spirit *alone* whom one must lean on and ultimately learn from ... irrespective of how the world, society, or even fellow 'Christians' might try and insult, persecute, or defame and consequently become stumbling blocks to that person who is following the very *teachings* of Christ – who is willing to listen to *His* Spirit that is given without prejudice to *all* who come to him – the Holy Spirit of Christ who teaches *all* things to those who are open and *willing* to listen. For as Jesus said,

> I will ask the Father, and He will give you another Helper [*Comforter, Advocate, Intercessor*], that He may be with you forever; that is the Spirit of Truth, whom the world cannot receive, because it does not see Him or know Him, but you know Him because He abides with you and will be *in* you. I will not leave you as orphans; *I* will come to you... Peace I leave with you; My peace I give to you; not as the world gives do I give to you. Do not let your heart be troubled, nor let it be fearful.
>
> JOHN 14:16-18, & 27

Furthermore, Christ also told his followers – both present and future, that:

> When the Spirit of truth comes, he will guide you into *all* the truth... He will glorify me, because He will take what is mine and declare it to you.

JOHN 16:13-14

But as many popular religious ideologies and fads – whether 'Christian'-based or not – have in some ways become stumbling blocks to the faith of many *more* innocent fellow Christian followers who have unintentionally become trapped in *some* – but thankfully not all – churches that oftentimes care much more about their own image and monetary standing, who care more about shouting the loudest about their latest target to perform a witch hunt on in front of the media and world stage as they are more concerned with appearing "righteous before man"[12] irrespective of who they might trample on, hurt, or drive away from the church[13] – while on the other hand others feel it a modern-day badge of honor

---

[12] As Christ told us:

> Beware of practicing your piety before others in order to be *seen* by them; for then you have no reward from your Father in heaven. Matthew 6:1.

[13] See also Chapter 14 on page 307.

to accommodate a degradation of the name of the living Christ for the sake of a form of so-called "global religious harmony" that has the real potential to contrarily become much more oppressive and freedom-stifling than any other world religion that has ever existed in the history of mankind, and that will kill any rightful notion of *genuine* freedom of religion for *all*[14] – and this at the expense of those who stand up for the simplicity of a faith that is in many instances all but lost, as well as at the expense of other faithful followers in *non*-Christian-based religions as well – the following outline is provided to remind followers of Christ just *who* they follow, and just who has their back in this brave new world where the Gospel of Christ has in many instances been replaced by the Christianity of legalism, dogma, and needless and never-ending debate; and where Christ himself is being replaced by illusions of religious piety, false 'spiritual' leaders, and even false christs[15] throughout the globe.

---

[14] See also Chapter 10 on page 187; as well as Appendix A on page 357, regarding the dangers of attempting to forcibly impose upon the world the *globalized* unification of differing religions at *any* cost.

[15] See Appendix A on page 357.

**The Deity of Jesus Christ is declared in Scripture:**

(i) The Old Testament both intimates and explicitly predicts His Deity:

(a) The theophanies intimate the appearance of God in human form, and His ministry in this form to man [GENESIS 16:7-14; 18:2-23, especially verse 17; compare 32:28 with HOSEA 12:3-5; EXODUS 3:2-14].

(b) The Messiah is expressly declared to be the Son of God (PSALM 2:2-9), and God [compare PSALM 45:6-7 with HEBREWS 1 :8-9; PSALM 110:1 with MATTHEW 22:44; ACTS 2:34 and HEBREWS 1:13; PSALM 110:4 with HEBREWS 5:6; 6:20; 7:17-21; ZECHARIAH 6:13].

(c) His virgin birth was foretold as the means through which God could be Immanuel, God with us [compare ISAIAH 7:13-14 with MATTHEW 1:22-23].

(d) The Messiah is expressly invested with the divine names (ISAIAH 9:6-7).

(o) In a prophecy of His death He is called the "man, My Associate" [compare ZECHARIAH 13:7 with MATTHEW 26:31]; and

(f) His eternal Being is declared [compare MICAH 5:2 with MATTHEW 2:6; JOHN 7:42].

(II) Christ *Himself* affirmed His Deity.

(a) He applied to Himself the Jehovistic "I AM" (JOHN 4:26; 6:20; 8:24,28,58; 18:5,6). The pronoun "He" appears in translation (4:26 and 18:5,6), but not in the Greek. In 8:56-59 the Jews correctly understood this as the Lord's claim to full Deity (compare JOHN 10:33).

(b) He claimed to be the *Adonai* of the Old Testament (MATTHEW 22:42-45. See GENESIS 15:2, note).

(c) He asserted His identity with the Father (MATTHEW 28:19; MARK 14:62; JOHN 10:30). That the Jews so understood is shown by JOHN 10:31-33; 14:8-9; 17:5.

(d) He exercised the chief prerogative of God – the forgiveness of sins (MARK 2:5-7; LUKE 7:48-50).

(e) He asserted omnipresence (MATTHEW 18:20; JOHN 3:13); omniscience (JOHN 11:11-14, when Jesus was fifty miles away; MARK 11:6-8); omnipotence (MATTHEW 28:18; LUKE 7:14; JOHN 5:21-23; 6:19); mastery over nature, and creative power (LUKE 9:16-17; JOHN 2:9; 10:28); and

(f) He received and approved human worship of Himself (MATTHEW 14:33; 28:9; JOHN 20:28-29).

(III) The New Testament writers ascribe divine titles to Christ (JOHN 1:1; 20:28; ACTS 20:28; ROMANS 1:4; 9:5; II THESSALONIANS 1:12; I TIMOTHY 3:16; TITUS 2:13; HEBREWS 1:8; I JOHN 5:20).

(IV) The New Testament writers ascribe divine perfections and attributes to Christ (MATTHEW 11:28; 18:20; 28:20; JOHN 1:2; 2:23-25; 3:13; 5:17; 21:17; HEBREWS 1:3, 11-12 with HEBREWS 13:8; REVELATION 1:8,17-18; 11:17; 22:13).

(V) The New Testament writers ascribe divine works to Christ (JOHN 1:3,10; COLOSSIANS 1:16-17; HEBREWS 1:3).

(VI) The New Testament writers teach that supreme worship should be paid to Christ (ACTS 7:59-60; I CORINTHIANS 1:2; II CORINTHIANS 13:14; PHILIPPIANS 2:9-11; HEBREWS 1:6; REVELATION 1:5-6; 5:12-13).

(VII) The holiness and resurrection of Christ confirm His Deity (JOHN 8:46; ROMANS 1:4).[16]

---

[16] The above outline has been reprinted from Cyrus I. Scofield, *Scofield Reference Bible*. Oxford University Press, 1917.

The New Testament describes it well, when it explains:

> He [*Christ*] is the image of the invisible God, the firstborn of all creation; for in him *all* things in heaven and on earth were created, things visible and invisible, whether thrones or dominions or rulers or powers—all things have been created *through* him and *for* him. He himself is *before* all things, and in him all things hold together. He is the head of the body, the church; he is the beginning, the firstborn from the dead, so that he might come to have first place in *everything*. For in him all the *fullness* of God was pleased to dwell, and *through* him God was pleased to reconcile to himself all things, whether on earth or in heaven, by making peace through the blood of his cross... For in him the whole fullness of deity dwells bodily, and you have come to fullness in him, who is the head of every ruler and authority. [17]
>
> COLOSSIANS 1:15-20 & 2:9-10

But what about the *Trinity* – the concept of God being the Creator of the Universe, *as well as* Christ himself, *and* also being the Holy Spirit – also referred to as the Counselor, Helper, or Spirit of Truth who Jesus stated he would send to those who placed their trust on him?[18] Though

---

[17] See also John 1:1-14, as in Chapter 1 on page 19.
[18] John 14:16-17, & 16:13-15.

this concept might seem complicated to some, it really is not. *Not* to say, of course, that we can *fully* understand God – but we *can* understand those secrets that God allows. As such, a good analogy can be taken from water itself.

As we are all very well aware, water is made up of the chemical compound consisting of two parts hydrogen and one part oxygen: $H_2O$. Water can take three forms: liquid (water), gas (vapor), and solid (ice) – and yet it always *remains* a single substance: $H_2O$. Likewise, one can look at God as taking three forms: the Creator of all (Father), the Son (Christ), and the Holy Spirit (some might say, the Spirit of God through Christ). And yet, like our water analogy, God is *still* a single entity. That is why – to those who believe – Christ is consistently shown to be Lord of *all* throughout scripture – and *this* to the glory of God the Father, as is for instance stated:

> Let each of you look not to your *own* interests, but to the interests of *others*. Let the *same mind* be in you that was in Christ Jesus; who, though he was in the form of God, did not consider equality with God as something to be used to his own advantage; rather, he made himself nothing by taking the very nature of a ser-

vant, being made in human likeness. And being found in appearance as a man, he humbled himself by becoming obedient to death— even death on a cross! Therefore God exalted him to the highest place and gave him the name that is above *every* name, that at the name of Jesus *every* knee should bow, in heaven and on earth and under the earth, and every tongue acknowledge that Jesus Christ is Lord, to the glory of God the Father.

PHILIPPIANS 2:4-11

Yes, how wonderful it would be if more modern-day, self-proclaimed Christians were to apply the above and truly *be* of the same mind as Christ, and look more at the interests of others as opposed to condemning, belittling, and judging those who they should instead love in action...as God through the human Christ *Himself* did. Not *all* self-confessed Christians are like this, of course, and many truly *do* have Christ's mindset of love and servitude – but many others have gotten bogged-down inside of organized religion and judgementalism, rather than on the power of the cross and the love that is behind it. So who *can* we trust? Maybe more should follow the examples of the early Christians and change the world around them instead of isolating themselves in their churches, as they take on an attitude of "see no evil, hear no evil", while those on the outside hardly see any light from them at all.[19]

Therefore, to those who have put their faith not in religion, but rather in Christ *himself* as the Son of God – as God incarnate who's love for you is greater than any other, and who's protection for you is a wall of fire around your and your family's lives, and *He* being the glory within it[20] – neither let the world, nor religion, nor religious hypocrisy, nor principalities and powers that may be, nor society and its intolerances, nor the media, nor your boss and work environment, nor radicals, nor terrors, nor crimes and persecutions, nor self-doubt or low self-confidence, nor riches, nor poverty, nor cults, nor denominations or books or manuals, nor divisive argument, nor peace, nor war – hinder your faith in your First

---

[19] As loosely paraphrased from the song *Rose Colored Stained Glass Windows* as by Classic Petra, *Back to the Rock album*. Sony Music Distribution, 2011. The viewing of the live DVD concert version – Petra, *Back to the Rock Live*. Provident, 2011 – is also highly recommended.

[20] As has been said:

> ...Jerusalem shall be inhabited like villages without walls, because of the multitude of people and animals in it. For I will be a wall of fire all around it, says the Lord, and I will be the glory within it. [Zechariah 2:4-5]

Love ... the best and most loyal friend you will *ever* know. Yes, He who formed you and *knew* you – *intimately* – before you were even born, and who loves you oh so *very* much – always and forever – *just* as you are.

To anyone who can accept Christ as the embodiment and earthly representation of God, and who *individually* chooses to follow Christ not out of religious compulsion nor dogmatic legalism, but out of *free will* and from the heart – in spirit and in truth – know that it is on Christ, and Christ alone, whom you can *always* depend upon. He is the same yesterday, today, and forever. He *never* changes. And never will. For the Christ that you speak to today is the *very same* Christ who walked this earth two-thousand years ago. Yes, the very same one! What he did *then* he can do *now*. As is rightly said in the New Testament:

> Jesus Christ is the same yesterday and today and forever. Do not be carried away by all kinds of strange teachings; for it is well for the heart to be strengthened by grace, not by regulations...
>
> HEBREWS 13:8-9

Yes, Jesus Christ – the God of the universe who stooped down to such lowly heights to *gladly* carry those like you and I on His shoulders – and all because of His undying love for each and every one of us... and love *alone*.

For as Jesus *the* promised Messiah has said – and, to the believer, as he *still* says to this very day:

> Very truly, I tell you, I am the gate for the sheep. All who came before me are thieves and bandits; but the sheep did not listen to them. I am the gate. Whoever enters by me will be saved, and will come in and go out and find pasture. The thief comes only to steal and kill and destroy. I came that they may have *life*, and have it *abundantly*. I am the good shepherd. The good shepherd lays down his life for the sheep... I know my own and my own know me, just as the Father knows me and I know the Father. And I lay down my life for the sheep. I have other sheep that do not belong to this fold. I must bring them also, and they *will* listen to my voice. So there will be *one* flock, *one* shepherd. For this reason the Father loves me, because I lay down my life in order to take it up again. No one takes it from me, but I lay it down of my own accord. I have power to lay it down, and I have power to take it up

again. I have received this command from my Father.

JOHN 10:7-18

Chapter Three

# The Authenticity of the Modern Bible

The reliability of the modern Bible cannot be disputed. We have original documents in tangible form strewn throughout the world in climate-controlled vaults, secure archives, internationally-known and globally-renowned museums, national library safes, banking institutions, and many other forms of well-publicized places; as well as in other locations undisclosed for reasons of security, and in order to adequately be able to physically protect such documentation.[1]

---

[1] See Kurt Aland et al., *The Text of the New Testament: An Introduction to the Critical Editions and to the Theory and Practice of Modern Textual Criticism.* 2nd edition. Wm. B. Eerdmans Publishing Co., 1995; David P. Barrett and Philip W. Comfort, *The Text of the Earliest New Testament Greek Manuscripts.* Tyndale House Publishers, 2001; as well as F. F. Bruce, *The Books and the Parchments: How We Got Our English Bible.* Fleming H Revell Co., 1984.

It is a modern-day common argument to state that the Bible has been translated so many times that it cannot be relied upon any longer. It is understandable when a lay person has doubts if they have not looked into this matter; but it is an altogether outright deception fueled by non-investigative recklessness and unfounded assumptions when such a claim is made by those in the media when they cannot be bothered to check their facts before broadcasting such utter misinformation. As a result, many, assuming the media's claims to be true, begin to believe such outright mass deceptions, and start to unnecessarily doubt the authenticity and reliability of priceless ancient documents and world treasures of human achievement – much like many now unbelievably do not accept that man walked on the moon. Such forms of misinformation only serve to devalue human accomplishment, and degrade the awesome history of mankind and its close-to-insurmountable feats.[2]

---

[2] See also Christina Tangora Schlachter, *Newsless: How the American Media is Destroying Democracy*. CIPP, 2009; Karl Kruszelnicki, *Great Mythconceptions: The Science Behind the Myths*. Andrews McMeel Publishing, 2006; Robert A. Braeunig, *Did We Land on the Moon? A Debunking of the Moon Hoax Theory*. Rocket & Space

Literally *thousands* of manuscripts exist in tangible and superior condition throughout the world dating back all the way to Genesis,[3] and the modern-day Bible reads pretty much as it did from when the various books that compose it were first written.[4] Furthermore, the modern-day Judeo-Christian Bible can be trusted and relied upon as reflecting the *original* manuscripts much more so than any classic literature *including* Homer, Aristotle, Pliny, and Tacitus.

For instance, the world has at its disposal more than 14,000 Old Testament manuscripts dating back several millennia. In addition to this, around 5,700 manuscripts of the New Testament exist today that go back all the way to the first century – yes, we actually *have* first century compositions as well as painstakingly-replicated word-for-word, hand-written copies that match up one-to-another precisely over both narrow as

---

Technology, 2012; as well as Charli Schuler, *Apollo 11 Experiment Still Going Strong after 35 Years*. California Institute of Technology.

[3] See also William E. Nix et al., *A General Introduction to the Bible*. Moody Publishers, 1986.

[4] See also F.F. Bruce, *The Canon of Scripture*. IVP Academic, 1988; and Norman L. Geisler, *Baker Encyclopedia of Christian Apologetics*. Baker Books, 2000.

well as wide timespans in history.[5] As has been stated:

> At last count, there are nearly 5,700 hand-written Greek manuscripts of the New Testament. In addition, there are more than 9,000 manuscripts in other languages (e.g., Syriac, Coptic, Latin, Arabic)... there is nothing from the ancient world that even comes close in terms of manuscript support. The next closest work is the *Iliad* by Homer, with 643 manuscripts. Most other ancient works survive on fewer than a dozen manuscripts, yet few historians question the historicity of the events those works describe.[6]

And in regards to manuscript support for other secular writings that are used and cited in our schools, universities, and research to this very day and that do not raise questions regarding their validity or accuracy to the original documents:

> In evaluating the significance of these statistics...one should consider, by way of contrast, the number of manuscripts which preserve the text of the ancient classics. Homer's Iliad...is

---

[5] See also Sir Frederic Kenyon et al., *Our Bible and the Ancient Manuscripts*. Harper and Row, 1962.

[6] Norman L. Geisler and Frank Turek, *I Don't Have Enough Faith to Be an Atheist* . Crossway, 2004.

> preserved by 457 papyri, 2 uncial manuscripts,
> and 188 minuscule manuscripts. Among the
> tragedians the witnesses to Euripides are the
> most abundant; his extant works are pre-
> served in 54 papyri and 276 parchment
> manuscripts, almost all of the later dating
> from the Byzantine period...the time between
> the composition of the books of the New Tes-
> tament and the earliest extant copies is rela-
> tively brief. Instead of the lapse of a millen-
> nium or more, as is the case of not a few clas-
> sical authors, several papyrus manuscripts
> of portions of the New Testament are extant
> which were copies within a century or so after
> the composition of the original documents.[7]

Even secular historians going back *before* the
second century AD make direct references to and
quote biblical text – and furthermore speak of
Christ in great and meticulous detail.[8]  These
include Josephus the famous Jewish historian,
Tacitus, Suetonius, and Pliny Secundus, who was
a Roman governor; as well as Irenaeus, Julius
Africanus, Tertullian, and Clement of Rome.[9]

Furthermore, archaeological evidence that support biblical stories, peoples, and history abound

---

[7] Bruce Metzger, *The Text of the New Testament: Its
Transmission, Corruption, and Restoration.* 4th edition.
Oxford University Press, 2005.

[8] See also Ibid..

[9] See Geisler and Turek (as in n. 6 on the preceding
page).

to such an extent that even archaeologists such as Sir William Ramsay who have previously set out to initially *disprove* biblical claims have as a result of their extensive research become believers in both biblical accuracy as well as in the very faith that is contained within its pages. For even many a skeptic has become a believer on realizing that specific biblical predictions dating all the way back to the Old Testament have so far come true; including prophecies concerning Israel, Babylon, the Phoenician city of Tyre, Sidon... as well as prophecies about governments, kingdoms, and individuals such as Christ himself to statistical probabilities that affirm the impossibility for the fulfillment of said prophecies to have occurred by sheer accident.[10]

Another common argument that people oftentimes make is that, with "so many" versions of the Bible out there, we cannot know whether the original message has been changed. But again, these "various versions" are strictly differentiated only as based upon the historical time

---

[10] See also Bruce M. Metzger, *The Canon of the New Testament: Its Origin, Development, and Significance.* Oxford University Press, April 1997; as well as Chapter 2 on page 23.

of translation with consideration to the audience's native language style, dialect, and pre-
ferred manner of speaking; and do not modify, as
some erroneously state, original meaning whatsoever.    Furthermore, current-day versions of
scripture are based *not* on contemporary versions
of each other, but on aforementioned manuscripts
and their *original* language – as has always been
the case throughout biblical translation history.[11]
As a simple example, let us say that one wants to
express this book's title in different ways.  One
can do so, for instance, through the following
derivatives without changing original meaning:

- The Good News in accordance to Christ
- The Good News as per the Christ
- The Gospel as taught by the Messiah
- The Gospel as based on Ha'Mashiach
- The Good Doctrine of Christ the Messiah
- The Fine Announcement as spoken of by Christ
- The Gospel as based on Christ's teachings
- The Gospel as focusing on the words of Christ
- Christ's awesome teachings

---

[11] See also Kenyon et al. (as in n. 5 on page 56).

As one can see, all of the above say essentially the same thing in different ways. In like manner, the various modern 'versions' of the Bible do the same, in that original meaning is retained even though scholars might choose to express it in manners more assimilative to current cultural norms of expression – in the same way that one may choose to revise a document or sentence to better come across to the intended audience, culture, and ways of modernity without changing the original message in any way. And so are the various "modern versions" of the Bible: they are *not* hard versions that change meaning, but rather *express* as accurately as possible the *same* original manuscripts of scripture in the reader's proper native linguistic form of speaking that he or she might more easily understand as based on current-day ways of expressing the *same* thing.

Furthermore, all of the earliest, as well as later copies, of biblical manuscripts agree in 99.5% of the text – which is a great accomplishment on the part of scribes and scholars throughout the ages who had meticulous techniques to both copy as well as check and re-check for errors. From the .5%, most arguable discrepancies involve either word order or spelling – but even this is *minuscule* on considering just how robust history has been able to keep later copies of the Judeo-Christian Bible so true to original manuscripts – especially as many other secular ancient manuscripts cannot often make such a claim – not to 99.5% accuracy at least. Furthermore, any said discrepancies or questions of meaning are usually now contained in footnotes in most of today's Bibles.[12] Furthermore,

> In order to address the issue of accuracy, we need to clear up misunderstandings many critics have concerning "errors" in the biblical manuscripts ... First of all, these are not "errors" but variant readings, the vast majority of which are strictly grammatical (i.e., punctuation and spelling). Second, these readings are spread throughout nearly 5,700 manuscripts, so that a variant spelling of *one* letter of *one* word in *one* verse in 2,000 manuscripts is counted as 2,000 "errors" ... No other ancient book is so well authenticated. The great New Testament scholar and Princeton professor Bruce Metzger estimated that the *Mahabharata* of Hinduism is copied with only about 90 percent accuracy and Homer's *Iliad* with about 95 percent. By comparison, he estimated the New Testament is about 99.5

---

[12] See also the short, comprehensive, exceptional, and easy to digest Frederick Fyvie Bruce, *The New Testament Documents: Are They Reliable?* Wilder Publications, 2009; as well as Bart D. Ehrman, *The New Testament and Other Early Christian Writings*. Oxford University Press, 1998.

> percent accurate. Again, the 0.5 percent in
> question does not affect a *single* doctrine of the
> Christian faith.[13]

Hence, the reliability of the Bible *cannot* be disputed. Mankind is not so ignorant as to be incapable of doing a competent job at passing down both original manuscripts through thousands of years, as well as accurately copying the same verbatim into other languages. Furthermore, the ancient documents we have include the Old Testament Hebrew and New Testament Greek manuscripts, to where any dispute regarding language translation is *easily* able to be compared and put to rest with the same – as it always is on producing third-language translations of any ancient work throughout the world.

As one of the most prominent authorities on ancient manuscripts has rightly stated in regards to biblical translations throughout the ages:

> It cannot be too strongly asserted that in
> substance the text of the Bible is certain:
> Especially is this the case with the New Tes-
> tament. The number of manuscripts of the
> New Testament, of early translations from it,
> and of quotations from it in the oldest writers

---

[13] Geisler and Turek (as in n. 6 on page 56).

of the church, is so large that it is practically certain that the true reading of every doubtful passage is preserved in some one or other of these ancient authorities. This can be said of no other ancient book in the world.[14]

Furthermore, it is interesting to note that Athanasius, the bishop of Alexandria, first listed twenty-seven documents of scripture to be declared as orthodox in AD 367; meaning that they were considered to be in accordance to what was widely seen as Christian doctrine and theology by around the 4th Century by the *then* newly established Roman Catholic Church; and this after certain groups of believers had within the previous centuries slowly developed the faith into a more hierarchical structure – one could say into what eventually became somewhat of an organized form of religion – though this must be differentiated from *the faith* itself.[15]

It must also be remembered that these documents had at that time already been around 250 - 300 years old, so that the *earliest* believers in Christ essentially had nothing to do with the

---

[14] Kenyon et al. (as in n. 5 on page 56).

[15] See Chapter 9 on page 161, regarding the difference between *the faith* as Christ taught it, as opposed to organized religion as we see it in this day and age.

*process,* or *approval,* of canonization (of choosing which letters and manuscripts to be included in an 'official' Christian collection... or Bible). *Even so,* these *same* early Christians *did* in fact hold to most of what would eventually become officially canonized documents as authoritative and inspired from as early as the 1st Century – *especially* the Gospels. The Council of Hippo then recognized a final agreed-upon list in AD 393, and the Third Council of Carthage re-affirmed this list, which now comprises the current New Testament, in AD 397. As Ehrman states:

> It [*the New Testament*] comprises twenty-seven diverse books brought together under one cover for particular religious reasons and under specific historical circumstances. It is *not fully* representative of the views and writings of the early Christians.[16]

Furthermore, although other very similar lists that included most of what makes up today's canon of New Testament scripture had been considered beforehand, this list is what essentially stuck to this day; where such things as Paul's letters where included and were thus deemed

---

[16] See Ehrman (as in n. 12 on page 61).

to be inspired and authoritative. It certainly made sense to include the Gospels – again, the books of MATTHEW, MARK, LUKE, and JOHN – as they are eye-witness accounts of Christ's quoted sayings, teachings, and deeds – and also because these are what *some* would rightly consider to be the preeminently authoritative books in regards to any possible gray areas on issues of faith.[17] Likewise, it seemed a proper decision to also have included the books of REVELATIONS and I, II, and III JOHN – all of which were written by the apostle John – as well as JAMES, I and II PETER, and JUDE – all of which having been written by *eye-witnesses* to Christ's life, while also being harmonious with his teachings – and the book of ACTS as having been a historical account of the initial spread of Christianity as derived from the early followers of Christ in and of itself, and as also having been written by Luke – to name but a few. Yet Paul's letters, and miscellaneous others should, I believe, be taken *in context*[18]

---

[17] See also Chapter 1 on page 3.

[18] Ernst-August Gutt, a linguistics specialist in Biblical translations, puts it this way on showing the importance of considering context as well as intended reader's knowledge about said context by the words being used – and how

to time, purpose, and audience[19] – these being letters to the early believers as under specific circumstances, and to specific groups that were going through specific challenges.[20]

Therefore, we *have* the very words of Christ available to us in this day and age, so that anyone can easily discern what he *himself* taught, and compare it to what modern Christianity teaches in regards to a myriad of current-day issues and gray areas of conscience. Thus, what many should probably be disputing is *not* the faithfulness of the current Bible to original scrolls, but rather the faithfulness of modern-day doctri-

---

said words are used – with the following example dialogue between a mother and her daughter:

> Mother: "What's your new teacher like?"
> Daughter: "He rides to school on a motorbike."

If the daughter liked men who rode motorbikes, the mother would know that her daughter liked the teacher. However, if the daughter did not like men who rode motorbikes, the mother would know that the daughter disliked the teacher. Ernst-August Gutt, *Relevance Theory and Translation: Toward a New Realism in Bible Translation.* International Meeting of the Society of Biblical Literature, 2004.

Hence the importance in taking both the intended reader's background knowledge and context of scripture into account.

[19] See also F. F. Bruce, *New Testament History.* Doubleday, 1983.

[20] See also Metzger (as in n. 10 on page 58).

nal claims from many newly-found "religions" to common sense[21] – and most importantly, to the teachings of Jesus Christ himself – especially as detailed in the Gospels.

---

[21] See Appendix A on page 357; as well as Chapter 14 on page 307.

# The Simplicity of the Gospel of Christ

Chapter Four

# *What Does it Mean to Believe?*

During his earthly ministry, Christ stated:

> Indeed, just as the Father raises the dead
> and gives them life, so also the Son gives
> life to whomever he wishes. The Father
> judges no one but has given all judgment
> to the Son, so that all may honor the Son
> just as they honor the Father. Anyone who
> does not honor the Son does not honor the
> Father who sent him. Very truly, I tell you,
> anyone who hears my word and believes
> Him who sent me has eternal life, and
> does not come under judgment, but has
> passed from death to life.
>
> JOHN 5:21-24

The Greek word for *believe* as used in the New
Testament portion of the Judeo-Christian Bible –
that being translated from the Greek verb *pisteuo*

– simply means to place one's "faith in", to "put one's *trust* in", and to "place one's *reliance* upon" – so that a *belief* in Christ simply means to place one's reliance and trust on Christ.

Furthermore, as has aptly been said in regards to the word *believe* in context to scripture:

> In sum, to believe in someone means to place one's confidence or trust in that person. But that confidence and trust must be informed, and the content that informs one's confidence and trust in Christ (in order to be saved) is what the Bible refers to as the Gospel. The Bible states that "*The Gospel is the power of God for salvation to everyone who believes*" (Romans 1:16). Being a Christian involves an *informed confidence* in Jesus Christ (the God-Man Savior). A person is *informed* about His death as a satisfactory payment for their sin (the Gospel), and that person places their *confidence* or *trust* in that payment. That informed confidence and trust is what the Bible means by the term *believe*. Anyone who places their confidence or trust in Jesus Christ for the forgiveness of sin and eternal life is a Christian.[1]

Therefore, as stated, *believing* in Christ simply means to place one's reliance or trust in him –

---

[1] As in G. Harry Leafe, *Muddy Water*. Scriptel.

which is accomplished by the simple act of faith in welcoming Christ into one's life, trusting that he is who he said he is, and accepting that he has paid the penalty for one's wrongdoings through taking all of mankind's place on the cross – and *not* by being "religious", nor by following religious law or tradition. It is an act of *will*, as well as an act of the *heart* – and this with the mere humble *faith of a child*. Yes, the faith of a child in that:

> People were bringing little children to him in order that he might touch them; and the disciples spoke sternly to them. But when Jesus saw this, he was indignant and said to them, 'Let the little children come to me; do not stop them; for it is to such as these that the kingdom of God belongs. Truly I tell you, whoever does not *receive* the kingdom of God as a little child will never enter it.' And he took them up in his arms, laid his hands on them, and blessed them.
>
> MARK 10:13-16

...to where, to come to Christ with the faith of a child is to be *willing* to humble myself before God, letting go of 'adult' ways of thinking if for a moment – whether about structured religiosity, deep philosophical theory, complex dogma, and such – and to simply *accept* that Christ is there, *waiting* for me to turn to his loving arms; and to straightforwardly accept him by *entrusting myself* to him – receiving, by this simple act of faith, the forgiveness and renewal of life and heart that he has for me – and all through a child-like, *uncomplicated* faith. No religion, ritual, sacrifice, or priestly confession necessary. It is to be able to *humble oneself* enough to acknowledge that one does not know everything, that one is blemished, and that one *needs* God as one's Heavenly Father for a renewed life, soul, and heart. Only a humble *acceptance* of Christ by a simple, elementary, and uncomplicated act of faith will do. Again,

> At that time the disciples came to Jesus and asked, 'Who is the greatest in the kingdom of heaven?' He called a child, whom he put among them, and said, 'Truly I tell you, unless you change and become like little children, you will never enter the kingdom of heaven. Whoever *humbles himself* like this child is the greatest in the kingdom of heaven. Whoever welcomes one such child in my name welcomes me.'
>
> MATTHEW 18:1-5

It all starts to make sense – that God calls those who are consciously *willing* to humble themselves before Him, while putting aside pride, the complications of theology and religion, and one's own ego – in order to become poor, or humble, in spirit – in order to finally be able to *let* God come rushing in and do *His* marvelous, miraculous work from within. And that is why one comes to Christ by *believing* – which simply means that one consciously makes the personal *choice* to places one's trust on him – to *surrender*, if you will, to him.

Thus a person comes to Christ just as one finds oneself – at *whatever* state one may find the self in conduct, behavior, lifestyle, or whatever it might be...*just as I am*. This is because Christ made very clear, through his teachings, that God *already* loves and accepts *us* unconditionally – just as we are. As has aptly been said:

> Define yourself radically as one *beloved* by God. This is the true self. Every other identity is illusion.[2]

---

[2] As in Brennan Manning, *Brennan Manning, Abba's Child: The Cry of the Heart for Intimate Belonging*. NavPress, 2002.

Yes, our Heavenly Father *already* loves us right where we find ourselves at in life – in the same ways that Christ *himself* actively attended to, befriended, loved, and unconditionally accepted those who were considered the rejects, the outcasts, and the black sheep of society.  This includes *us* as well – with all of our imperfections, failures, mistakes, sins, regrets – *just as I am*. In *whatever way* we may presently find ourselves at in this great big game of life. Any improvements to be made, it is God *Himself* – through *His* Holy Spirit – that gently makes them in *His* perfect timing – and this from the inside-out.

Therefore, one does *not* need to clean up one's life before coming to Christ. It is Christ, through *his* Spirit, who does the work *from within*. All *we* need to do is simply follow him, and let God do the work in us that may need doing. And that is why Christ explicitly says:

> Blessed are the *poor* in spirit, for theirs is
> the kingdom of heaven.
>
> MATTHEW 5:3

The phrase "poor in spirit" literally translates from the Greek as "those who are not spiritually arrogant" – or the "humble in spirit".[3] Further-more, *blessed* translates into *happy, fortunate,* or *blissful* – to where those who are *willing to* hum-ble themselves before God, while leaving self-righteousness to one side (an oftentimes much too common but justifiable complaint towards those who place religion before God Himself) are therefore happy and fortunate from within their very core as a result, to where the kingdom of God *belongs* to such as these.

Furthermore, Christ *himself* described rules made by hierarchical religions in general as null and void, unnecessary, legalistic, and having come from the "traditions of man"[4] – or traditions

---

[3] A full explanation of the same can also be found as referenced from the NASB regarding the phrase "poor in spirit" as used in this verse [NASB; LockmanFoundation, editor, *Updated New American Standard Bible.* Zondervan Publishing House, 1999].

[4] As Christ himself clearly said in Mark 7:6-9 & 13:

"Isaiah prophesied rightly about you hypocrites, as it is written,'THIS PEOPLE HONORS ME WITH THEIR LIPS, BUT THEIR HEARTS ARE FAR FROM ME; IN VAIN DO THEY WORSHIP ME, TEACHING HUMAN PRECEPTS AS DOCTRINES.' You abandon the commandment of God and hold to human tradition... You have a fine way of rejecting the commandment of God in order to keep your tradition!... thus making void the word of God through your tradition that you have handed on. And you do many things like this."

of *organized* religion – and that we are not bound by them any longer – to where every single one of us, *without exception*, is free to come to God *personally* and *directly* as He *Himself* draws us[5] – and this *without* ever having to follow nor adhere to official religion, imposed-upon tradition, or doctrinally-legalistic obligation.[6]

Can *organized* religion say the same thing in this day and age of political correctness, hypocritical taboos, pious tradition that leaves the soul empty, religious observance at the cost of the oppression of those who do not follow, the beheading of those who do not submit while blocking the path and persecuting the few who truly love their God – organized religion's legalities that oftentimes result in self-repression, confusion, mass murders, world-wide terror, the oppression of the sexually-realistic, the envy towards the sexually-active innocent – and the stifling of spiritual liberty, ultimate truth, and a personal faith and trust in our Heavenly Father who has *absolutely nothing* whatsoever to do with such man-appointed and man-made things...as

---

[5] See also Chapter 10 on page 187.
[6] See also note 19 on page 409.

Christ himself stated? Sorry to seem so over-the-top, but it *is* true, is it not?

The "Holiness Code"[7] were Jewish religious laws that the Hebrew people had to follow. Essentially, they had to follow religion and tradition before their Messiah arrived. Yet, with Christ's arrival, these 613 Old Testament Torah-based laws were *all* sweepingly done away with through Christ's *separating* mankind from the *religiosity* of religious law by his finished work for all on the cross, to where a relationship with God is now formed by our sincerely turning to Him by faith alone and simply asking Him – as a child would ask a parent for comfort and safety through a child-like faith – to become a *part* of our lives and be involved in our daily living; and believing (placing our trust) on Him who He has sent – and *not* by such frivolous works of obedience to mankind's rule – *nor* through being pious or enchained to the noose of doctrinal rule of *any* form. To come to Christ is to be *set free* from such earth-bound idiosyncrasies and enchainments.

So what must one *do*? What good works, how many church services, what religion must one

---

[7] See more on the Code in Appendix C on page 459.

follow? What must I *do*? Well, here is how Christ responded to similar questions:

> Therefore they said to Him, 'What shall we do, so that we may work the works of God?' Jesus answered and said to them, 'This is the work of God, that you *believe* in Him whom He has sent.'
>
> JOHN 6:28-29

Therefore, there really is no *doing*, but rather *believing* – specifically, placing one's trust in Christ, inviting him into one's life, and letting *him* take over. For as he himself said:

> While you have the Light, *believe* in the Light, so that you may *become* sons of Light.
>
> JOHN 12:36

Chapter Five

# No One is Ever Rejected

Christ calls each and every one of us to himself – regardless of one's race, religion, sex, sexual preference, social standing, family background, personal history, or whatever the case may be. He does not filter people out like religions, corporations, nations, governments, or anyone else might do. He spoke, healed, and attended to people of *all* backgrounds and social standings, and never discriminated, but wholly *accepted* those who were *willing* to come to him, and to follow him. For as Jesus clearly stated:

> Come to me, all you who work to exhaustion and are heavy-laden, and I will give you rest. Take my yoke upon you and learn from me, for I am gentle and humble in heart, and you will find rest for your souls. For my yoke is *easy* and my burden is *light*.

> MATTHEW 11:28-30

Christ promises that everyone – *without excep-tion whatsoever* – who is burdened, weary, bro-ken, and shattered; may come to him for peace. An inner peace that this world *cannot* give, and one that no one can *ever* take away. As he put it:

> Peace I leave with you; my peace I *give* to you. I do not give to you as the world gives. Do not let your hearts be troubled, and do not let them be afraid.

> JOHN 14:27

He does not tell anyone to become 'religious', cer-emonial, or outwardly pious. No. He invites *all* to come to him, irrespective of religious background, political stance, creed, race, economic standing, geographic location, sexual orientation,[1] or sex-

---

[1] Yes, *even* homosexuals. For it is Christ *himself* who said in Matthew 19:12:

> For there are eunuchs who were *born that way* from their mother's womb; and there are eunuchs who were made eunuchs by men; and there are also eunuchs who made themselves eunuchs for the sake of the kingdom of heaven. He who is able to accept this, let him accept it.

...the word *eunuch* having *also* referred to gay people at that time – as Christ himself defines eunuchs here in three categories – the first of which being in reference to homosexuality. Christ *allowed for* as well as *defended* homosexuality as a birth trait. See also Appendix C on page 433 for a more detailed explanation as to how

ual lifestyle.[2] Yes, he invites *all* to follow him. *All* – without any exception. But how can we know that he accepts all of the above – and everyone else who will come? Because when we open our door to Christ, his Holy Spirit comes to live *in* us – the Great Comforter, the Spirit of Truth who testifies *to us* that we are indeed children of God. But to receive Him, you must receive Christ – for Christ and the Spirit, in the same way that Christ and the Father, *are* One. For, as it is written:

---

the Judeo-Christian Bible is actually very positive and affirming in regards to homosexuality, along with an entire and thorough study on the same in M.W. Sphero, *The Gay Faith: Christ, Scripture, and Sexuality.* Herms Press, 2011.

[2] See Appendix B on page 397, regarding how premarital sex is not against the Bible, and why one does not need to abstain from sex in order to have a relationship with God. Many stumble on their way to God because they wrongly see Christianity as a conservative and 'prudish' religion – whereas it is in fact the exact opposite. Sex is physical. Faith is from the heart. The only time they could clash is in regards to how one treats other people that they might be sexually active with (and how one allows others to treat him- or herself if one is being abused or mistreated by them) – particularly in regards to respecting others that could be involved or affected; and not abusing, deliberately mistreating, nor forcing anyone into anything. Otherwise, sex is sex, and faith is faith that must be applied through compassion and respect towards other's personal choices – as well as towards the self.

> By this we *know* that we abide in him and
> he in us, because he has given us of *his*
> Spirit.
>
> I JOHN 4:13

Christ does not call anyone to be *religious*, nor
does he want one's religiosity. No. He calls all
who are, out of free will, *willing* to hear his voice,
to simply *"follow me, and let the dead bury their
own dead"*.[3] Nothing more. No strings attached.
No complications. No confusion. Just peace. *His*
peace. *And* his eternally-cleansing forgiveness.
*No one* is refused. Nobody! As he himself has
clearly and rightly declared:

> I am the bread of life. Whoever comes
> to me will *never* be hungry, and whoever
> believes in me will *never* be thirsty. But I
> said to you that you have seen me and yet
> do not believe. Everything that the Father
> gives me will come to me, and *anyone* who
> comes to me I will *never* drive away.
>
> JOHN 6:35-37

Are you burdened, stressed out, on the edge
– in some form of earth-bound despair? Have
you been carrying around heavy yokes around
your neck all of your life in the name of societal

---

[3] Matthew 8:22

expectations, in order to please others, or to appease those who don't even seem to care? Well, maybe you are, and than again, maybe you're not. Even so, *everyone* needs Christ, because everyone needs God – for that is how He has created us. And only *He* holds the key to the core of our hearts. If He does not fill the gap inside that only *He* can adequately fill, something else that never satisfies – whether it be some kind of excess, workaholism, boredom, depression, low self-esteem or self-confidence, monetary obsession, or even religious fanaticism – will attempt to... which will ultimately only lead to *more* frustration than it is worth.

But Christ promises that, if you are *willing* to exchange your heavy yoke and baggage for his, you *will* find out for yourself – apart from and completely *without* organized religion and the myriad types of repressive expectations of this world – that he truly *is* gentle and humble in heart, and that his yoke is oh so much *easier,* and so much lighter, to bear. You *will* find rest for your soul. I promise you you will! For as Christ has himself said:

> Everything that the Father *gives me* will
> come to me, and *anyone* who comes to me
> I will *never* drive away; for I have come
> down from heaven, not to do my own will,
> but the will of Him who sent me. And
> this is the will of Him who sent me, that
> I should *lose nothing* of all that He has
> given me, but raise it up on the last day.
> This is indeed the will of my Father, that
> *all* who see the Son and *believe* in him may
> have eternal life; and I will raise them up
> on the last day.
>
> JOHN 6:37-40

With Christ, a promise is a promise. He's absolutely and totally the very same this very day,
as he was two thousand years ago – and as he
was from the beginning of time. He created us,
and knows just what we long for from the depths
of our being. In fact, it is he who puts our most
keen desires within us. For He truly *is* our heart's
desire, and He truly *is* all that we need...

> 'Martha, Martha,' the Lord answered, 'you
> are worried and upset about many things,
> but few things are needed—or indeed only
> one. Mary has chosen the better part, and
> it will not be taken away from her.'
>
> LUKE 10:41-42 NIV

Christ promises each and every one of us –
whomever we are – that:

> Those who love me will keep my word,
> and my Father will love them, and *we* will
> come to them and make our home *with*
> them.
>
> JOHN 14:23

The Spirit of Truth is calling – will you listen?

Chapter Six

# Only in Spirit and in Truth

Christ was speaking to a Samaritan women at a well who inquired as to how one should come to God and have a relationship with Him – should it be by being religious, partaking in religious ceremonies, and sacrificing oneself out of piety? And *where* should one worship God? What religious *sect* should one follow to *get* to God? As reiterated herein, the meeting went like this:

> The woman said to him, 'Our ancestors worshiped on this mountain, but you[1] say that the place where people must worship is in Jerusalem.' Jesus said to her, 'Woman, believe me, the hour is coming

---

[1] The Greek for the word *you* here is plural, as she was referring to the Hebraic Jewish religion not involving the quasi-Judaic-Samaritan sect.

when you will worship the Father neither
on this mountain nor in Jerusalem. You
worship what you do not know; we worship what we know, for salvation is *from*
the Jews. But the hour is coming, and is
now here, when the *true* worshipers will
worship the Father in spirit and truth, for
the Father seeks such as these to worship him. God is spirit, and those who
worship Him must worship in spirit and
truth.' The woman said to him, 'I know
that Messiah is coming' (who is called
Christ). 'When he comes, he will proclaim
all things to us.' Jesus said to her, '*I am*
he,[2] the one who is speaking to you.'

JOHN 4:20-26

Herein lies the major difference between faith
and religion. Faith liberates the soul; religion
limits it. The difference lies in perspective and
a sincere mind and spirit. Are you seeking God
and hearing His word as He speaks to you on a
*personal* level – or are you letting the 'religious'
explain to you how you should or should not live?
Are you seeking God through religion, striving to
be pious, keeping religious traditions created by
a church, or doing good works; or have you come

---

[2] *I Am* in the Greek, to where Christ used the Jehovic
"I Am" in this context – thus calling himself God. See also
Chapter 2 on page 23.

to God, *just as you are*, with all your fallacies and shortcomings, with the simple faith of a child, in spirit and in truth and *apart from* trying to *be* religious? For even Paul rightly states,

> But God, who is rich in mercy, out of the great love with which he loved us *even when* we were dead through our trespasses, made us alive together with Christ — *by grace*[3] *you have been saved* — and raised us up with him and seated us with him in the heavenly places in Christ Jesus, so that in the ages to come he might show the immeasurable riches of his grace in kindness toward us in Christ Jesus. For *by grace* you have been saved *through faith*, and this is not your *own* doing; it is the gift of God — *not* the result of [*good, or religious*] works, so that no one may boast.
>
> EPHESIANS 2:4-9

...and in regards to those who wrongly place their trust on their religion, tradition, ceremonial rule, and church law – rather than on a child-like faith in God – Paul rightly states:

> Brothers and sisters, my heart's desire and prayer to God for them is that they may be saved. I can testify that they *have*

---

[3] *Grace* being God's unmerited, undeserved favor and unconditional love to *all* of mankind.

*a zeal* for God, but it is not enlightened.
For, being ignorant of the righteousness
that comes from God, and seeking to *es-*
*tablish their own*, they have not submitted to *God*'s righteousness. For Christ is
the end of the law so that there may be
righteousness for *everyone* who believes.

ROMANS 10:1-4

Simply put, having a relationship with God is for
everyone who places their trust in Christ, who
opens their door to God from within their heart;
and this *not* through being religious – as Paul
rightly says in the above – but rather in spirit and
in truth alone; and this with the humble faith
of a child who *does not need* to figure everything
out, knowing that his Heavenly Father will take
care of, unconditionally love, and accept him just
as he is – even when his earthly parents, priest,
society, co-workers, the hypocrisies of political
correctness, or mankind in general might not.

Where does *your* perspective lie?  Are you
focusing on your *own* personal relationship with
God, or on the dictates and demands of a rogue
preacher or other religious leader of whatever
sort?  On intuition guided by God's voice and
common sense, or on church guidelines and harsh
religious law (whatever religion that may be)?

Herein lies the meaning of seeking God in spirit and in truth – for God *is* spirit, and not a temple, church, synagogue, book, rites and rituals, traditions of man, preacher, guru, rabbi, supervisor, director, regulator, prosecutor, mob, taboo, news anchor, professor, theologian, or religiously-controlling group blindingly 'guiding' the dead into a pit of dullness and apathy.

Christ taught us that we do *not* need to be religious to get to God. In fact, organized religion is oftentimes a *stumbling block* to God. For as Christ said, in regards to the religious leaders of his day:

> The scribes and the Pharisees sit on Moses' seat; therefore, do whatever they teach you and follow it; but do not do as they do, for they do not practice what they preach. They tie up heavy burdens, hard to bear, and lay them on the shoulders of others; but they themselves are unwilling to *lift a finger* to move them. They do all their deeds to be *seen* by others... But woe to you, scribes and Pharisees, hypocrites! For you lock people out of the kingdom of heaven. For you do not go in yourselves, and when others are going in, you stop them. Woe to you, scribes and Pharisees, hypocrites! For you cross sea and land to make a single convert, and you make the

new convert twice as much a child of hell as yourselves...Woe to you, scribes and Pharisees, hypocrites! For you tithe mint, dill, and cummin, and have neglected the weightier matters of the law: *justice and mercy and faith.* It is these you ought to have practiced without neglecting the others. You blind guides! You strain out a gnat but swallow a camel!...Woe to you, scribes and Pharisees, hypocrites! For you clean the outside of the cup and of the plate, but inside they are full of greed and self-indulgence. You blind Pharisees! First clean the *inside* of the cup, so that the outside also may become clean...So you also *on the outside* look righteous to others, but *inside* you are full of hypocrisy and lawlessness.

MATTHEW 23:2-5, 23-26, & 28

On the other hand, it is *Christ's Holy Spirit* who calls us to Himself, and who *teaches* us, and *guides* us. All we have to do is simply be *willing* to open the door – in spirit and in truth – and we are His, *forever.* Again, no religion necessary. No, not at all! But rather – *in spirit and in truth.* It really *is* as plain and simple as that. No gimmicks. No strings attached.

As Christ has said,

> Behold! I stand at the door and knock; if
> you hear my voice and open the door [*the
> door to your spirit in sincerity of truth*], I
> will come to you and eat with you, and you
> with me.

REVELATION 3:20

and again, Jesus states:

> My sheep hear my voice. I know them, and
> they follow me. I give them eternal life,
> and they will *never* perish. No one will
> snatch them out of my hand. My Father
> who has given them to me is greater than
> all, and no one can snatch them out of the
> Father's hand. The Father and I are one.

JOHN 10:27-30

To the believer – does your reliance and relationship with God depend on following orders from
the structured spheres you might find yourself
in, or do you worship and love Him directly and
without earthly intervention – in spirit and in
truth? Either way, He loves you and cares for
you. But oh the fruit you could bear *through Him*
towards those around you – as well as *for yourself*
– by choosing to come to Him *not* out of obligation
nor man-induced guilt – but through love, and
this by coming to Him from *within* your spirit,

and by loving and gratefully – *joyously* – rejoicing in Him in truth.

To the dear reader that might not believe – as you have probably known all along, Christ taught mankind about a spiritual, *non-religious* love and connection with God on an *individual* basis that is custom-made for each and every one that may come; and he taught us to walk the walk not through compulsion nor obligation – but rather in love... and in truth. Is that how you see your believing friends live their faith? If not, keep loving them, for I'm sure they are wonderful and loving, albeit possibly sometimes rather inflexible, people – God bless'em. Believe me, they *need* your love and understanding! But please don't assume that that is how Christ taught them to walk – again, you may already know that. Maybe *you* could be the best example they themselves need! Just go with the flow, baby – and don't get your feathers too flustered when they get *overly* preachy with you. Go with the flow. By your own kindness they might one day chill out a bit, and at last learn to lean on God's everlasting peace and love. For God uses *everyone* – even those who might not necessarily 'believe'. So, hey there! Smile.

Chapter Seven

# The Light of the World

For God so loved the world that He gave His one and only Son, that whoever believes in him shall not perish but have eternal life. For God did not send his Son into the world to condemn the world, but to save the world through him. Whoever believes in him is not judged, but whoever does not believe has already been judged because they have not believed in the name of God's one and only Son. This is the verdict: Light has come into the world, but people loved darkness instead of light because their deeds were evil. Everyone who does evil hates the light, and will not come into the light for fear that their deeds will be exposed. But whoever lives by the truth comes into the light, so that it may be seen plainly that what they have done has been done through God.

JOHN 3:16-21

Imagine for a moment that you are seated in a huge, *completely* darkened arena – you know, that gigantic kind that puts on music concerts for globally-renowned bands and performing icons, the kind that holds sporting events that are broadcast live throughout the world, and that have the capacity to support tens of thousands of screaming, fun-loving spectators that just never want it to end. Imagine that you are sitting in one of its seats off to the side – such as those nose-bleed balconies where you have to struggle to actually *see* what's going on on-stage, on the court, or in the field below. Now imagine that, amidst the total darkness, you begin to see a small light opposite from where you are – at a great distance, but you see the light shinning. Someone just lit a match, and you see that light, as well as some people who are immediately around it. All else is hidden in pitch darkness. All except that small distant light that you now see.

Similarly, even if one walks in darkness in this world, and becomes perplexed at all of the different voices, opinions, admonitions, and philosophies going around – one can *still* see a light. The warm, compassionate, and loving light of Christ. The Light that itself *is* Christ, in the midst of a broken world. Can you see it? Can you see it shimmer?  Can you feel its warm welcome to all who are willing to come to it?  Can you see its love, and its open acceptance for *all* who may come?  For, as Christ himself declared to all who would listen:

> I am the light of the world.  Whoever follows me will *never* walk in darkness but will have the light of life.
>
> JOHN 8:12

Yes, even in darkness, the Light still shines forth, and can *never* – nor *will* ever – be quenched.  It overcomes the darkness.  It reveals itself to any who will look for it – no matter how far they may be from where it is – and its source, that which shines brighter than anything else around it, makes clear that the overshadowing darkness surrounding it cannot stop it from burning brightly, consistently, and without shifting of shadows.  When one has tried everything else – wealth, world philosophies, opinions, traditions, religions, sacrifices, and works – the Light of the world still remains, and will *never* surrender.  Yes, Christ is *indeed* the light of the world.  The Light of mankind.  And he *is* the Light of life.

Coming to the Light does not mean you have to give up your individuality, self-esteem, and ambitions.  In fact, if someone tells you otherwise, do *not* believe them, and do not let them and their restrictive notions make you stumble and consequently deprive you from personally *knowing* Christ in the intimate manner in which he *calls you* to Himself through His unending and unconditional love for you, respectively and individually.  Again, no religiosity necessary – just a simple, childlike faith that will *never* give up.  For it is not through some sort of "religious experience", nor through some kind of "devout obligation" that one comes *into* the light, but rather, as the first portion of scripture in the beginning of this chapter states; it is when one "lives by the truth", when one is *hungry* for the truth – it is than that they *will* come to the light – and this they will have done "through God" alone. Even one of Christ's beatitudes states it, when he said:

> Blessed are those who hunger and thirst for righteousness, for they *will* be filled.
>
> MATTHEW 5:6

So when *some* attempt to impose rule and ritual on your soul – claiming that your personal and sincere relationship with God the Son is not enough, and that you still need to do x, y, or z – do not let them. For it is not they that you need to answer to, but Christ, and Christ alone. For their hypocrisies, un-Christ-like judgementalisms and condemnations, and the self-righteousness that supersedes their *own* relationship to Christ – whatever may exist of it – precedes their self-imposed complexities. Don't allow them to give you guilt trips, nor make you stumble with doubt as to your walk with Christ. For, to those who have answered, you *have* the light of Christ, even in those bad days when it seems like nothing is working out – yet *still* he is there, by your side, and *carrying you* as no one else can. The light may look a bit dimmer to you, but he is there. Just like that small light in the arena. It may be faint, but it *is* there.

And then there are days where his light shines forth like a 10,000 watt floodlight in your life. Yea, those days are awesome as well! But whatever the days – or nights – in your life, he is there. Always faithfully shining, never wanning – always consistent in its shimmer. So when they try and beat your door down, keep your *eyes* on that light – not on their flapping. Listening always to *him* – not to *them*. Again, as Christ said: "whoever follows me will *never* walk in darkness but will have the light of life." Let them bury their *own* cats – and lovingly tell them to leave yours alone! And move on – with the Light of the world always by your side.

And then there are others who – though religious in practice – *also* follow the Light as you do – and this not through self-righteousness, nor through a reliance on tradition – but by an unshakable confidence on Christ, the Light of mankind. They *too* are your brothers and sisters in Christ – to those who believe – so always encourage them, and take care not to make *them* stumble – whatever 'denomination', church, or *non*-church-goer it might be. Whatever sexual preference they might be of, and however many 'dates' they might rightfully enjoy (for it is no one's business but their own anyway). For we're talking spirit here, not the passing idiosyncrasies of life.  For if they practice truth, and have thereby come to the Light of Christ, they have come *through* God – and in God they *will* remain.

Christ was one day walking amongst a multitude of people, being pressed by the crowds, and a woman who had had a hemorrhage for twelve years came up behind him and touched him. He turned around and stated that *someone* had touched him. His disciples said that *many* were pressing against him as he walked, to where it would be *impossible* to know who he was referring to as having 'touched' him. But he stated that he had felt power leave him, especially in reference to a particular person having *deliberately* touched him. The woman, trembling, came up to him and stated that it was she, and told how she had been *immediately* healed when she had in fact touched him out of her *own* faith and conviction that she would *in fact* be healed if she would merely touch the hem of his garment.

Christ told her that her faith had made her well, to go in peace.[1] He did *not* say to her that she now had to join some religious group, or jump through dogmatic hoops and practices, or that she now was obliged to live by a set of do's and don'ts. He simply stated that her faith was

---

[1] Luke 8:40-48

*sufficient* – and to go in peace. *That* is the Light of the world.

Christ is all about a *personal* faith. Much – but certainly *not* all, not in the least – of modern-day Christianity, on the other hand – as is the case with most other religious establishments of today – is about dull *religion* and its varied dogmas, theologies, traditions, dictates, and politics. I hope that you might understand this significant difference by now – thought you probably have already known this for quite some time at this point in life.

Christ is the Light of the world. And it is he *alone* – *as* the Light of mankind – who provides that rock-solid and unbreakable peace, innermost joy, and enduring satisfaction and self-fulfillment at the very *core* of the simple, no-fluff-added believer. Yes, it is these things that He alone *freely* provides to any and all who will come, and which can *never* be snatched away – these essential elements to being *fully* human, and fully *alive,* on which many have sought to reach by other means through ineffective personal effort: such as attempts at self-enlightenment, ritualistic practices of self-sacrifice; and the deification of man-made objects, philosophies, and re-invented dogmas of every sort. But such as these can only be had by Him alone – the one and only Creator of all who is the *sole* source that can ever *genuinely* fill the void within that others have attempted to fill through cheap substitutions, dissipation, and the approval of others – and yes, even by dry and self-imposed religiosity itself. For, concerning light, Christ also stated that:

> The eye is the lamp of the body. So, if your eye is healthy, your whole body will be full of light; but if your eye is *unhealthy*, your whole body will be full of darkness. If then the light in you is darkness, how great is the darkness!
>
> MATTHEW 6:22-23

So don't waste your time with silly things. Keep looking to the Light, and you will *never* go wrong. For only the Light of Christ *alone* can fill the void, as a key can only fit the lock it has been made for. In turn, we ourselves as individuals are *made* for God, and for the Kingdom of God, in the same unique manner that no one else can substitute nor take the place of...just like no one can ever take *your* place. Do you believe it? Tis so true, you know. For, as has been rightly illustrated:

> The mold in which a key is made would be a strange thing, if you had never seen a key: and the key itself a strange thing if you had never seen a lock. Your soul has a curious shape because it is a hollow made to fit a particular swelling in the infinite contours of the divine substance, or a key to unlock one of the doors in the house with many mansions...
>
> But God will look to every soul like its first love because He *is* its first love. Your place in heaven will seem to be made for you and you alone, because you were made for it – made for it stitch by stitch as a glove is made for a hand...Now God, who has made us, knows what we are and that *our happiness lies in Him*.[2]

For on Christ – the Son of the Living God as well as *the* Son of Man – you *can* depend on. The Light of the world, on whom *billions* have set their hope on. On him one can depend on - fully and absolutely. Utterly, and without rival. For he *is* the only key that can fill the void within. And we are, individually, the keys that fit his everlasting love – all of us uniquely and without any other substitution on which he patiently waits to unlock his love for – that love that comes

---

[2] As in C.S. Lewis, *The Problem of Pain*. HarperOne, 2001.

*rushing in* when we are finally willing to trust enough to *let* in. And when we *finally* let go of ourselves, and let the Light shine in, we become children of light, as Christ termed it:

> While you have the light, *believe* in the light, so that you may *become* children of light.
>
> JOHN 12:36

As has rightly been stated in the aforementioned quote regarding the lock and key, Christ is *indeed* the First Love[3] to those who have accepted his invitation to come and follow him. This term, *First Love*, was used in the book of REVELATIONS in the New Testament, where Christ says to the church in Ephesus that, although they have been eager in following rules of religiosity, and in protecting Christian doctrine against false teachers, that they have nonetheless lost sight of their First Love – that being Christ *himself*. For as has been rightly said:

> Even though they were doing a lot of right things, many lost sight as to who they were called into a relationship with.

---

[3] As per Revelations 2:4. See also the song, *First Love*, as recorded by the Christian rock band Stryper, *Soldiers Under Command album*. Hollywood Records, 1985.

> While struggling to defend against doctrinal corruption, they lost sight of the most important aspect of their Christianity—Jesus Christ Himself. While it is essential to remain faithful to the teaching once delivered (Jude 3), Christians must remember their relationship with Christ is paramount... Jesus Christ did not want His followers to merely embrace yet another religion and primarily be concerned with lists of dos and don'ts. Colossians 2:20-22, summarizes the typical legalistic and ascetic religions of the world... [4]

These referred-to verses in the New Testament book of COLOSSIANS stating that:

> If with Christ you died to the elemental spirits of the universe, why do you live as if you still belonged to the world? Why do you submit to *regulations*, 'Do not handle, Do not taste, Do not touch'? All these regulations refer to things that perish with use; they are simply *human commands and teachings*. These have indeed an *appearance* of wisdom in promoting self-imposed piety, humility, and severe treatment of the body, but they are of *no value*, serving only to indulge the flesh.
>
> COLOSSIANS 2:20-23

---

[4] As in Tom Damour, *Do You Still Have Your First Love?* . Volume 9, 3rd edition. Virtual Christian Magazine, March 2007.

It is interesting to note, in regards to the oppressive and unnecessary religious regulations that were being spoken against in the above scriptures, that:

> There is much plausibility in this; and this has been the foundation of the appointment of the fasts and festivals of the church; of penances and self-inflicted tortures; of painful vigils and pilgrimages; of works of supererogation, and of the merits of the 'saints.' A large part of the corruptions of religion have arisen from this plausible but deceitful argument... The effect of these observances, on which so much stress is laid as if they would promote piety, is merely to gratify pride, self-righteousness, the love of distinction, and the other carnal propensities of our nature. There seems to be a great deal of humility and piety in them; there is really little else than pride, selfishness, and ambition.[5]

Even so, *not* everyone who follows such strict religious observances are either prideful or selfish – not in the least! But there are the few who do in fact do such religious things out of a desire to appear more righteous than others, and it is they who make the rest who are involved in such things stumble in their faith and doubtful

---

[5] As in Barnes (as in n. 1 on page xviii).

of the worthiness or 'correctness' of their walk with God. That is why it is vital to keep one's eyes on the Light, rather than on either religious practice or "exceedingly religious" people. Again, it is Christ who is the Light of man, and not piety, religious observance, nor those who most grossly fixate on it. To look to such as these for approval, rather than on Christ himself, only places one on the path of either abandonment of faith, or spiritual self-destruction.  For the follower of Christ – always let your focus be on the Light of the world, rather than on the dry and unfulfilling morsels of forced religious observance.

> ...Jesus Christ came to introduce a new way of living motivated by a unique relationship between God and the believer. That relationship, when properly understood would radically alter the way people respond to each other and the world. 'By this all will know that you are My disciples, if you have love for one another' (John 13:35). The message to the church at Ephesus remains relevant after almost two millennia.  It warns God's people against losing sight of the importance of having a proper relationship with Him. It warns us to not confuse legalism (supposing salvation is earned by works) with true Christianity. We are warned against

confusing knowledge about God with the
righteousness of God.[6]

So, therefore, it is not religion, nor religious piety,
nor ritual and self-sacrifice, nor knowledge of God
in place of how He may deal with and lead us
personally and individually by His Holy Spirit
of Truth – it is not bland works and humdrum
ritual that *reveal* the Light of the world. Not at
all. Rather, it is Christ *himself* who gives light,
and is *himself* Light. For, in respect to Christ:

> The light shines in the darkness, and the
> darkness did *not* overcome it.
> JOHN 1:5

Thus, it is implored that the reader not waste
time allowing those who have exalted religiosity
above God Himself to steal your faith and make
you into yet *another* Pharisee or Sadducee – a
religious *slave* – of modern-day religion. Look
to Christ, instead of on organized religion and
its many rules, regulations, and devices, and you
will not go wrong. For it is only the faith of a
child that matters – in fact, it is all that *really*
counts to God – *not* being religious for the sake
of it, nor bearing its countless entanglements. So

---

[6] As continued from Damour (as in n. 4 on page 108).

go ahead – reach out, by faith, and touch the hem of his garment directly as the woman who boldly pressed through the crowd did with the faith of a child that she *would* be healed, and this *without* the need for religiosity to be your channel to God. And he *will* heal you. No religion necessary. Just a simple faith and the willingness to just *go for it*. You can do it right where you are – right here, right now. You don't have to wait for anything, anybody, or any approval.[7] It doesn't matter if you're currently on a crowded bus, if you're at your work desk, if you're on a plane, if you're with your family, if you're in a bar, if on your porcelain throne, or if your alone. He *will* hear you, and touch you, and heal you – because *he is* the Light of the world.

Whatever religion, whatever background or upbringing, whatever culture or nation or sex or sexual preference you may be of, *whomever* you are or *whatever* you are. . . everyone *needs* Christ in their life – for He *is* the Light of the World.

---

[7] As loosely paraphrased from the song *Reach Out*, as per Rance Allen, *Front Row Live: The Rance Allen Group*. Tyscot Records, 2007; the viewing of which is highly recommended.

Then Jesus cried aloud: 'Whoever believes in me believes not in me but in Him who sent me. And whoever sees me sees Him who sent me. *I have come as Light into the world, so that everyone who believes in me should not remain in the darkness.* I do not judge anyone who hears my words and does not keep them, for I came *not* to judge the world, but to *save* the world. The one who rejects me and does not receive my word has a judge; on the last day the word that I have spoken will serve as judge, for I have not spoken on my own, but the Father who sent me has Himself given me a commandment about what to say and what to speak. And I know that his commandment is eternal life. What I speak, therefore, I speak just as the Father has told me.'

JOHN 12:44-50

# The Particulars of
# the Gospel of Christ

Chapter Eight

# *Who Can You Trust?*

So therefore, if one can accept that the modern Bible is authentic and true to its original manuscripts, if Jesus is in fact the Messiah long-awaited from days of old, and if the Gospels should thereby be heeded as principle authorities on what Christ said and what he did – even *when* modern Christianity has at times taken on tangents that are oftentimes not completely in sync with who Christ was, what he taught, and what examples he gave his followers to follow – than who *can* we trust in this day and age to reflect the heart, love, and instructions of Jesus Christ?

Some say all written scripture is God's authority, and – to the believer – they tell the truth when even Christ quoted the Old Testament, and in addition to this clearly stated that we must listen to *him*, because *he* has the words of life,[1] and he himself *brings* about life, and *is* life.[2] For even the Father is said to have stated of Christ,

> This is My beloved Son, in whom I am well pleased. Listen to *Him*.
> MATTHEW 3:17; 17:5; LUKE 3:22; & MARK 9:7

Of course, He did *not* say "listen to Paul", or to your church leader, or to popular theological opinion in the place of Christ, or to religious fads or politically-correct dogma, or anything of the sort. No. He said, "Listen to *Him*".

Thus neither Christ, nor the Father, nor anyone else in the Bible, ever mention letters written by anybody coming *after* Christ as their words being considered the exclusive and unadulterated

---

[1] As Jesus said,

> It is the spirit that gives life; the flesh is useless. The words that I have spoken to you are spirit and life.

[2] As Jesus said, right before he raised Lazarus from the dead – one of many accounts where he did the same on other occasions:

> I am the resurrection and the life. Those who believe in me, even though they die, will live; and everyone who lives and believes in me will never die. Do you believe this? [John 11:25-26]

words of God – though God *does* inspire mankind, as He does even today. For even Paul himself stated that "all scripture is inspired by God"[3] when he clearly referred to the Old Testament scriptures; as he was not so arrogant as to consider his *own* letters to the early churches to be the unadulterated words of God – though they *too* were inspired and enrich Christ's followers with much understanding of who Christ was, why he came, and why we are justified for our sins – for *"all* have sinned and fallen short of the glory of God"[4] – and this not through being 'religious' or doing 'religious things' ... as Paul aptly put it – "not by works, so that no man can boast".[5]

Thus, to those who believe, we are justified before God, as Paul himself correctly explained, by the simple yet very much *personal* choice of accepting Christ's gift for us on the cross, in that "God proves His love for us in that while we were

---

[3] II Timothy 3:16

[4] Romans 3:23

[5] As stated by Paul:

> For by grace you have been saved through faith, and this is not your own doing; it is the gift of God— not the result of works, so that no one may boast. [Ephesians 2:8-9]

still sinners, Christ died for us"[6] – his having
taken the place of everyone who has ever and
who *would ever* live, onto the cross of Calvary –
God incarnate becoming the sacrificial lamb that
would take our place much like a loving father
might choose to take the place of his adult child
in a court case that has pronounced the sentence
of death for the crimes his child committed... and
all that the child has to do is simply *accept* his
father's undeserved gift of death in exchange for
his own life by a humble, child-like trust through
an accepting faith that is *willing* to receive such
an undeserved act of love that has no strings
attached and that is freely given for the taking.
And what *is* faith? As the Bible describes it:

> Now faith is the assurance of things hoped
> for, the conviction of things *not* seen.
> HEBREWS 11:1

For the believer, the *acceptance* by faith of Christ's
sacrifice on the cross as his having taken our
place for what we deserve as sinners against
God's righteousness is all there is to it in order to
*become* a child of God. That's all that's required
in order to have a direct, non-religiously tainted,

---

[6] Romans 5:8

relationship *with* God.  Nothing more, nothing less.  That *is* the Gospel – the Good News – of Christ.

But why would God do such a thing?  And why should He do such a thing to mere mortals who, compared to God, are nothing but meager, worthless ants?  Well, apparently, in God's eyes, we are so much *more* than just mere ants.  We are *His* creation.  Created in *His* image.  We are *His* children.  *His* creation.  *His* pleasure.  The *love* of His life.

But come on!  How can God give a care about such worthless creatures?  Be realistic!  Well ... we are *His* children.  *His* image.  *His* love.

Are you a parent?  Maybe you can somewhat see what I'm talking about.  Would you not do just about *anything* for your kids?  No matter *what* kind of trouble they might get into?  No matter *who* they are, or what they might one day grow up to become?  Well, God's love is just that, only magnified immeasurably to such an extent that we cannot even *begin* to know its full scope as it relates to every single one of us as unique individuals.  Yes, *that* is His ever-empowering, never-ending love for us all.  For you.  For me.  For your neighbor.  For your sad, conniving boss.  For the terrorist on the news. For the weird homeless guy in your neighborhood. For your nagging partner. For your eye-wandering husband. For your parents. For your children. For *you*. And he would do it all over again even if you were the *only* person on earth. For God *is* love. He is *pure* love ... and He is pure *justice*.

Yes, He *is* pure justice. For, how would one feel if someone like Hitler could get away with what he did to millions of God's people unless he truly had *in sincerity* turned with the honest trust and humility of a child and *genuinely* accepted God's offer of forgiveness that applies to any and all without reservation? God *is* just.

Yes, Christ took the place of death on the cross for people like Hitler as well. But without receiving Christ's having taken their place – much like that child sentenced to death who, out of free will, *chose* to accept his own father's unreserved and undeserved substitution for his execution – well, I don't know. Only God can say. Even so, the *beatitudes* that Christ spoke during his ministry on earth seem, to me at least, to be *universal* laws that apply to everyone regardless of who they might be. Maybe I'm wrong, but it seems that a promise is a promise, and God certainly never goes back on His word. Therefore, I just assume the following beatitudes, as Christ spoke them, apply to everyone for whom each may be relevant to without exception – these being, as he stated:

> Blessed [*or, happy, fortunate, blissful*] are the poor [*or, humble*] in spirit, for theirs is the kingdom of heaven.
> Blessed are those who mourn, for they will be comforted.
> Blessed are the meek, for they will inherit the earth.
> Blessed are those who hunger and thirst for righteousness, for they will be filled.
> Blessed are the merciful, for they will *receive* mercy.
> Blessed are the pure in heart, for they *will* see God.
> Blessed are the peacemakers, for they will be called *children* of God.
> Blessed are those who are persecuted *for righteousness' sake*, for theirs is the kingdom of heaven.
> Blessed are you when people revile you and persecute you and utter all kinds of evil against you falsely on *my* account. Rejoice and be glad, for your reward is great in heaven, for in the same way they persecuted the prophets who were before you.
>
> MATTHEW 5:3-12

Furthermore, in the Gospel of Luke, Christ also states:

> Blessed are you who are poor, for *yours* is the kingdom of God. Blessed are you who are hungry now, for you *will* be filled. Blessed are you who weep now, for you will *laugh*. Blessed are you when people hate you, and when they *exclude* you, revile you, and defame you on account of the Son of Man. Rejoice in that day and leap for joy, for surely your reward is *great* in heaven; for that is what *their* ancestors did to the prophets. But woe to you who are rich, for you have received your consolation. Woe to you who are full now, for you will be hungry. Woe to you who are laughing now, for you will mourn and weep. Woe to you when all speak well of you, for that is what their ancestors did to the *false* prophets.
>
> LUKE 6:20-26

Furthermore, Christ's teachings primarily revolved around compassion, faith, mercy – and, of course, love. As such, what James wrote makes a lot of sense when he says:

> So speak and so act as those who are to be judged by the law of liberty. For judgment will be without mercy to anyone who has shown no mercy; for mercy triumphs over judgment. [JAMES 2:12-13]

And Christ taught about *justice*. And God *is* just, to where someone *must* pay the penalty for our sins – for we are all sinners, one way or another. If it's not murder, it is hatred, unforgiveness, or vindictiveness. If it is not religious self-righteousness, it is arrogance. If not unprovoked violence, than it is the condemnation and judgement of the innocent from within our hearts. We're *all* sinners in one way or another. Yes, God *is* just, as He is merciful, compassionate, and unconditionally loving to one and all. And someone must pay the penalty... or He would not be pure justice, would He? And His justice, if not seen in this life, *will* be seen in the next. Yes, someone must pay the price. But His justice is absolutely fair, and utterly balanced – and will never be in any way *inferior* to the very best that we ourselves would do – even thought we ourselves are imperfect.

In the same way, *because* God is just, and because there is no wavering nor change in Him, He *will* balance everything out ... for everyone who *has* ever, and who *will* ever live. He *will* give you the justice you seek – even if you never seem to get it in *this* life.

As such, when one is persecuted for the sake of righteousness – as we see in the above beatitudes – Christ says that that person should *rejoice*, for their reward will be great in heaven. He will level *everything* out. For all that is secret *will* be made know. As Christ put it bluntly:

> So have no fear of them; for *nothing* is covered up that will not be uncovered, and nothing secret that will not become known.
>
> MATTHEW 10:26

When it's all said and done, and we exit this life, *everyone* will know *everything* about everybody and everything else – everything that God allows to be known, at least. And that is why "vengeance is *Mine* to take, says the Lord",[7] to where – to those who believe – we *can* "turn the other cheek" and love our enemies in action if not in sentiment[8] – that's *our* job. *His* job is to do the vengeance part, not us. For He *will* – without

---

[7] Romans 12:17-19

[8] As Christ said:

> If anyone strikes you on the cheek, offer the other also; and from anyone who takes away your coat do not withhold even your shirt. Give to everyone who begs from you; and if anyone takes away your goods, do not ask for

even the smallest passing shadow of a doubt –
bring about justice to those who put their trust on
Him[9]...*oh* so guaranteed! So when you do not see
justice being done on this earth, just "wait upon
the Lord";[10] for, as my super-awesome loving
mother says, "God *never* sleeps". And go ahead
and, with boldness, *pray* for your enemies[11] –

---

them again. Do to others as you would have
them do to you. [Luke 6:29-31]

[9] As Christ stated,

And will not God grant justice to his chosen
ones who cry to him day and night? Will he
delay long in helping them? I tell you, he will
quickly grant justice to them. And yet, when
the Son of Man comes, will he find faith on
earth? [Luke 18:7-8]

[10] As is rightly said:

...but those who wait for the Lord shall renew
their strength, they shall mount up with
wings like eagles, they shall run and not be
weary, they shall walk and not faint. [Isaiah
40:31]

[11] As Christ said:

But I say to you that listen – Love your
enemies, do good to those who hate you, bless
those who curse you, pray for those who abuse
you. [Luke 6:27-28]

even if that prayer merely consists of you asking God that at the very least they wake up and *genuinely* turn to the Light someday. That's praying for your enemies, is it not?

Yes, God never – *ever* – sleeps, and He *will* bring about justice for those who call to Him day and night, and this He will do *quickly* – in *His* perfect timing... as He *always* does.[12] For God will *never* contradict Himself. He *is* pure love. He has given every single one of us – past, present, and future – a way out. He *is* pure justice. He will *not* allow those who hurt His children – that's *you* – to get away with it.

Yet He *is* abundantly merciful. And He is ever *faithful* to forgive those who sincerely turn to Him and accept the gift of salvation that He has provided to anyone and everyone who accepts it in spirit and in truth by His Son's death on the cross, and life through his resurrection from the stench of death that just could *not* hold him down. God is *Spirit*... so that those who accept Him will do so "in spirit and in truth". For as Christ himself said:

---

[12] Luke 18:7-8; as per note 9 on the preceding page.

> But the hour is coming, and is now here,
> when the *true* worshipers will worship the
> Father *in spirit and truth*, for the Father
> seeks such as these to worship him. God
> is spirit, and those who worship him must
> worship in spirit and truth.
> JOHN 4:23-24

Not through being religious, not by balancing out
the good and the bad that one has done (for it
will *never* balance out in comparison to God's
righteousness), and not by being a prude. No.
This is *God's* undeserved gift to any and all who
are *willing* to come to Him...from within our
spirit, and in sincerity of heart...*just as we are.*
With *all* of our imperfections, sins, doubts, fears,
troubles, stubbornness, and hangups. *Just as
we are.* He takes care of the rest. His gift of
total and complete forgiveness is given to any
and all – without having to somehow "clean up"
our lives beforehand – for *only* God can do that.
And without needing to go to a church to do
it. Without having to become 'religious', nor
having to somehow *appease* "religious people".
Ha! They're just like anyone else, or have you not
already noticed long ago? We are *all* the same
in one way or another. Imperfect, fallible, often
wrong, and in need of something greater than

our *own* selves. Just as we find ourselves at this precise moment in time. You could even open your door to Him now, and just *let* Him in. No need for ceremony, location, or mood. All it takes is a simple *turn* – just a slight shift in attitude – towards His love. Nothing more. Nothing less. In spirit and in truth.

Yes indeed – *only* in spirit – *your* spirit with God's Spirit – and in truth. Why do we complicate such a simple invitation to come with such things as religiosity and man-made religious obligation, man-made tradition, rules, regulations, and oppressions of every sort;[13] when we can *instead* have it all just by opening our doors to follow *Him*, and Him *without* religion... in spirit and in truth? Again – no prerequisites, no experience needed. Just as you are. In spirit and in truth.

If you saw a colony of ants in your garden and wanted to communicate with them, how would

---

[13] As Jesus Christ himself stated in Matthew 23:4-7, on speaking about religious leaders of his day who behaved in similar manners as we see many – but certainly *not* all – in organized religion likewise doing today:

> They tie up heavy burdens, hard to bear, and lay them on the shoulders of others; but they themselves are unwilling to lift a finger to move them. [Matthew 23:4-7]

*you* do it? Could you scream and shout at them in the hopes that they might *somehow* understand you? Good luck with that!

But think about it for a second – how *would* one go about communicating with a whole colony of ants? Well, maybe if you *became* an ant yourself, than *maybe* you could get something accomplished. *Maybe.* I guess the rest would be up to the ants, and whether they would accept you as their own or not.

But hold on a minute! Are you saying that God became an *ant* in order to communicate with us? Well, not exactly, but somewhat in that line of thinking. To the believer, God's love for the world – His precious and unique creation, His children, His kids – was so great that he became like one of *us* Himself. And in addition to this, He took it upon *Himself* to be the sacrifice who would take *our* place of death in order that we might *have* life, and have it *abundantly*[14] – in other words,

---

[14] So again Jesus said to them, "Very truly, I tell you, I am the gate for the sheep. All who came before me are thieves and bandits; but the sheep did not listen to them. I am the gate. Whoever enters by me will be saved, and will come in and go out and find pasture. The thief comes only to steal and kill and destroy. I came that they may have life, and have it abundantly." [John 10:7-10]

so that we would be *fully* human as God intended
by being fully fulfilled, fully loved, fully at peace,
and fully forgiven, justified, and made right – and
this not by *anything* we might try to do, but by
who we *belong* to. Well, maybe some don't want
to *belong* to anybody. But when you are *connected*
to the Creator and Perfecter of the Universe ...
watch out world! Because nothing can beat that!
*Nothing*.

Yes – as imperfect as we are, we can *all* be
connected to the Creator of it all. No questions
asked. He wipes the slate clean, to where what
God sees in us is the cleansing blood of Jesus,
*without* our imperfections and sins. He wipes the
slate clean. A new beginning. And one that can
*never* be taken away from us. No, not *ever*. Even
when we stumble and fall – and we always will,
for we are but *human*. No, not even then. All
we need to do is to *just keep following*. Just don't
quit. Just keep at it, and this possibly with my
motto in mind, if you will:

Faith in God – *Always* Forward

Don't let them get you down, baby. Don't worry
about what 'they' might say. When one comes
to Christ, one is made totally clean before Him –

like a spotless lamb that is completely blameless in His sight, as the Christian rock song *Clean* rightly says.[15] And *because* He lives, and because we know He holds the future – we *can* face tomorrow, all fear dissipates, and life does *indeed* become worth the living.[16] To those who believe, He *is* walking in your shoes, reaching out with *your* hands, smiling with *your* face, and will continually show you the way – because He lives *in* you.[17]

It *is* an undeserved gift, and this in order that His perfect and unconditional Agape love and unchanging justice be manifest *fully* in our own lives. And what *is* God's Agape love? On defining the Greek word *agape* – one of the terms often used to describe God's unconditional love for us – much like the unconditional love between a parent and child – it is rightly said that:

---

[15] As paraphrased from the song *Clean*, as by Petra, *Beat the System album*. 1985; the listening of which is highly recommended.

[16] As paraphrased from the song *Because He Lives*, as per Bill Gaither and Gloria Gaither, *Because He Lives*. Warner/Chappell Music, 1971.

[17] As paraphrased from the song *He's Walking in My Shoes,* as per B.J. Thomas, *You Gave Me Love [When Nobody Gave Me A Prayer] album*. Myrrh Records, 2010; the listening of this album being highly recommended.

> If we could imagine the love of one who
> loves men purely for their own sake, and
> not because of any need or desire of his
> own, purely desires their good, and yet
> loves them wholly, not for what at this
> moment they are, but for what he knows
> he can make of them because he made
> them, then we should have in our minds
> some true image of the love of the Father
> and Creator of mankind.[18]

Yes, we've *all* fallen short of God's expectations.
But to the believer, Jesus Christ came to communicate God's good news – *His* Gospel – yes,
the Gospel *according to* Christ – His undying
and eternal love for you and I. He came to take
our place under the penalty of death in order to
give *us* life ...  and so that we *could have* life.
A spring of living water from within that would
*never* dry up. Not in *this* life, and certainly not in
the next. Living water that would flow eternally
from within, to where we would *never* die. For,

> On the last and greatest day of the festi-
> val, Jesus stood and said in a loud voice,
> 'Let anyone who is thirsty come to me and
> drink. Whoever believes in me, as Scrip-
> ture has said, rivers of living water will

---

[18] As in O.C. Quick, *Doctrines of the Creed*. Scribners,
1938.

flow from within them.' By this he meant
the Spirit, whom those who believed in
him were later to receive.

JOHN 7:37-39

And He rose again on the third day so that we
might live...because *He* lives. No good works
required. No religion necessary. No piety, compulsion, strings attached, sacrifice, or obligation.
Just a simple *acceptance* of God the Father's love
– and the ultimate price His Son was totally
and unreservedly – *freely* – willing to pay in
exchange for the road we were headed on from
within – protecting us *from ourselves*, loving us
*unconditionally,* whomever we are ... *just as we
are*. Nothing more. Nothing less. As has been
aptly put by C.S. Lewis, again in regards to God's
unconditional *Agape* love for us:

> God has no needs. Human love, as Plato
> teaches us, is the child of Poverty – of want
> or lack; it is caused by a real or supposed
> goal in its beloved which the lover needs
> and desires. But God's love, far from being
> caused by goodness in the object, causes
> all the goodness which the object has,
> loving it first into existence, and then into
> real, though derivative, lovability. God is
> Goodness. He can give good, but cannot
> need or get it. In that sense, His love is,

as it were, bottomlessly selfless by very
definition; it has everything to give, and
nothing to receive.[19]

And that is why there truly *is* goodness in everyone – if we look hard enough for it, as sometimes
we must. But it *is* there. It is so very true,
that God "causes all the goodness which the
object has" – as stated above by C.S. Lewis –
because God Himself *is* good – and He Himself
*is* Goodness. Likewise, I would add, God causes
*faith* within us – whether we choose to use it
or not. It is there as well, so that no one can
truly state that they "have no faith". Rather, one
chooses, out of free will, whether one will *use* the
faith that God has given him, or not. But that
in and of *itself* is a personal choice – much like
it is a personal choice whether one will use the
goodness that they have within themselves, or
not. For God is also *freedom*. And He will not
run His Universe like a clan of robots that are
destined to do His will – for that would not be
genuine, unconditional love now, would it?

But again, in regards to the word of God,
and who we can trust if *even* certain self-labeled

---

[19] As in Lewis, *The Problem of Pain* (as in n. 2 on
page 106).

Christians *themselves* seem not to truly reflect the love of Christ, while at the same time claiming to follow the word of God – are they *indeed* doing the very thing they oftentimes zealously claim to be doing? For even scripture clearly states that it is Christ *himself* who is the Word of God. Christ is the *Living* Word of God.[20] We must be careful not to substitute this for something else. To do so, I believe, is to commit idolatry...placing man's words and traditions above God's, as the Jewish leaders commonly did in Christ's day – and as many preachers, self-proclaimed "gurus", "yogi masters", religious speakers, denominations, and religions still do today. For only Christ can make such a claim – considering what we have seen in Chapter 2 as his having been the undisputed Messiah that was talked about in the Old Testament, knowing of the works he performed, and realizing the Deity that was inherent within him *exclusively* and without rival...God in man, in the literal sense – to those who believe, of course.

That is why we must take care what we listen to – be it current religious opinion regarding

---

[20] As seen from Chapter 1 on page 19 in John 1:1-14.

homosexuality[21] or premarital sex;[22] be it your
preacher, teacher, or church leaders; be it popular
opinion or the latest religious craze[23]... or be it
this very book even. For on Christ we *have* the
Word of God – to those who are believers – and by
the guidance of his Spirit of Truth are we set *free*
from the confusions of contradictory theology, as-
sorted religions, innumerable philosophies, and
volatile opinions. For as Christ himself said:

> Therefore, everyone who hears these words
> of Mine and *acts* on them, may be com-
> pared to a wise man who built his house on
> the rock. And the rain fell, and the floods
> came, and the winds blew and slammed

---

[21] See Appendix C on page 433 for a fuller explanation
of why homosexuality is a characteristic from birth as
allowed by one's Creator, so that homosexuals must not be
condemned for being who they were meant to be from the
beginning.

[22] See Appendix B on page 397 in regards to how
premarital sex is *not* adultery, and how the Bible seems to
never *explicitly* condemn premarital sex... despite all that
you might have heard before.

[23] See Appendix A on page 357 regarding how new and
*seemingly* lovely and ever-welcoming community groups,
short classes, and philosophies marketed under the guise of
*spirituality* have in many instances taking the place of God,
while exalting the self *as* God – which, of course, is idolatry;
as well as Chapter 14 on page 307, which provides the
reader with the tell-tale signs of controlling and oppressive
cults that likewise attempt to subtly *replace* God with pulp
fiction and the traditions of man.

against that house; and *yet* it did not fall, for it had been founded on the rock. Everyone who hears these words of Mine and does *not* act on them, will be like a foolish man who built his house on the sand. The rain fell, and the floods came, and the winds blew and slammed against that house; and it fell – and great was its fall.

MATTHEW 6:24-27

Why else would he have told us not to call anyone on earth our teachers,[24] as those who have opened their hearts to him already *have* a teacher and leader – the Holy Spirit of the *living* Christ himself – who can *never* be substituted for either religion or the fallacies of man. To do so – to hold to someone else's teaching over and above that of Christ's, and over what his Spirit may testify to those who have *turned* to Christ – is to risk turning what Christianity is meant to

---

[24] As having been quoted from Chapter 1 on page 3:

But you are not to be called 'Rabbi' [*spiritual leader, teacher, and guru*], for you have only one Master and you are all brothers. And do not call anyone on earth 'father' [*'spiritual father'*], for you have one Father, and He is in heaven. Nor are you to be called 'teacher', for you have one Teacher, the Christ. [Matthew 23:8-10]

stand for from its very *origin* as the good news of God drawing mankind to Himself through a simple child-like faith – and into an *organized* and oftentimes imperfect form of religion that is based on man's opinions, traditions, and dogmas – most likely organizational, judgemental, and rigid in style, as opposed to Christ-like in spirit and purpose. For Christ did not come to burden man's souls with yet *another* organized form of religion... but to *free* them *himself*, as he *alone* does the work in our lives.[25]

And herein lies the critical and most obvious difference between any *religion*'s irrational and very much *burdensome* demands regarding the subjugation to a set of behaviors and rules within a predetermined list of recommendations, long-held traditions, and man-made inventions – as opposed to Christ's teaching of a simple, *child-like* faith and completely surrendered *reliance* on

---

[25] For as Christ himself explained,

> Come to me, all you that are weary and are carrying heavy burdens, and I will give you rest. Take my yoke upon you, and learn from me; for I am gentle and humble in heart, and you will find rest for your souls. For my yoke is easy, and my burden is light. [Matthew 11:28-30]

our Creator; as well as a self-acceptance that does not oppress the ego – but rather expands and matures it into what God meant for mankind to be *from the beginning* – free, and without man-made enchainments nor fragile dependencies to rigid and uncompromising systems and traditions of man.

In essence – to the believing reader – let Christ *himself* be your authority. *Trust* him. Trust him above all others. For he *is* the Living Word of God – the Holy Spirit being *his* Spirit within each and every one who opens their door to him *just as they are* and at *whatever point* in life that they might find themselves at – whether good or bad, happy or sad, victorious or tragic, isolated or within a crowd, intelligent or plain, religious or not. It is *his* Spirit of Truth who reminds us of everything that he taught the world in the Gospels. And it is *his* Holy Spirit who leads us all – without *any* exclusion or exception whatsoever – into *all* truth in a day and age where empty hearts and minds abound, and where multiple voices will often tear down those who would quickly put too much trust in their words and philosophies...yet they never *can* overcome.

For he himself has said,

> These things I have spoken to you, so that
> in Me you may have peace. In the world
> you have tribulation, but take courage, I
> have *overcome* the world.
>
> JOHN 16:33

For that *is* the Gospel of Christ. As was rightly
stated by Paul, "Let God be true and every man a
liar."[26]

I believe that it is *not* Paul – nor his words,
opinions, and occasional admonishments – nor
anyone else who has ever – or *will* ever – live, who
is truth. For it is only Christ – God incarnate who
stooped down so low in order to *unconditionally*
love a weary soul such as I – who has plainly said,

> *I* am the way, and the truth, and the life.
> No one comes to the Father except through
> me.
>
> JOHN 14:6

---

[26] As expressed by Paul himself in Romans 3:3-4,

> What then? If some did not believe, their
> unbelief will not nullify the faithfulness of
> God, will it? May it never be! Rather, let God
> be found true, though every man be found a
> liar.

Hence, it is my *personal* conviction that those who *genuinely* come to God in spirit and in truth – irregardless of what 'religion' (or *no* religion) they might claim to ascribe to, come to and *through* Christ, because Christ and the Father *are* one. Again, this is only my own *personal* opinion. And if they therefore came *through* Christ, than they should praise him for who he is – for if those who have heard his voice have come to the Father *through* him, than it is *He* who is worthy of our love and praise – not some man-made god, concept, philosophy, prophet, or whatever the case might be. And anyone who honors the Son and what He stands for honors the Father who sent him. Only you and God know if you have ever done so yourself... maybe you don't even *realize* that you have, I don't know. No one can judge you. Nor should you *let* anyone judge you. It is not their place, and it is not on them that you have placed your trust on. For only *He* sees your heart, and nobody else. Yet such lasting assurance, peace, and rock-solid stability from *within* cannot be had by anything else, nor through any form of *religiousness* nor self-defining '*righteousness*' that this world has to

offer – as when one comes to the Son of the Living
God *directly* and says:

> Jesus, thank you for your unconditional
> love for me. I don't have anything to offer
> back to you. But I *welcome you* into my
> life. Thank you for making me yours.

It becomes a *personal* experience – an *intimate*
one-on-one... without *any* sign or notion of religion, without the approvals of mankind, and
without doctrine and theology. But those who
have *somehow* – in simplicity of spirit and sincerity of truth – turned to the Father and honor the
Son – in whatever unique way that God reaches
out to each and every one of us – I believe in
my *own* humble opinion are part of the family
of Christ. For those who do *not* honor the Son
obviously do *not* honor what he stands for – for
he stands for love, hope, peace, compassion, and
mercy – and therefore cannot in their hearts
honor the Father who sent him. For, as Jesus
plainly said,

I and the Father are *One*. [27] [JOHN 10:30]

------

[27] Or literally translated to *one essence*, or *unity* – herein
referring *not* to some 'New Age' concept that makes *all*
equal to God, no; but rather an *explicit declaration* as made
by Christ that both he and God are in fact *one and the same*,

Furthermore, *all* judgement has been handed over to Christ from the Father, who has the legitimate *right* to judge because it is he who *walked* with us, *knows* our weaknesses, and was as fully human as we all are – and who *is* fully God. He has that right to judge, because he walked as *we* walked – and was yet without sin – to where he is able to *genuinely* judge with mercy, compassion, understanding, and *true* justice. Not the sort of 'justice' that we see on earth, and that very often turns out to be injustice instead. No. True, pure, *untainted* justice. I would certainly hope for *his* justice rather than the sort of 'justice' we often see in our court systems, that's for sure! But thank God it is *He* who is the final judge, or else every single one of us would surely be in hot water otherwise! For, as Christ himself stated:

> For just as the Father raises the dead and gives them life, even so the Son also gives life to whom He wishes. For not even the Father judges anyone, but He has given *all* judgment to the Son, so that all will honor the Son even as they honor the

---

and this without any other rival – whether in heaven or on earth… this being one of many instances where Christ declared himself as God, the Creator of all that is and that shall ever be. See also Chapter 2 on page 41 regarding the incarnate *deity* of Christ.

> Father. He who does not honor the Son
> does not honor the Father who sent Him.
> Truly, truly, I say to you, he who *hears*
> My word, and *believes* Him who sent Me,
> has eternal life, and does *not* come into
> judgment, but has passed *out of* death *into*
> life.
>
> JOHN 5:21-24

And as Christ said:

> Blessed [*happy, fortunate, blissful*] is he
> who does not take offense at Me.
>
> MATTHEW 11:6

Again, it is a *personal* experience. Without
religion. Without ceremony. Without preconditions. Jesus Christ *is* the *only* way to the Father
because he *is* the Father. Paul is not the way,
and neither is any self-proclaimed cult or religious "guru", nor religious teacher, nor preacher,
nor biblical commentaries, nor whatever form
of organized religion there may be. So why
should we even put our trust on them? It is the
difference between a *genuine* follower of Christ
and what she stands for, as opposed to merely
calling oneself a "Christian". And he is *worthy*
of our trust.

And that is why I would personally rather simply be called a *follower* of Christ. For than, even if I stumble and fall, the religious cannot judge nor condemn me, because my spiritual connection is not with *them*, but with *Him*. And thus, if and when I *do* falter – as I do every single day of my life in one way or another – still I see him there with outstretched arms saying:

> Wipe your tears away, and do not fear. See,
> I *never* left you, and never will. I love you.
> Get back up, and just keep following *me*.

All that is required is that one *continues* to follow with a sincere heart. For if you are on an elevator going up, and you stumble and fall, are you *still* going up? Of course you are. So *pick yourself back up*, and just keep following! *Keep going up. Never quit*, though you may falter. *Never quit*, for you're a follower of Christ – for he will *never* leave you alone on that elevator. Even though your partner, your friends, your family, your co-workers – or even the *entire world* – may turn their backs on you, Christ will *always* be there, and will *never* let you go. *Ever*.

For, as it has been said,

> Do not rejoice over me, O my enemy; when
> I fall, I shall rise; when I sit in darkness,
> the Lord *Himself* will be a light to me.
>
> MICAH 7:8

Anyhow, that is what *I* believe as based on both the Gospels and the words of Christ, and *especially* based on *my* personal experience. For when the religious, the non-religious, the traditionalists, and even my own self had condemned me and had left me high and dry, it was Christ who stood by me through thick and thin – and this without religion ever being involved.

As it happened, I sat down one day, and decided to do what to me had been unthinkable to *ever* do for years, as over a decade before I had become *completely* turned off to anything to do with Christianity – though I dabbled in completely opposite spheres instead – mainly as a sign of protest against God Himself, though I now realize He had nothing to do with what I had gone through. So I sat down that day, and decided to read the Gospels once more after such a long time – for I had followed Christ from the age of nine, having been known to spend hours comparing scripture with literal Greek translations, going to Bible study groups, and preaching to anyone who would put up with me – not because I had to, but because it gave me pleasure in doing so.

But soon after I entered my twenties, I had now become disillusioned by those who, though claiming to follow Christ, did nothing but continually judge and oppress others through their own religiosity and self-serving hypocrisies – defaming the name of Christ through religious commercialism, and misrepresenting him by their own impositions to control any and all who got in their way. By then I had forgotten my First Love, as he now became overshadowed by the very ones who, though claiming to follow and love him, by their own actions seemed more like they had *never* known him – not the historic Christ of the Bible, that's for sure! And so, after having gone through near tragedy in my own life years later – years after I had left Christ, when I thought I did not need God because I could rely on the many diverse and rather (and I truly mean this with humility) somewhat amazing achievements I had accomplished in life in such a short time – none of what I achieved through education, career, and so on and so forth – none of it was enough for me anymore, and I truly *did* hit rock bottom. But as Christ had said to a man *desperate* to see his daughter healed:

> All things can be done for the one who believes.
> MARK 9:23

– to where this man, somewhat like myself in my greatest hour of despair and utter emptiness, cried out:

> I believe; *help* my unbelief! [MARK 9:24]

I simply realized just how much, to what extent, I had genuinely gotten tired of it all. Tired of life. Tired of everything and everybody. And so I looked back on my childhood and teenage years, when I had walked with Christ *without* all the complications of religion, and all the dull and hypocritical nonsense that oftentimes comes with it. So now, at my greatest hour of need, as I read Christ's words in the Gospels, I simply decided to *forget* about the religious, to *let go* of all the mire, suffering, self-doubt, and self-condemnation that they had put me through years before, and finally began to look to Christ instead, and him *alone*. As a result of having once again realized, after so many

years, that the Christ of the Gospels was *not* the
Christ that much of modern Christendom claims
to represent, but in many ways the complete
opposite – I fell on my knees, and said something
in the likes of this:

> Jesus, if your there, give me hope, and
> save me from myself. I can't promise you
> anything, and I can't promise I'll change
> x, y, or z – and I'm certainly *not* going to
> become religious. But I come to you *just as
> I am*. So if you're really who you say you
> are, than I need you. Forgive me for how I
> have treated you all these years. Take my
> fears away – and give me your light, and
> pull me from this darkness. I give you my
> life, and I give you my *trust*. Thank you
> for your love.

Well, after having blasphemed his name for a
decade and a half – this very one I had initially
and completely loved as a child – I now felt
an overwhelming peace after having said that
prayer – knowing that he had *indeed* listened –
that he had indeed wiped the slate clean, and
that he had indeed given me a new life. *I just
knew*. And that is when I looked back and
realized that, though I had left him, though I had
cursed his name for years – I now realized that

he had *never*, *ever* left me. Not for a second! He
never did!

I had walked away from him, deliberately
turned my back to him – but he just *kept* watching over me for all those years. I had insulted
his name, but he just kept right on *loving* me.
Even though many had condemned me, he was
always there, consistently fighting *for* me – yes,
even *when* I was fighting against *him*. That is
the type of God I serve. That is the type of God
I love. Yes, I love him, because he first loved me.
Selfish, I know. But that is Agape love. Even in
my most rebellious state, he still *cared* for me.
Unconditionally, and without strings attached.
That *is* Jesus Christ. That is the Christ of the
Gospels. For he *himself* is the gospel – the *good
news* – according to Christ.

It is oh so *very* true. For he truly *is* the same
yesterday, today, and forever. And from then on,
I was a changed man. And I finally believed
in *myself* again, instead of looking to anyone
else (whether the religious, the non-religious, the
corporation, the schooling, the many philosophies
of man, and so forth) for some sort of 'approval'.
He *alone* became my approval. And I became *free*.

It really was as the song states: something had indeed happened – when I stopped looking at everyone else, including myself, and had simply come to him with the faith of a child – to where I now realized that he *had* touch me and had pretty much *instantly* made me whole again[28]... much like when Christ had touched the blind and made them see, the deaf and made them hear, the sick and cured them, the dead and raised them, the demonically oppressed and released them – and me, the utterly *desperate-hearted* who in addition had become fed up with anything to do with religion and life itself – and loved me. Yes, the very same Jesus who did these things two thousand years ago, is the very same one who *still* loves today as he loved then.

Believing in Christ is not about bland, stale, hypocritical, and dead religiosity – but about a *relationship*. A *personal* relationship. A walk of faith. It's a matter of the heart. Religion, on the other hand, *whatever* religion it might be, is for the birds. Who *can* you trust? Well, you *can* trust

---

[28] As paraphrased from the song *He Touched Me*, as per Bill Gaither Trio, *He Touched Me*. Gaither Music Company, 1963.

*him*.  He won't forsake you.  For he truly *is* the
friend that sticks closer than a brother!

> One who has unreliable friends soon comes
> to ruin, but there *is* a friend who sticks
> closer than a brother.
> PROVERBS 18:24

Yes, he kept his promise. He *gave* me his peace. A
peace that since then has *never* left me.  Even in
times of frustration, anxiety, and doubt – neither
that  peace,  nor  the  comforting  inner  joy  that
comes from his Spirit – appropriately also known
as the great *Comforter* – has *ever* left me.

No religion necessary.  No church attendance
required. And to paraphrase the Christian-based
rock song *Shadows*, he *indeed* took the shadows
away  from  me,  and  gave  me  hope  and  a  clear
sense of an unconditional, prodigal-son sort of
love – and saved me from *myself*.[29]   The sense

------

[29] As loosely paraphrased from the song *Shadows*, as
per  the  Christian  rock  band  Rez  Band,  *Between Heaven
'N Hell album*. Sparrow Records, 2008 – also known as
*Resurrection Band*, and who's entire music catalog is *highly*
recommended.      Furthermore,  this  band  started  Jesus
People  USA,  which  houses  the  homeless,  takes  care  of
the  elderly,  assists  those  wishing  to  leave  street  gangs,
and  essentially  walks  the  walk  as  Christ  taught.    Their
Christian  example  is  truly  Christ-like,  and  has  proven  to
be  the  Gospel  according  to  Christ  in  modern-day  *action*

of an undeserved love for a black sheep who had squandered his time with stuff that does not matter in the end, and that only stressed me out and made my life progressively more and more complicated as the years went by – but who was being welcomed back home by a loving Father with open arms, and who was simply just *glad* to see me again, as I now rested on His mighty shoulders. Yes, He truly *is* worthy of my trust. He is worthy of *anyone's* trust.

And now I realize just what people mean when they say that Christ never came to bring the world yet *another* religion. I slowly started to see this as I continued to read Christ's words *alone*. I wanted to see what I would get out of reading the words of Christ *for myself*. And I slowly began to realized that he *did* come to bring life, and life *abundantly*. For *me* – just as I was, and right where I was at. And that is good enough for me – because it was good enough for *him*.

And that's what he did for me. What's *your* story? You may not feel that anyone is interested – but *God* is. Will you tell *Him* your story?

---

and practice. See JPUSA, *Jesus People USA*. ⟨URL: http://jpusa.org⟩.

Will you let Him tell you *His*? Don't worry. No 'conversion' required. The only thing one can get converted *into* is religion. God wants *you* – *not* your religion. He wants love – not self-condemnation, self-doubt, or religious fanaticism. That's what Jesus taught, you know. That *is* the Gospel of Christ – despite everything else you might have already heard before.

Right... it *is* such a personal experience that only you and God can truly know. God sees straight *past* one's religious beliefs, dogmas, traditions, fears, doubts, errors, wrongs, and intentions... and straight *into* the heart. How is *your* heart with God? If you are not sure, go ahead and simply *ask* Him to show Himself to you, and He *will* reveal Himself to you... guaranteed. For, as Christ proclaimed:

> ... anyone who comes to Me I will *never* drive away.
>
> JOHN 6:37

And, as the magnificent Book of Proverbs states:

> ... those who diligently seek Me *will* find Me.
>
> PROVERBS 8:17

Yes, religion can really be a downer – especially when God is nowhere to be seen in the picture! And Christ warned us that there would be *many* false prophets, false teachers, and false religions who would appear and mislead *many* – even the elect[30] – before his return. These many diverse (and oft-times *divisive*) religious voices whom billions would look to for answers while taking their focus away from the Spirit of God – and that we must be careful and discerning, and not run after them; but that we must *personally* keep our focus on *Him* alone without either being fearful or confused by what we see and hear in the world today. But, to paraphrase a song by the late great Keith Green, we must *rest* in our faith, even though we are constantly being flooded by many diverse and conflicting voices – and when we hold on to what Christ has taught us, his peace *will* come to us.[31] So, therefore, who *can* you truly trust in a world where love is lost, and where even those who profess to follow God often turn out to be charlatans, disingenuous, or good-

---

[30] See Matthew 24:23-27.

[31] Paraphrased from the song, *When I Hear the Praises Start*; as per Keith Green, *For Him Who Has Ears to Hear Album*. Sparrow Records, 1977. Yes, all of his musical catalog also being *highly* recommended.

hearted but misled? On Christ you *can* trust. On
him you *can* depend on.  For he *never* changes,
nor ever will.

So, therefore, boldly *place* your trust on Christ,
and Christ *apart from* organized religion and all
the time-wasting nonsense that comes with it –
and you will *never* go wrong –

> whatever your self-perceived quantity
> of faith,
>
> whatever your religious or *non*-religious
> background,
>
> whatever your sexuality,
>
> wherever you come from,
>
> whatever the world might say,
>
> whatever your doubts,
>
> whatever your fears,
>
> whatever mess you're in,
>
> whatever you have done,
>
> whatever you've been through,
>
> *whoever* you are!

Look to the One who is the same yesterday,
today, and forever – who's love for you is eternal
and without any earthy comparison – and leave
the rest to wallow in their own self-imposed

constraints. For genuine, steadfast happiness and lasting contentment comes *not* from religion, rule, tradition, nor money – but from the Creator of *all* – exclusively and without rival – for *that* is how He has created us.

On Christ, and Christ alone, you can trust with your *very life* in the here-and-now, and in the place that awaits you when you have finally finished your *own* race. Can't say the same about anyone or anything else, *can* we? Yes, not even in terms of our very *own* selves or our own efforts, sacrifices, or works. But he saves us from all things – *including* ourselves – so that we can love again. So that we can unconditionally love, accept, and forgive *ourselves* again.

For as Jesus Christ – God *Himself,* who stooped down to love unreservedly and without judgement nor condemnation – said to *all* who would freely place their trust and hope on him:

> Do not let your hearts be troubled. Trust [or, *you believe*] in God; trust [*believe*] also in me...Peace I leave with you; *My peace* I give to you. I do not give to you as the world gives. Do not let your hearts be *troubled*, and do not let them be afraid.
> [JOHN 14:1 & 27]

Chapter Nine

# *No Religion Necessary to Get to God*

> But you are not to be called 'Rabbi',[1] for
> you have only one Master and you are all
> brothers. And do not call anyone on earth
> 'father',[2] for you have one Father, and He
> is in heaven. Nor are you to be called
> 'teacher', for you have one Teacher, the
> Christ.
>
> Matthew 23:8-10

Considering what Christ told his apostles in the
above statement, it is important to comprehend
that he *never* stated – nor intended – that humanity must come to God through *belonging* to
an organized regime, submitting to a church, nor
by being a sexually-repressed 'puritan'; never did
he hinder those who are different, free-spirited,

---

[1] Or, *spiritual leader, teacher,* or *religious guru.*

[2] Or, *a spiritual father* or *superior.*

or decidedly disconnected from such regimes of oppression from becoming children of God.

On the contrary, Christ stated that no one can approach God except through a childlike, simple faith alone; and this only as God draws him or her to Himself. This applies to *all* religions under the sun. For, as he again said, and as has previously been cited:

> Truly I say to you, unless you turn and become *like children*, you will not enter the kingdom of heaven. [3]
>
> Matthew 18:3

and as Christ *also* said,

> No one can come to Me unless the Father who sent Me *draws* him. . . For this reason I have said to you, that no one can come to Me unless it has been *granted him* from the Father.
>
> John 6:44 & 65

As we have seen, no one gets to God acting as an 'adult' doing some business deal to where they follow a regime of theology, a dogma created by others, a set of repressive and contradictory rules, and belonging to some fanatical

---

[3] See also Chapter 4 on page 71.

*religious* group or commune; while excluding others as 'sinners', 'heretics', 'infidels', and "the misguided". Only as a little child seeking his or her parent for love, nourishment, and support – without any knowledge of what parental responsibilities are supposed to be, or of the fact that he or she is a child at all – but simply by coming to the parent for comfort, love, guidance, and affection – yes, as a vulnerable child humbles herself and turns to her parent for love – this is how one approaches God.

Christ's definition of what "true religion" is is to love the widow, to feed and cloth the poor, to visit the prisoner and the sick; to be a friend to the emotionally, mentally, and physically despairing; and in essence, to make the effort to *be there* (in love and active support) for those who are down and who cannot help themselves out of dark and difficult circumstances in life... whether friend or foe[4]. Thus, *genuinely* being religious is an *action* of loving others – not in sentiment, but in assistance, mercy, and compassion.

---

[4] To where it is the job of true faith, free and apart from religiosity, to befriend, support, and carry the desperate-hearted through as our Heavenly Father does – to those who accept this – carrying us through such circumstances when no one else seems to listen or care.

Furthermore, Christ himself stated that to do these things to others is to do it to him *directly*,[5] and thus to do it to God. For this is what Christ clearly taught when he spoke of how it would be on his return some day in the probably not-too-distant future:

> When the Son of Man comes in his glory, and all the angels with him, then he will sit on the throne of his glory. All the nations will be gathered before him, and he will separate people one from another as a shepherd separates the sheep from the goats, and he will put the sheep at his right hand and the goats at the left. Then the king will say to those at his right hand, 'Come, you that are blessed by my Father, inherit the kingdom prepared for you from the foundation of the world; for I was hungry and you gave me food, I was thirsty and you gave me something to drink, I was a stranger and you welcomed me, I was naked and you gave me clothing, I was sick and you took care of me, I was in prison and you visited me.' Then the righteous will answer him, 'Lord, when was it that we saw you hungry and gave you food, or thirsty and gave you something to drink? And when was it that we saw you a stranger and welcomed you, or naked and gave you clothing? And when was it that we saw you sick or in prison and visited you?' And the king will answer them, 'Truly I tell you, *just as you*

---

[5] Matthew 25:31-46

*did it to one of the least of these who are*
*members of my family, you did it to me.'*
Then he will say to those at his left hand,
'You that are accursed, depart from me
into the eternal fire prepared for the devil
and his angels; for I was hungry and you
gave me no food, I was thirsty and you
gave me nothing to drink, I was a stranger
and you did not welcome me, naked and
you did not give me clothing, sick and in
prison and you did not visit me.'  Then
they also will answer, 'Lord, when was it
that we saw you hungry or thirsty or a
stranger or naked or sick or in prison, and
did not take care of you?'  Then he will
answer them, 'Truly I tell you, *just as you*
*did not do it to one of the least of these,*
*you did not do it to me.'*  And these will
go away into eternal punishment, but the
righteous into eternal life. [MATTHEW 25:31-
46]

The root of 'religion' is *supposed to be* grounded
on loving one's neighbor, and being there for
the one who needs someone to turn to.  For, as
scripture tells us:

Those who consider themselves religious
and yet do not keep a tight rein on their
tongues deceive themselves, and their religion is worthless. Religion that God our
Father accepts as pure and faultless is
this:  to look after orphans and widows
in their distress and to keep oneself un-
stained by the world. [JAMES 1:26-27]

Yes, true religion is love *in action* – rather than ritualistic piety, sacramental observance, or submission to dogmatic tradition. For it is oftentimes not easy for one to turn to God when his whole life is in tethers. And it is the job of those who consider themselves 'religious' to *apply* their religion in the real world; not by standing on street corners or knocking on doors to 'convert' and preach *down* to someone, but to be *a friend* to the friendless, *a haven* to the outcast, *a companion* to the 'non-religious', and *a confidant* to the controversial – without condemning nor mocking – and without strings attached. *That* – and that alone – *is* true religion in theory and in practice.

Even the Old Testament attests to this notion of what *genuine* religion really is – not the leading of a congregation in song and prayer – though fellowship with the right people who are non-judgemental, loving, accepting, and Christ-like *can be* very important to some for spiritual development and maturity, as well as to be present in such places as a support for others – nor the institutionalization of ritual, practice, and theology – but rather the active practice and real-world applicability of kindness, mercy, love and patience towards all – and this *especially* for the broken and desperate hearts of the contradictory and selfish world in which we find ourselves in. As scripture states:

> The word of the Lord came to me: 'Son of man, prophesy against the shepherds of Israel; prophesy and say to them: "This is what the Sovereign Lord says: Woe to the shepherds of Israel who only take care of themselves! Should not shepherds take care of the flock? You eat the curds, clothe yourselves with the wool and slaughter the choice animals, but you do not take care of the flock. You have not strengthened the weak or healed the sick or bound up the injured. You have not brought back the strays or searched for the lost. You have ruled them harshly and brutally. So they were scattered because there was no shepherd, and when they were scattered they became food for all the wild animals. My sheep wandered over all the mountains and on every high hill. They were scattered over the whole earth, and no one searched or looked for them... I *Myself* will search for my sheep and look after them." ' [Ezekiel 34:1-6 & 11 NIV]

So where does organized religion and its varied rules, dogmas, teachings, and discriminations towards certain groups and favoritism towards others come into this – into *finding* God – into believing in Christ as the Son of God who can lead one to the Father for *all* who open their

door to Him, without favoritism or exception –
in our own analysis? *It doesn't*. You *cannot* find
God through organized religion and becoming
a member of a church – much like you cannot
become rich simply because you might sleep in
a luxurious mansion overnight – for that is what
*adults* do. You find God on your *own* free will,
by simply *coming to Him* in whatever way He
draws you to Himself – by simply going to your
Heavenly Father – by coming to Christ as a child
would seek his or her own earthly mother or
father – and nothing more.

There is no 'conversion' into *anything* here.
That's for 'adults' doing 'adult-like' things and
obligations; not for a child seeking his or her
loving parent. And to those who did not have a
loving parent – God *is* a Father, *your* Father – if
you so accept Him as such – the kind of father
who will *never* betray, abuse, nor humiliate you –
the kind of father who will *never* let you go nor
turn you away. For, as the Old Testament states:

> With what shall I come before the Lord,
> and bow myself before God on high? Shall
> I come before him with burnt offerings,
> with calves a year old? Will the Lord be
> pleased with thousands of rams, with ten
> thousands of rivers of oil? Shall I give my

> firstborn for my transgression, the fruit
> of my body for the sin of my soul?  He
> has told you, O mortal, what is good; and
> what does the Lord *require* of you but to *do
> justice*, and to *love kindness*, and to *walk
> humbly with your God.*
> MICAH 6:6-8

For religion does *not* get you to God – but rather
it is God *alone* that gets you to *Himself.* To those
who believe – detach from those in organized
religion that hinder your soul and deprive you
from the joy of having God in your life, and
stick to those – whether within it or not – who
*genuinely* follow Christ. Or, simply follow him on
your own if you so choose – depending on how
God's Holy Spirit may lead you at this point in
time in your life.

For even Paul *himself* admits to having set
himself apart from early church leadership for
seventeen years – aside from having spent fifteen
days with Peter three years after having come
to Christ – in order to allow himself to grow
spiritually *in* Christ while acting as a missionary
throughout the land – though he *did* fellowship
with followers during that time.[6]  Not that I am

---

[6] For Paul himself admits: "But when God, who had
set me apart even from my mother's womb and called me

advocating that one isolates oneself from church leadership – but sometimes, depending on the person, this can be beneficial for self-growth and spiritual independence – even *if* for a brief time, or for however long God may lead one to do so. It is certainly better than getting involved with the *wrong* church that may bog one down, restrict the fruits that she could bear in Christ, and

---

through His grace, was pleased to reveal His Son in me so that I might preach him among the Gentiles, I did not immediately consult with flesh and blood, nor did I go up to Jerusalem *to those who were apostles before me*; but I went away to Arabia, and returned once more to Damascus. Then three years later I went up to Jerusalem to become acquainted with Cephas [*that is, Peter*], and stayed with him fifteen days.    But I did not see any other of the apostles except James, the Lord's brother... then after an interval of fourteen years I went up again to Jerusalem with Barnabas, taking Titus along also. It was because of a revelation that I went up; and I submitted to them the gospel which I preached among the Gentiles, but I did so in private to those who were of reputation, for fear that I might be running, or had run, in vain... but from those who were of high reputation (what they were makes no difference to me; God shows no partiality) – well, those who were of reputation *added nothing* to my message.  On the contrary, they recognized that I had been entrusted with the task of preaching the gospel to the uncircumcised, just as Peter had been to the circumcised... All they asked was that we should continue to remember the poor, the very thing I had been eager to do all along." [Galatians 1:15-19 & 2:1-2 & 6-7 & 10 NIV]

possibly even make her stumble from the faith altogether.[7]

Fellowship with others who love Christ can *definitely* be extraordinarily enriching, but so can following Christ *without* any outwardly 'religious' connections. What matters is that one *follows* Christ in their personal lives, and this in spirit and in truth. Anything else – so long as it is healthy and is not a noose around one's neck – is secondary. For *organized* religion is highly influenced by man – whereas the soul, and its relationship *with* God, comes directly from its Creator and true Lover. True religion is spirit, love, justice, mercy, and truth – organized religion is oftentimes (but certainly *not* always) a rut of fear-riddled guilt and codependencies of every kind.

Not all *within* organized religion are trouble waiting to happen, but one must *choose wisely* if one is to delve into spiritual communion with a group – though there *are* in fact very good, sensible, caring, loving, and genuine churches out there that are a pure *joy* to be involved in, and

---

[7] Please see Chapter 14 on page 307 for details.

to serve others through.[8]    What's important is to use one's common sense as guided by God's Holy Spirit.   And if one finds such a group – more power to you!   But nothing – not even a church, pastor, minister, priest, congregation, denominational theology, or opinionated dogma – must *ever* take the place of Christ in one's heart. So use your head, as well as your heart.

But to continue, it must be noted that Christ himself *never* used the word 'conversion' to describe how one comes to God – much like he never used the world 'church' as an institution to submit to in any way.   In fact, although Christ stated that "...on this rock I will build my church [or, *assembly*], and the gates of Hades will not prevail against it",[9] he was speaking of the *global* fellowship and family of Christ, and all who would on their *own* initiative freely choose to follow him throughout the world irrespective of denominations, sects, church attendance, as well as *non*-attendance – and *not* in regards to

---

[8] See also Chapter 14 on page 307, which includes valuable advise on choosing the right church or group for one to attend *if* one so chooses.

[9] Matthew 16:18

religious institutions, denominations, or sects. For, as is well explained:

> The word 'church' (Gk. *ekklesia*, from a verb meaning *to call out*) is used of *any* assembly and in itself implies no more than a gathering of people who have been called forth, e.g. the town meeting at Ephesus (Acts 19:41), and Israel, called out of Egypt and assembled in the wilderness (Acts 7:38). Israel was a 'church,' but not in any sense the N.T. church–the primary point of similarity being that both were 'called out' and by the same God.[10]

Furthermore,

> The Gospels do not develop the doctrine of the Church. The word 'church' occurs in Matthew only [*on considering the Gospels alone*].[11]

As such, though the word *church*, as used in the New Testament letters, was primarily utilized in reference to various geographically-located *assemblies* of Christ's followers – it was ultimately used to refer to the assembly of the *spiritual* body of Christ as a universal entity in regards to those

---

[10] As in NASB; C.I. Scofield, editor, *The New Scofield Study Bible: New American Standard Bible*. World Bible Publishers, 1988; p. 1351.

[11] As per Ibid.; p. 1314.

who – whether part of an *actual* assembly or not – follow him in spirit and in truth wherever they might be throughout the globe, and *irrespective* of whether they attend a church or not.[12]

---

[12] For instance, references to the church as the universal body of Christ can be seen in scriptures such as:

> Husbands, love your wives, just as Christ loved the church and gave himself up for her. [Ephesians 5:25]

as well as,

> He is the head of the body, the church; he is the beginning, the firstborn from the dead, so that he might come to have first place in everything... I am now rejoicing in my sufferings for your sake, and in my flesh I am completing what is lacking in Christ's afflictions for the sake of his body, that is, the church. [Colossians 1:18 & 24]

and,

> For I am the least of the apostles, unfit to be called an apostle, because I persecuted the church of God. [I Corinthians 15:9]

Furthermore, the word *church* was also commonly used in reference to localized assemblies of believers in Christ, wherever they might be found, as seen in scriptures such as:

> ...to Apphia our sister, to Archippus our fellow soldier, and to the church in your house... [Philemon 0:2],

as well as,

Therefore, instead of Christ using words such as 'convert' or 'church', he used terms such as "*come* to me",[13] "follow me",[14] "he who *believes*",[15] "*believe* in the Light",[16] "in spirit and in truth",[17] and "*your* faith", "*by* your faith", and "according

---

Greet also the church in their house. Greet my beloved Epaenetus, who was the first convert in Asia for Christ. [Romans 16:5]

[13] Such as in Matthew 11:28 and 19:14; Mark 10:14; Luke 18:16; as well as in John 5:40, 6:37, 6:44, 6:65, and 7:37.

[14] Such as in Matthew 4:19, 8:22, 9:9, 10:38, 16:24, and 19:21; Mark 1:17, 2:14, 8:34, and 10:21; Luke 5:27, 9:23, 9:59, 14:27, and 18:22; as well as in John 1:43, 10:27, 12:26, 21:19 and 22.

[15] Such as in Matthew 18:6, Mark 5:36, 9:23, and 16:16; John 3:15-16 & 36, 5:24 & 46, 6:29, 35, & 40, 6:47, 7:38, 8:24, 9:35 & 38, 10:38, 11:25-26, 12:36, & 44-46, 14:1, & 11-12, 16:31, 17:20-21, 20:27, and 20:29. As Christ said, "Truly, truly, I say to you, he who believes has eternal life" [John 6:47]. See also Chapter 4 on page 71 for a thorough explanation of what the word *believe* is defined as in scripture.

[16] As Christ said, "While you have the Light, *believe* in the Light, so that you may *become* sons of Light" [John 12:36]. See also Chapter 4 on page 71 for a thorough explanation of what *believe* is defined as in scripture.

[17] Such as in John 4:23-24. See also Chapter 6 on page 89.

to your faith"[18] – rather than "convert into" and the like.

Nor did Christ ever teach anyone to be religious or ritualistic; nor to be repetitively prayerful just for the sake of it;[19] nor to tithe one's earnings to a religious institution as some form of obligatory act; nor to entrust one's faith life to a church leader as some form of "spiritual guide"

---

[18] As in Matthew 8:13, 9:2, 22, & 29, 15:28, 17:20, and 21:21-22; Mark 2:5, 5:34, 10:52, 9:23, and 11:23-24; Luke 5:20, 7:9, 7:50, 8:48-50, 17:6 & 19, and 18:42. For as Christ stated:

> All things can be done for the one who believes. [Mark 9:23]

[19] For instance, Christ taught us not to be *continually* repetitive when we pray – as this is ritualistic, and oftentimes is done to be *seen* by others, rather than as it ought to be – a normal conversation with God that can be done anytime and anywhere one might be. As he put it:

> And whenever you pray, do not be like the hypocrites; for they love to stand and pray in the synagogues and at the street corners, so that they may be *seen* by others. Truly I tell you, they have received their reward... When you are praying, do not heap up empty phrases as the Gentiles do; for they think that they will be heard because of their many words. Do not be like them, for your Father *knows* what you need *before you ask Him*. [Matthew 6:5-8]

who has the last word on matters of faith when it is Christ's Holy Spirit that one must listen to and learn from above all else (as he himself stated in MATTHEW 23:8-10, and as clearly quoted in the very beginning of this chapter); nor to "speak in tongues" as some sort of evidence of one's 'holiness'; nor to allow oneself to become trapped in confusions on doctrinal matters that do not include the simplicity of the Gospel and of following Christ as one's ultimate authority on questions of belief; nor to condemn and make stumble fellow followers on legitimate gray areas of faith; nor to be baptized[20] as a *prerequisite* for

---

[20] Though Christ *did* instruct believers – but *without* this ever being obligatory – to be baptized as a *public* and *symbolic* act of the rebirth that has taken place from *within* – as seen in Mark 16:16; and Christ himself was present as his own disciples baptized others as in John 3:22 and 4:2 – likely leaving it to them to do so as an example of what his followers should do to each other as a symbol of love and servitude for one another, as he commanded as per John 13:34-35 and Mark 9:35.

In fact, contrary to what some churches state, being baptized has never been a requirement for coming to Christ. Even so, water baptism as a *symbolic* ritual is a powerful outward act of faith as done in public in that it testifies of what has *already occurred* on the *inside* of the believer from the very moment they came to Christ by faith, and faith *alone* – that they have on their own free will *accepted* Christ in their hearts, have been filled with his Holy Spirit, and have had their sins washed away through

salvation – as some modern groups erroneously demand – just as going to church is *not* a prerequisite to following Christ or coming to God – nor anything else of the sort! Such things are for 'adults'. The kingdom of heaven, on the other

---

his cleansing blood – and have thus been spiritually born *again*. Furthermore, it was Christ himself who said that those who would accept him would be baptized *not* in water, but rather by the Holy Spirit of God, as he said: "...for John baptized *with* water, but you will be baptized *by* [*or, with*] the Holy Spirit." [Acts 1:5]

Furthermore, even John the Baptist stated the same during his ministry in preparation for Christ's arrival, as he himself said: "I baptize you in water for repentance, but one who is more powerful than I is coming after me; I am not worthy to carry his sandals. He will baptize you *with* [*or, in*] the Holy Spirit and fire." [Matthew 3:11 – this also found in Mark 1:8, Luke 3:16, and John 1:26 & 33]

Lastly, in Christ's use of the phrase "water and the Spirit" in John 3:5, water referred to *natural birth* (water from a mother's *womb*), as the context of discussion included references to being born a *second* time (as per v. 4); to where being born from *above* (v. 3 & 7) attests to a second *spiritual* birth through the Holy Spirit. Furthermore, Christ clarifies the same when he states that "What is born of the flesh is flesh, and what is born of the Spirit is spirit." as per v. 6. Furthermore, even Paul *consistently* speaks salvation by faith alone *without* the physical need for baptism, as he did not make it a habit of baptizing new converts (see I Corinthians 1:13-17), and in addition affirms "For Christ did not send me to baptize but to proclaim the gospel," as per v. 17. See also Matt Slick, *Baptism and John 3:5*. Christian Apologetics & Research Ministry CARM ⟨URL: http://carm.org/baptism-and-john-35⟩.

hand, is for – and *belongs* to – the humble in spirit who, with an honest heart, make a *personal* decision to turn to and come to the Light of the world *apart from* relying on religiosity and man's traditions – yes, these the seekers of Light who come to Christ "in spirit and in truth".[21] For, as we have seen, and as Christ stated:

> God is spirit, and those who worship Him must worship in spirit and truth.
> John 4:24

It's truly just as simple as that. Christ *did* in fact tell the world – both than as well as now, for He never changes, and his words today are as authoritative and applicable as when he first said them – he *did* say that "my yoke is easy and my burden is light".[22]

For religiosity in itself is irrelevant. What matters is that one have a personal relationship, and direct communication, with God. Yes. This, and love. Not some sort of "New Age"-based counterfeit of a form of esoteric love that is supposed to unify, excuse, and apologize for all things – while rejecting all that it imitates, and

---

[21] See Chapter 4 on page 71.
[22] Matthew 11:30

that in itself has become the early foundations
of a globalized but ultimately repressive religion
in its own right – the 'new' religion of New
Age-ism, that is.[23]   No.   But rather the honest, nonreligious but ever pure, unconditional,
always present though often subtle, consistent
and patient love that only comes from above,
and that *never* fails.   No modern-day 'religion'
nor cheap-copy philosophy can ever provide such
genuine, honest, and *consistent* love.   For those
that have run after such man-made counterfeits
of truth have always become sorely disappointed
and disheartened soon after.   But God *is* love.
*True* love. The *original* love – that can *never* be
duplicated, though many have tried. As it is said:

> Dear friends, let us love one another, for
> love *comes from* God. Everyone who loves
> has been *born* of God and knows God.
> Whoever does not love does not know God,
> because God *is* love.

> I JOHN 4:7-8

What *is* true religion?   A proactive love for
God, for others, for self – and the humble faith

---

[23] See Appendix A on page 357, regarding how New Age-
related philosophies oftentimes attempt to copy the things
of God, while denying Him altogether, and neglecting His
power.

of a child that worships God in spirit and in truth. *This* is what true religion – the religion of God – is. For even Christ stated that such a spiritual rebirth as this comes not through religious observance, but rather from the Spirit of the Living God directly and utterly, when he said:

> Very truly, I tell you, no one can enter the kingdom of God without being born of water[24] and Spirit. What is born of the flesh is flesh, and what is born of the Spirit is spirit. Do not be astonished that I said to you, 'You must be born from above.' The wind blows where it chooses, and you hear the sound of it, but you do not know where it comes from or where it goes. So it is with everyone who is born of the Spirit.
>
> JOHN 3:5-8

That was Christ's message...if you believe in it, and if you can accept it. He did not create, nor did he advocate for, the creation of an *organized* form of religiosity – mankind in his traditions and

---

[24] Water herein referring first to a natural (physical) birth – hence water from the womb; the Spirit referring to being born a *second* time through the Spirit of God by placing one's faith and surrender to Christ – hence: "What is born of the flesh is flesh, and what is born of the Spirit is spirit." as per v. 6. See also note 20 on page 177.

rules of engagement did.[25] He did not advocate for the creation of certain rigid religious traditions, repetitions, and man-made edicts. And he never stated that if one goes to a church, follows the Bible as some rulebook, and tries as hard as one might to be 'righteous' in the eyes of man – that they would get closer to God – no, this is seeking God as an adult and not as a little child... mankind did. Remember – God is greater than *any* organized religion – and He is greater than anything mankind has ever written down – and He is greater than rules and regulations, factions and doctrines.

"No one can ever receive God but as a little child" – however way He might lead you and talk to you within your heart through Christ's Holy Spirit, whom he promised he would give to *all* who place their trust on Him. As Jesus said:

> But when He, the Spirit of truth, comes,
> He will guide you into *all* the truth.
> John 16:13

and as again Jesus promised:

---

[25] See Chapter 3 on page 53 regarding the slow organization of *the faith* as taught by Christ and into a form of organized religion over early centuries after his death and resurrection.

> If you than, being evil, know how to give
> good gifts to your children, how much
> *more* will your heavenly Father give the
> Holy Spirit to those who *ask* him?
>
> Luke 11:13

Again, one can plainly see that organized religion has nothing at all to do with it! Don't let them destroy the good that God has created in your heart. Don't let them hinder you from being who God has preappointed and created you to be in the fullness and richness of life. Don't let them deprive you from a joyous relationship with your Creator. Don't let them be a stumbling block between you and God. Don't let them defame God by their self-righteous and hypocritical religiosity. Don't let them confuse you nor hinder your soul. If you believe, come to God *boldly* and with confidence just as you are and at *whatever* point you find yourself in your life, knowing that His unconditional love and mercy covers *all* sin and imperfection...knowing that He would rather have *you* – and not your religiosity – to love and care for forever. All that is required of you is to say, "God, if you are there, come to me, and *reveal* yourself to me." And He *will* do it...guaranteed.

For as has rightly been said in regards to God's unconditional and incomprehensible love for us:

> The Love of the Father for his children plunges us into mystery, because it is utterly beyond the pale of human experience.[26]

If God through *His* Son does not condemn you, than how can man? If God is for us, who can be against us?[27] Keep your eyes on *Him* alone, and not on organized religion. Put your trust in *Him*, and *not* on the ever-wavering mood swings of mankind, nor on opinionated dogma – whether from preachers, teachers, texts – nor even from this very book. Speak to Christ *directly*. You don't *need* religion for that. And listen to *His* voice – in spirit and in truth... and you will *never* go wrong.

Christ spoke a parable on comparing self-righteousness and religious hypocrisy as opposed

---

[26] As in Brennan Manning, *A Glimpse of Jesus: The Stranger to Self-Hatred*. HarperOne, 2003.

[27] As Paul himself rightly stated:

> What then shall we say to these things? If God is for us, who is against us? ... Who will bring a charge against God's elect? God is the one who justifies; who is the one who condemns? Who will separate us from the love of Christ? [Romans 8:31-35; abridged]

to the non-arrogant and child-like faith that God seeks from those who wish to follow him – as recorded in the Gospel of Luke:

> He also told this parable to some who trusted in themselves that they were righteous and regarded others with contempt: 'Two men went up to the temple to pray, one a Pharisee and the other a tax collector. The Pharisee, standing by himself, was praying thus, "God, I thank you that I am not like other people: thieves, rogues, adulterers, or even like this tax collector. I fast twice a week; I give a tenth of all my income." But the tax collector, standing far off, would not even look up to heaven, but was beating his breast and saying, "God, be merciful to me, a sinner!" I tell you, this man went down to his home justified rather than the other; for all who exalt themselves will be humbled, but all who humble themselves will be exalted.'
>
> LUKE 18:9-14

For those who believe: Do you follow the risen Christ, or do you follow the religion that has been built up around him? Only you can know.

# Chapter Ten

# *It is God Who Chooses Us*

> At that time Jesus said, 'I thank You,
> Father, Lord of heaven and earth, because
> You have hidden these things from the
> wise and intelligent and have revealed
> them to infants. Yes, Father, for this
> way was well-pleasing in Your sight. All
> things have been handed over to Me by
> My Father; and no one knows who the
> Son is except the Father; nor does anyone
> know who the Father is except the Son,
> and anyone to whom the Son *chooses* to
> reveal Him.'
>
> LUKE 10:21-22.

A primary difference between all *other* religions and the Christian faith is that other religions attempt to get to God by works – such as being ritualistic, sacrificial, meditative, ceremonial, and repetitive through many religious practices and self-sacrifices – while Christianity explicitly teaches, by Christ's own words as well as through the rest of scripture, that it is God *Himself* who comes directly to each and every one of us, and it is *He* who invites all who are *willing* to listen to His voice to open their door to form a relationship with Him on an *individual* level. As has been said in regards to Christianity as standing alone in respect to all other faiths in world history on bringing forth *good* news:

> A gospel is an announcement of something that has happened in history, something that's been done for you that changes your status forever. Right there you can see the difference between Christianity and all other religions, including no religion. The essence of other religions is advice; Christianity is essentially news. Other religions say, "This is what you have to do in order to connect to God forever; this is how you have to live in order to earn your way to God.' But the gospel says, 'This is what has been done in history. This is how Jesus lived and died to earn the way to God for you.' Christianity is completely different. It's joyful news.[1]

---

[1] From Timothy Keller, *King's Cross: The Story of the World in the Life of Jesus*. Dutton Adult, 2011.

Even so, most people (including self-confessed Christians themselves) still mistake Christianity as the faith of love and freedom that it has always been, with *religion* itself. Yes, many *Christians* are in fact very religious, but have forgotten that Christ did not come to bring mankind yet *another* religion. No. He came that we might have life, and have it *abundantly* and to the full,[2] which has nothing at all to do with ceremony, repetition, obligation, earthly permission, ritualistic slavery, or any form of mandatory sacrifice.

A parable about a Seeker of Truth as told herein describes this difference between mankind attempting to get to God by his *own* efforts, works, and religious practices – versus God coming to mankind on *His own* initiative and by His unconditional love. It goes something like this:

\* \* \*

A man, herein named as the *Seeker of Truth*, sought to find meaning in life, and decided to set about traveling throughout the world in order to answer three basic questions:

---

[2] As Christ stated: "The thief comes only to steal and kill and destroy; I have come that they may have life, and have it abundantly [or *to the full*]". John 10:10

Who am I?

Why am I here?

Where am I going?

The man went to a distant land, where he observed its natives devout in meditation in order to purify their minds so that they might one day reach what they said was a release from a never-ending cycle of reincarnation. They told the man that, if he himself devoted enough time and energy doing likewise, that he would eventually reach ultimate enlightenment where the fires of desire, habit, self, and delusion would be extinguished – nirvana. All suffering would cease. The Seeker tried with all his might to achieve this through dedicated meditation, but was left without his questions being answered. He never did find the answer to where he was headed after reaching such a state, other than that he would cease from having to be reincarnated over and over again should he reach such enlightenment – though he never understood how he would even realize whether he had reached it or not.

The man decided to continue to seek, and went to yet another distant land, where he was told he did not even exist in the first place – that he merely lived in a philosophical illusion – possibly even a parallel universe! Well, this did not help him any, so he continued to seek.

On reaching yet another distant land, the man was told to perform as many good deeds as possible in order to balance out his karma. He was told that, by his mere existence, he could see how he had come from another life where his karma had not balanced out enough towards the positive, and that he was alive in order to do as many good deeds as possible so that he might remove himself from the never-ending cycle of reincarnation – though this gave him no guarantee that he would not yet again have to return as another earthly form in the next life should he fail to perform enough good deeds. Disillusioned, the man kept seeking for answers.

As he arrived in another land, the man was told that he must pray five times a day facing a particular geographic location, perform a pilgrimage to yet another land, fast regularly, and follow religious law as strictly as humanly possible. He was told he was on earth for such purposes, but that he had no guarantee as to where he was headed in the afterlife – as it all depended on whether his devotion to religious law, as well as whether his good works on earth, would be strong enough for him to pass the test of life that he was now living. He knew full well he could never be that perfect, and furthermore was looking for a guarantee as to where he was headed. He thanked his informants, and continued on to yet another land.

When he arrived, he was told that he was one with the Universe, that God was a part of all, and that he himself was a part of God. Certainly this seemed like a very kindly notion – that he was from God, and that he was on earth as a god himself – as was every other human, animal, plant, and cosmic body – for each and every one of them were also considered to themselves be gods in one sense or another. But he was never able to get any assurance as to where he was headed, besides some claiming that he would one day simply return to a supreme cosmic being if he lived life well enough, and for the good of all. The man knew full well he was imperfect, that there must be a being greater than himself, and that such attractive concepts did not genuinely guarantee where he was heading to. For he realized that these philosophies, though attractive, seemed more like pulp fiction, and the inventions of mankind without solidity nor evidential precedence. And so, now weary and disillusioned from his many travels, he simply gave up and returned to his home.

On arriving back home, he put his feet up, decided that he was just going to forget about answering any of the questions that he had originally set out to answer, and just enjoy life as best he could. He certainly wanted to find meaning in life – but not through being religious, attempting to be someone he knew he could never be, nor by being told what to do. And though he had a certain emptiness from within, which he had tried to fill throughout his entire life through relationships, money, career, crutches of habit, and other such things – nothing really fulfilled him fully and wholly – certainly not in the way some had told him that they themselves had been fully fulfilled not through religion, sacrifice – nor by their own efforts – but simply by divine love, and that alone. But what *is* divine anyway, he thought – as he looked at an imperfect and broken world around him.

And as he was sitting on his couch, petting his dog, sipping a nice one, and getting on with life; he heard a knock on his door. He answered, and the smiling stranger boldly told him,

> I know that you've been seeking for answers to your questions, and I'm here to tell you that *I* am the answer that you seek, because *I am* the way, the truth, and the life.

The man replied,

> No one can be truth, for truth is a concept, and is relative to how one looks at it.

But the visitor again boldly, but gently, said,

> Truth is not a concept, but rather *a person*. Buddy, I am it. You're alive because I created you. You are here because I love you. And, if you invite me into your home, I'll make my home *with* you. I'll eat with you, and you with me. And I'll give you my Spirit of Truth, and will make all things known

to you in their perfect time. I'll guide you,
protect you, and will *never* leave you. Do
you believe this?

The man, now rather flustered, responded,

I don't believe in anything anymore. I've
traveled throughout the world, and all I have
been told from everyone I meet is that I have
to jump through hoops just to be happy. I'm
fed up, so if you please excuse me. But
thank you for your advice.

The visitor said,

Alright than, I'll always be here at the door
if you ever want to invite me in. In the
meantime, please know that I love you. I
proved it by what I did for you quite a while
ago, and if you let me, I'll flood you with the
peace and joy you have been looking for for
so long. I'll fill your emptiness to where your
innermost being will flow rivers of living water
that will never end. And you will enter into
eternal life, not only when your time on earth
is up, but from the very second you willingly
invite me in.

The visitor extended his hand to shake the Seeker's hand.
The man saw a scar on each of the smiling visitor's wrists,
and immediately knew who it was that stood before
his door, asking to come in. He realized that the One,
the answers, and the lasting fulfillment he had traveled
the world to look for, to obtain with his own efforts and
sacrifices, had instead come to him on *His* own initiative,
and was not requiring anything of the man, but merely
that the man *welcome him* into his home, place his trust

on him, and follow. And so goes the story of the Seeker of Truth.

* * *

Yes, all other religions teach that the responsibility rests on each individual to get to God by one's own efforts, whereas Christ taught that it is God that, through His love for all, comes to each person and *invites* them, through His Spirit, to make Him part of their own lives instead. The Hindu must either bear the never-ending sufferings of multiple lives through reincarnation until he "gets it right", or else try by his own efforts through meditation and the worship of idols to get on one or more of many so-called mystic deity's good side in order to be saved. Muslims must constantly and without question comply with the five pillars of Islam which include praying five times a day and being selflessly dedicated to religion – often to non-negotiable extremes – in order to please God, even though in the end they still have absolutely no assurance that they will be saved – as they state that on judgement day God is said to weigh each person's 'good' works against the bad that they did in life before they can be saved.  As such, they can

never really be sure if they will ever be able to
enter God's Kingdom until it is all said and done.
Jewish people must comply with the letter of the
Old Testament Jewish law in order to be worthy
of salvation. Even agnostics, who leave it open
that there may or may not be a God, nevertheless
never have any assurance whatsoever of where
they might be going after they pass away. And
atheists generally don't even believe that our
souls continue on after this, such a short and
oftentimes difficult life, and often struggle with
the question of what the meaning of life is, and
why we are here.

But – as per the Gospel according to Christ –
it is Jesus Christ himself who has given *everyone*
on this earth (regardless of their religion, race, or
culture) – anyone who is willing to simply *open*
their door to him – an unwavering and solid *assurance* that they *will* be healed of their passed,
their wrong-doings washed away by his blood on
the cross, and that they *will* live eternally where
there will be no more tears, no more death, and
no more sorrow. For as Christ himself has said:

> I am the resurrection and the life. Those
> who believe[3] in me, even though they
> die, will live, and everyone who lives and
> believes in me will *never* die.  Do you
> believe this?
>
> JOHN 11:25

Furthermore, Christ also told the world that:

> My sheep hear my voice. I know them, and
> they follow me.  I give them eternal life,
> and they will *never* perish.  No one will
> snatch them out of my hand. My Father,
> who has given them to me, is greater than
> all; no one can snatch them out of my
> Father's hand. The Father and I are one.
>
> JOHN 10:27-30

Thus, when one places one's trust in Christ, one
can be *sure* that they will be with Him forever
when this life is over. They *can* be sure, without
a shadow of a doubt. No other belief system on
earth provides such an undisputed *assurance* of
the afterlife – *regardless* of whether one stumbles
on the way there or not. *None.*

Alrighty than.  But what about people from
all those *other* religions – or from none at all?
It is interesting to note that Christ mentioned

---

[3] See the definition of the word *believe* as used herein
in Chapter 4 on page 71.

that there are *individuals* to whom certain of
God's promises apply *regardless* of who they are
– and God *is* faithful, just, and merciful; and He
never breaks a promise. For instance, some of the
beatitudes that Christ spoke of include:

- Blessed [*or happy, fortunate, blissful*] are the
poor [*humble*] in spirit, for theirs is the kingdom
of heaven.

- Blessed are the merciful, for they will *receive*
mercy.

- Blessed are the pure in heart, for they *will* see
God.

- Blessed are the peacemakers, for they will be
called *children of God*.

- Blessed are those who are persecuted for *righteousness'* sake, for theirs is the kingdom of
heaven.

MATTHEW 5:3-10

Furthermore, Christ stated that ...

> Whoever welcomes you welcomes me, and
> whoever welcomes me welcomes the one
> who sent me. Whoever welcomes a prophet
> in the name of a prophet will receive a
> prophet's reward; and whoever welcomes

a righteous person in the name of a righteous person will receive the reward of the righteous; and whoever gives even a cup of cold water to one of these little ones who is my disciple—truly I tell you, none of these will lose their reward.

MATTHEW 10:40-42

... and as Jesus *also* said,

Very truly, I tell you, whoever receives one whom I send receives me; and whoever receives me receives Him who sent me.

JOHN 13:20

In addition, on speaking directly to His apostles, it is again told that:

He [*Christ*] sat down, called the twelve, and said to them, 'Whoever wants to be first must be last of all and servant of all.' Then he took a little child and put it among them; and taking it in his arms, he said to them, 'Whoever welcomes one such child in my name welcomes me, and whoever welcomes me welcomes not me but the one who sent me.'

MARK 9:35-37

Lastly, Christ also told us that:

But they will do all these things to you on account of my name, because they do

not know Him who sent me.  If I had
not come and spoken to them, they would
not have sin; but now they have no excuse for their sin.  Whoever hates me
hates my Father also.  If I had not done
among them the works that no one else
did, they would not have sin.  But now
they have seen and hated both me and
my Father.  It was to fulfill the word that
is written in their law, 'They hated me
without a cause.'  When the Advocate [*the
Holy Spirit*] comes, whom I will send to
you from the Father, the Spirit of Truth
who comes from the Father, he will testify
on my behalf.  You also are to testify
because you have been with me from the
beginning.

JOHN 15:21-27

Yes, it is the Spirit of Truth – the Holy Spirit
of Christ – who testifies on his behalf to *all* who
will listen – whomever they may be.[4]  And every
single one of us, at some point in each of our own
individual lives, *will* make a choice – whether we
are consciously aware of it or not – on whether we
will respond to the calling of God's Holy Spirit,
or whether we will reject the Spirit of the Living
God as He gently urges us to *become* a part of

---

[4] See also John F. Walvoord, *The Holy Spirit*.
Zondervan, 1991.

our lives. But it must be realized that no one can
state what will be of this or that person when
they have not – in our eyes – come to Christ.
For only God, who is spirit, knows the heart, and
He does *whatever* He wills. As has been aptly
explained in regards to the heart as referred to
by scripture:

> Of all the words to be found in the Bible
> that describe man, the term *heart* pro-
> vides the most complete characterization.
> The term heart (Gr. *kardia*; Heb. *leb*),
> denotes the 'inner man' (cf. Eph. 3:16),
> the essence of personality; the seat and
> center of all life. The heart is that central
> essence of man with which God is primar-
> ily concerned – He looks upon it (I Sam.
> 16:7), searches it (Prov. 10:8), and tries
> it (Jere.11:20; 17:10: 20:12). Further, the
> heart is the center and source of all belief
> and faith (Luke 24:25; Rom. 10:10)...
> Every person lives by faith – whether
> believer or unbeliever. The difference lies
> in what each believes. The beliefs that
> we have about God, ourselves and the
> world in which we live – which ultimately
> become the basis of all acts of volition –
> center in the heart: 'And He said to them,
> "O foolish men and slow of heart to believe
> in all that the prophets have spoken!"'

(Lk. 24:25); '... for with the heart man believes, resulting in righteousness' (Rom. 10:10).[5]

Yes, God indeed looks at the heart. And as rightly said, our beliefs regarding God, ourselves, and others does indeed center on the heart. Furthermore, as C.S. Lewis himself states:

There are people in other religions who are being led by God's secret influence to concentrate on those parts of their religion which are in agreement with Christianity, and who thus belong to Christ without knowing it. For example a Buddhist of good will may be led to concentrate more and more on the Buddhist teaching about mercy and to leave in the background (though he might still say he believed) the Buddhist teaching on certain points. Many of the good Pagans long before Christ's birth may have been in this position. And always, of course, there are a great many people who are just confused in mind and have a lot of inconsistent beliefs all jumbled up together. Consequently, it is not much use trying to make judgments about Christians and non-Christians in the mass.[6]

Similarly, the renowned global evangelist Dr. Billy Graham has stated,

---

[5] As in G. Harry Leafe, *The Heart of Man*. Scriptel.

[6] As per the classic *Mere Christianity*, Lewis, *Mere Christianity* (as in n. 3 on page xix).

I think that everybody that *loves* Christ or knows Christ, whether they're *conscious* of it or not, they're members of the *body* of Christ.   And that's what God is doing today.  He's calling people out of the world for *His* name – whether they come from the Muslim world, or the Buddhist world, or the Christian world, or the non-believing world – they are members of the body of Christ because they've been called by *God*.  They may not even know the *name* of Jesus; but they know in their *heart* that they need *something* that they don't have – and they turn to the only light that they have – and I think that they're saved, that they're going to be with us in heaven... I've met people in various parts of the world in tribal situations, that they have never seen a Bible or heard about a Bible, and never heard of Jesus, but they've believed in their hearts that there was a God, and they've tried to live a life that was quite apart from the surrounding community in which they lived. [7]

Yes, God will do *whatever* He wills – in *His* time, and in *His* pleasure.  It is *His* prerogative, and *His* alone.  We cannot make the judgement.  For only *He* knows the heart, and only He draws all of mankind to Himself.  If they listen and have genuinely responded to His voice – which is the voice of Christ Himself, for "I and the Father are

---

[7] As per Billy Graham, *Hour of Power - Crystal Cathedral: Robert Schuller*. May 31, 1997 broadcast.

One", who are *we* to judge. And if he is "the way, the truth, and the life", to where "no one comes to the Father but by Me", than if some have legitimately come to the Father in spirit and in truth, have they not come *through* Christ? Of course, if this is so, than it is hoped that they recognize it as such and praise Christ for who he is – for he *is* worthy of our praise. Furthermore, even scripture states:

> Therefore God also highly exalted him and gave him the name that is above *every* name, so that at the name of Jesus every knee should bend, in heaven and on earth and under the earth, and *every* tongue should confess that Jesus Christ is Lord, to the glory of God the Father.
>
> PHILIPPIANS 2:9-11

All we can do is trust Him, and follow Him individually and without condemnation. For who are *we* to condemn? Whatever one's own opinions regarding the above two latter quotes from two of the most respected Christian leaders in modern times, one nonetheless cannot *legitimately* make a blank statement and say that "all religions lead to the same path", or that "all religions are essentially the same at their core" – which of

course the above quotes do *not* say nor insinuate
at in the least. Not in the slightest. They only
acknowledge the fact that God will do what He
chooses to do, to where we must be open to such
possibilities. For Christ is sovereign over any and
all, and only He has the right to do what He
wills. We are to follow, to trust, to be a light to
the world, to love in action. . . and to walk humbly
with our God.[8] As Christ has said:

> Do not judge, so that you may not be
> judged. For with the judgment you make
> you will be judged, and the measure you
> give will be the measure you get. Why do
> you see the speck in your neighbor's eye,
> but do not notice the log in your own eye?
> Or how can you say to your neighbor, "Let
> me take the speck out of your eye," while
> the log is in your own eye? You hypocrite,
> first take the log out of your own eye, and
> then you will see clearly to take the speck
> out of your neighbor's eye.
>
> MATTHEW 7:1-5

and,

> Do not judge, and you will not be judged;
> do not condemn, and you will not be con-

---

[8] He has told you, O mortal, what is good; and what
does the Lord require of you but to do justice, and to love
kindness, and to walk humbly with your God? [Micah 6:8]

demned. Forgive, and you will be forgiven;
give, and it will be given to you. A good
measure, pressed down, shaken together,
running over, will be put into your lap; for
the measure you *give* will be the measure
you get *back*.

LUKE 6:37-38

No wonder much of modern Christianity has been
getting a bad rap. If we as believers followed
Christ word-for-word, than the world would see
Christ for who he *is*, rather than for how he has
been misrepresented in many ways. Yes, they
would more dearly see the light of Christ through
us, as was meant to be from the beginning –
because they would see truth, *with* mercy and
compassion and reason – and *without* the judgement, condemnations, nor political agendas. Yes,
we are in the world, but not *of* it[9] – granted. And
yes, the world will hate us because of the name
we so love and bear.[10] But those who *genuinely*

---

[9] "Do not be conformed to this world, but be
transformed by the renewing of your minds, so that you
may discern what is the will of God—what is good and
acceptable and perfect." [Romans 12:2]

[10] As Christ stated: "If the world hates you, be aware
that it hated me before it hated you. If you belonged to the
world, the world would love you as its own. Because you
do not belong to the world, but I have chosen you out of the
world—therefore the world hates you." [John 15:18-19]

seek the truth – and who live *by* the truth – *would* come, and would receive us as the followers of Christ that he called us to be.

Hence, it is not up to *us* to figure out what will be of person A in religion X, or person B who might hold to whatever belief that might be. That is *God's* territory, and only *He* sees the heart – *irrespective* of whatever religion (or *no* religion) one might follow – and must be left with Him alone. This is not watering down the Gospel. For Christ is sovereign, and he is the way, because he *is* God incarnate. And He *will* do what He pleases – whatever our feelings about it may or may not be. He *alone* is sovereign. And He *alone* draws all of mankind to Himself in *whatever way* that may be – through His Spirit, and on His initiative exclusively and respectively. Again, all *we* must do is trust and obey – to faithfully *follow*, to be a light to the world and salt of the earth[11]– and

---

[11] As Christ said: "You are the salt of the earth; but if salt has lost its taste, how can its saltiness be restored? It is no longer good for anything, but is thrown out and trampled under foot. You are the light of the world. A city built on a hill cannot be hid. No one after lighting a lamp puts it under the bushel basket, but on the lampstand, and it gives light to all in the house. In the same way, let your light shine before others, so that they may see your good

leave the rest up to *Him*. For He *is* worthy of our trust.

For, if we, though limited and fallible, can on our own initiative judge what is right, as Christ stated,[12] can we not *trust* the ultimate Judge of all creation to do what is right and fair by each individual being's life that is lived? Would he ever do something that is "less good" than what we ourselves would do? Will He do something *inferior* than the good that we ourselves would think *correct* to do? Or will He not make the fair and *just* judgement in relation to *this* person, or *that* person? God is truly a fair and *just* God – for He *is* pure justice. It is therefore not *our* job to judge, but rather to follow *Him*, to speak the truth, and to love *in action* – and to trust the judgement on any particular person's ultimate destiny to Him, and Him *alone*. Yes, it is *so*

---

works and give glory to your Father in heaven." [Matthew 5:13-16]

[12] As Christ stated: "When you see a cloud rising in the west, you immediately say, 'It is going to rain'; and so it happens. And when you see the south wind blowing, you say, 'There will be scorching heat'; and it happens. You hypocrites! You know how to interpret the appearance of earth and sky, but why do you not know how to interpret the present time? And why do you not judge for yourselves what is right?" [Luke 12:54-57]

true. God will *never* do anything that is *less* good, fair, or equitable than what we *ourselves* would do. Not in a trillion years. So consider your own destiny, *trust* in Him, and move on. Thank God that other people's ultimate destiny is *not* left up to us to ever decide.

In addition to this, it has also been said that:

> Because salvation is by grace through faith, I believe that among the countless number of people standing in front of the throne and in front of the Lamb, dressed in white robes and holding palms in their hands (see Revelation 7:9), I shall see the prostitute from the Kit-Kat Ranch in Carson City, Nevada, who tearfully told me that she could find no other employment to support her two-year-old son. I shall see the woman who had an abortion and is haunted by guilt and remorse but did the best she could faced with grueling alternatives; the businessman besieged with debt who sold his integrity in a series of desperate transactions; the insecure clergyman addicted to being liked, who never challenged his people from the pulpit and longed for unconditional love; the sexually abused teen molested by his father and now selling his body on the street, who, as he falls asleep each night after his last 'trick', whispers the name of the unknown God he learned about in Sunday school.

'But how?' we ask.

Then the voice says, 'They have washed their robes and have made them white in the blood of the Lamb.'

There they are.  There *we* are - the multitude who so wanted to be faithful, who at times got defeated, soiled by life, and bested by trials, wearing the bloodied garments of life's tribulations, but through it all clung to faith.

My friends, if this is not good news to you, you have never understood the gospel of grace.[13]

For, as has been said in scripture in regards to God's *perfect* justice and mercy:

Those who fear the Lord prepare their hearts, and humble themselves before Him. Let us fall into the hands of the Lord, but not into the hands of mortals; for equal to His majesty is His mercy, and equal to His name are His works.

SIRACH 2:17

Lastly, in regards to our *own* personal practice of mercy, as has previously been quoted, and as James rightly tells us:

---

[13] As per Brennan Manning, *The Ragamuffin Gospel: Good News for the Bedraggled, Beat-Up, and Burnt Out*. Multnomah Books, 2005.

> So speak and so act as those who are to be
> judged by the law of liberty. For judgment
> will be without mercy to anyone who has
> shown no mercy; for mercy triumphs over
> judgment.
>
> JAMES 2:12-13

All of this being said, it must also be noted that
any cursory look on attempting to compare –
or worse, to *assimilate*, as is often the case –
one religion to another in respect to each other's
values and beliefs will immediately show that no
two religions are the same – despite what might
now be the "politically correct" way to look at it in
this day and age. For just because an idea might
be popular or sound harmonious, 'universal', or
'unifying' as a sound bite does not necessarily
make it correct, truthful, or in any way valid. Any
student of logic will likely tell you the same.

In fact, the closest one can realistically come
to in regards to any sort of "religious symmetry"
with respect to world religions might be on considering that Buddha may have been regarded as
a Hindu guru who was the founder of what developed into Buddhism – though both are for the
most part now diametrically opposed in regards
to their belief structure despite the coincidental

history that they might have in common;[14] and likewise, in regards to Christianity and Judaism, that Christians could very well be viewed as *believing Jews* who have accepted that Jesus of Nazareth *is* in fact the prophesied-about and awaited Messiah of the Hebrew people[15] who are now not bound by religious law any longer,[16] but who have been redeemed by God's love and undeserved favor, and not by works, so that no one can boast, as Paul himself aptly puts when he states:

> But God, who is rich in mercy, out of the great love with which he loved us even when we were dead through our trespasses, made us alive together with Christ—For by grace you have been saved through faith, and this is not your own doing; it is the *gift* of God— not the result of works, so that no one may boast.

EPHESIANS 2:4 & 8-9

---

[14] See Hirakawa Akira, *History of Indian Buddhism: From Sakyamuni to Early Mahayana*. Motilal Banarsidass, 2007; Richard F. Gombrich, *How Buddhism Began: The Conditioned Genesis of the Early Teachings*. Routledge, 2005; as well as Heinrich Dumoulin, *Zen Buddhism: A History, India & China*. World Wisdom, 2005.

[15] See Chapter 2 on page 23 for a full explanation.

[16] See Appendix section C on page 459.

In addition, as has been rightly said:

> Different religions contradict one another. Logic says they could all be wrong, but logic says they can't all be right ... Most religions teach some form of works—if we do this, and that, and if we do it well enough, then we will eventually get to God. The gospel says that all such approaches don't work. People can never work their way to God. Rules can't save anyone, or get anyone closer to God. The gospel teaches a different path of salvation than other religions do. At the heart of the gospel is that our own works cannot save us—and that means that the gospel also says that religions can't save us. People in other religions need grace [*grace being God's unmerited, undeserved favor towards us*], just like we need grace, and grace is found only in the gospel of Jesus Christ ... God has come to us and saved us because we could not save ourselves. We need this kind of salvation, and the gospel of Jesus Christ teaches that God has given us what we need.[17]

Furthermore, as has been aptly put,

> Christianity, if false, is of no importance, and if true, of infinite importance, the only thing it cannot be is moderately important.[18]

---

[17] From Joseph Tkach, *Do All Religions Lead to God?* ⟨URL: http://www.gci.org/gospel/pluralism⟩.

[18] C.S. Lewis, *God in the Dock: Essays on Theology and Ethics*. Wm. B. Eerdmans Publishing Co., 1972.

And lastly, as Christ has *himself* said:

> I am the way, and the truth, and the life.
> No one comes to the Father except through
> me. If you had known me, you will have
> known my Father also. From now on you
> do know him and have seen him.

JOHN 14:6-7

Yet one might look at the many belief systems
and philosophies going around and, in sincere
perplexity, ask "but what *is* the truth". And it is
interesting to note that, no other religious leader
has ever said what Christ said, when he stated
that *he* is the truth.[19] Yes, to those who can
accept it, truth – from a spiritual sense – is not
a concept or idea, but is rather a *person*. Yes,
Christ *is* the truth. God is the truth. And when
one follows the Son of the Living God, one follows

---

[19] Again, as C.S. Lewis once stated, and as has been
shown within this work's Preface:

> A man who was merely a man and said the
> sort of things Jesus said would not be a great
> moral teacher. He would either be a lunatic
> — on the level with the man who says he is a
> poached egg — or else he would be the Devil
> of Hell. You must make your choice. Either
> this man was, and is, the Son of God, or else
> a madman or something worse. [As in Lewis,
> *Mere Christianity* (as in n. 3 on page xix)]

truth. Thus, taking the above statement made by him, when one places one's *trust* on Christ, one places one's trust *in* truth.

So therefore, taking all of the above into consideration, it is clear that when one places their trust on Christ – when one opens their door to Christ – when one is consciously *willing* to allow Christ to become a part of their lives irrespective of where one might be spiritually, morally, or whatever the case might be – for as we have seen, Christ accepts any and *all* who come to him, *just as they are*, and without strings attached – that person has a solid and undisputed *guarantee* that they have eternal life, and will be with God when they leave this earth. Don't worry. Any betterment to be done is done by God's Holy Spirit from the inside out – in *His* good timing, and in *His* way as depending on the individual in question – as He does so to all who have placed their trust on Him with a willing heart – even if such growth takes an entire *lifetime* to complete.

As has been well put:

> I may not be where I need to be, but I
> thank God that I am not where I *used* to
> be.[20]

As such, those who have genuinely accepted Christ
into their lives, he promises, will never come into
judgement after they pass on, for they *already*
have – while still alive on earth – been judged
and found clean before God through the cleansing
blood of Christ, and they *already* have entered
into eternal life in the here-and-now, and will
*never* die nor face judgement to find whether or
not they have "made it", so-to-speak.  For even
though they may die *physically* – they will *never*
die. For as Christ has said:

> Very truly, I tell you, anyone who hears
> my word and believes him who sent me
> has eternal life, and *does not come under
> judgment*, but has passed from death to
> life.

> JOHN 5:24

and, as Jesus affirmed:

> I am the resurrection and the life.  Those
> who believe in me, *even though they die,*

---

[20] As in Joyce Meyer, *Woman to Woman: Candid
Conversations From Me to You*. FaithWords, 2008.

> *will live*, and everyone who lives and be-
> lieves in me will *never* die.
>
> JOHN 11:25-26

Furthermore, it is said that,

> Indeed, God did not send the Son into the
> world to condemn the world, but in order
> that the world might be saved through
> him.   Those who believe in him *are not
> condemned*; but those who do not believe
> are condemned already, because they have
> not believed in the name of the only Son of
> God.
>
> JOHN 3:17-18

No other religion can give such a guarantee.
None other than Christianity – not as a religion,
but as a simple faith in Him who loved the world
so very much to have opened His door to all, so
that all might *possibly* – if they are willing within
their hearts – open *their* door to Him.   It's *so*
simple that many people will simply miss it – or
stumble over it, or not accept it at all – because
they feel there *must* be more, or that they need
to *do* more. But that *is* the Gospel of Christ. The
*simple* Gospel of Christ.  The *ease* of the Gospel
of Christ – without religious obligation, without

religious sacrifice, and without strings attached. As has been well said,

> I get the impression that many must think that believing is either too easy or too abstract. Too easy in that such an outcome – the total forgiveness of one's sins and the gift of eternal life – certainly must require more. Too abstract in that people must be able to objectify their belief in order for it to be real. This later concept usually involves belief plus something else – pray the sinner's prayer, raise your hand at an evangelistic meeting, walk down an aisle at church in response to an invitation to 'come to Christ', be baptized, live under Christ's lordship, etc. The list can go on and on...My point is this: Romans 10:9-10[21] do not present a different formula for personal salvation. A person is saved from the penalty of sin through faith in Christ *alone*.[22]

---

[21] As is written in scripture: " ... because if you confess with your lips that Jesus is Lord and believe in your heart that God raised him from the dead, you will be saved. For one believes with the heart and so is justified, and one confesses with the mouth and so is saved. The scripture says, *'No one who believes in him will be put to shame.'* For there is no distinction between Jew and Greek; the same Lord is Lord of all and is generous to all who call on him. For, *'Everyone who calls on the name of the Lord shall be saved.'*" [Romans 10:9-13]

[22] Leafe, *Muddy Water* (as in n. 1 on page 72).

And that is why it may truthfully be said that
Christ did not come to bring the world yet *another*
religion – but rather personal liberty and freedom
from the enchainments of mankind and its own
traditions, superstitions, unbeliefs, cynicisms, religions, and traps.  This is why Christ plainly
stated that his yoke *is* easy, and his burden is
*light*, when he told the world:

> Come to me, all you that are weary and
> are carrying heavy burdens, and I will
> give you rest. Take my yoke upon you, and
> learn from me; for I am gentle and humble
> in heart, and you will find rest for your
> souls. For my yoke is easy, and my burden
> is light.
>
> Matthew 11:28-30

As such, just because someone might be 'wrong'
about some matters does not mean they are not
going to see God, much as just because someone
might seem to be 'right' in the eyes of others does
not mean that that is how God sees it. Remember,
He *alone* is the judge – the just and righteous
judge – who's judgement will *never* be inferior
to the good that we *ourselves* would do with a
compassionate and good heart. For God looks at

the heart.[23] And as has been previously quoted elsewhere, Christ has himself stated:

> For just as the Father raises the dead and gives them life, even so the Son also gives life to whom He wishes. For not even the Father judges anyone, but He has given *all* judgment to the Son, so that all will honor the Son even as they honor the Father. He who does *not* honor the Son does *not* honor the Father who sent Him. Truly, truly, I say to you, he who hears My word, and believes Him who sent Me, has eternal life, and does not come into judgment, but has passed out of death into life.
>
> John 5:21-24

It's not even about belief in the strict sense of the word, but rather about a *change* of heart, a change of mind, and a *willingness* to *let God* be part of one's life – a life that *He* has given, and one that ultimately belongs to *Him*, and Him alone.

It is about God making the rules because He *is* the Creator of all and thereby has a right *to*

---

[23] As is said, "But the Lord said to Samuel, 'Do not look on his appearance or on the height of his stature, because I have rejected him; for the Lord does not see as *mortals* see – they look on the outward appearance, but the Lord looks on the heart.' " [I Samuel 16:7]

all. It's about letting God have what He's entitled to, because He gave us life in the first place, and is *Himself* life. It's about not insulting God with false gods made by man, nor through religions that oppress mankind – whom He loves and would defend unto death – *His* death on the cross. It's about free will, to where we ourselves choose whether we want Him to be a part of our lives, or whether we choose to be separate and apart from Him now and forever. And God honors our desire, whatever we choose. For with God there is *freedom*. And He does not oppress, man-handle, nor force anyone into anything – as religiosity, and as mankind in general, does one to another in myriads of ways. No. We are *free* to choose. And He will *always* honor our choices – choices that have consequences, one way or another. And that is why He looks at the heart, rather than our appearance or the masks we might put on for the benefit of others.

It's a matter of the heart, and a *choice* of the mind. The choice between Light and dark. Between good and evil. Between truth and deception. It's a matter of the soul. It's a matter of free will. It's a matter of love. It's a matter of who you freely choose to be – on the *inside* – in your *core* being. For, as has been said:

> All your life an unattainable ecstasy has hovered just beyond the grasp of your consciousness. The day is coming when you will wake to find, beyond all hope, that you have attained it, or else, that it was within your reach and you have lost it forever. [24]

So therefore, only Christ can judge. And only He knows what's in the heart of mankind – utterly and *individually*. We cannot truly speculate on what will happen to this person or to that person in our lives, or to those around us. Again, only *God* truly knows one's heart – and will never misjudge. We cannot know how God will handle *that* life that was lived, or the *other's* life that was lived. For those who truthfully *accept* Christ – irrespective of whatever religious title they might or might not use – are called to love, to be the salt of the earth, and to be a light to the world,[25] and

---

[24] As in Lewis, *The Problem of Pain* (as in n. 2 on page 106).

[25] As Christ said: "You are the salt of the earth; but if salt has lost its taste, how can its saltiness be restored? It is no longer good for anything, but is thrown out and trampled under foot. You are the light of the world. A city built on a hill cannot be hid. No one after lighting a lamp puts it under the bushel basket, but on the lampstand, and

not to judge nor condemn others – but to speak the truth when it is called for. [26]

But what remains is the knowledge and blessed *assurance* that, those who have opened their door to Christ already *have* eternal life, and will *never* die. Christ *is* the guarantee ... the *ultimate* guarantee. As the Reverend Billy Graham once said:

> Someday you will read or hear that Billy Graham is dead. Don't you believe a word of it! I shall be more alive than I am now.

---

it gives light to all in the house. In the same way, let your light shine before others, so that they may see your good works and give glory to your Father in heaven." [Matthew 5:13-16]

[26] So – to those who believe – tell the truth as based on what Christ has said. Not on what *religion* has said, no – lest you want to muddy up the waters and bring forth confusion into the mix. No. Speak what Christ is saying. And tell the truth in regards to other spiritual viewpoints. But do so in a Christ-like fashion, for those you speak to are also God's creation and are made in His image, and therefore deserve dignity and respect. For even Paul showed respect for Pagan idol worshipers when he was preaching to the crowd in Athens as per Acts 17:16-34. Even so, the truth *must* be told. If one does not receive it, simply move on, and pray that one day even *they* might see the love of God in the midst of opinionated religiosity (or of no religiosity), and that they might open their own door to Him if they have not done so already.

> I will just have changed my address. I will
> have gone into the presence of God. [27]

Yes, we *shall* be more alive than we are now.
For we will then finally be *fully* human – something that many seek to find through ritual, self-
sacrifice, suffering, meditation, and the like – to
reach 'enlightenment', so to speak – though this
will only come when it is all said and done. For
as has been said:

> To enter heaven is to become more human
> than you ever succeeded in being on earth;
> to enter hell is to be banished from hu-
> manity. What is cast (or casts itself) into
> hell is not a man: it is "remains." To be a
> complete man means to have the passions
> obedient to the will and the will offered
> to God: to have been a man – to be an
> ex-man or "damned ghost" – would pre-
> sumably mean to consist of a will utterly
> centered in its self and passions utterly
> uncontrolled by the will. [28]

One mustn't look to others, nor to what is considered to be "politically correct" or acceptable at the
time, nor to other's approvals in regards to one's
own convictions – for only God is the judge, and

---

[27] From Franklin Graham, *Billy Graham in Quotes*.
Thomas Nelson, 2011.

[28] As per Lewis, *The Problem of Pain* (as in n. 2 on
page 106).

no one else. It is between the self and God, and that alone. For, to the believer – one must look *only* to Christ – for it is *he* who is our hope and unwavering promise of our salvation. The rest will follow by the examples we set, by the truth we speak while showing dignity and respect for all, and by the love we abundantly show in our actions. But it is God who ultimately does *all* the work . . . and *is* all the work.

Yes, God wants to have a relationship with you – *apart from* religion. All you need to do is open your door to Him by placing your trust in His ever-loving hands. Again, God does not want – nor need – your religion. No. God wants *you*. . . just as you are, with all your baggage, mistakes, wrong-doings, shortcomings, faults, unbelief, stubbornness. . . whatever it may be. Don't worry, He does the rest from the inside out.

If God has beckoned for you, than you are very privileged indeed! For how can you compare having the Creator of the Universe caring for you enough to say, "I love you so very much and want to be part of *your* life" – with anyone else on this earth who might tell you the same thing? For truly nobody is capable of accepting that there *is* a God who unconditionally loves and accepts them without reservation or preconditions *unless* God reveals this to them directly. For, as Christ said:

> No one can come to Me unless the Father who sent Me *draws* him; and I will raise him up on the last day. It is written in the prophets, 'AND THEY SHALL ALL BE TAUGHT OF GOD.' Everyone who has heard and learned from the Father comes to Me.
>
> JOHN 6:44-45

It is the Spirit of the Living God *Himself* who makes the choice to come to the Seeker of Truth in the parable at the beginning of this chapter – and not the Seeker who suddenly chooses to come to God, no matter how hard he might try, nor how religious and self-sacrificing he may be. As has been rightly said:

> No matter how deep of a pit you are in, God's arm is never to short to reach down and pull you up. Grace will meet you where you are at, but grace will never leave you where it found you.[29]

---

[29] As in Joyce Meyer, *Enjoying Everyday Life broadcasts.* Joyce Meyer Ministries ⟨URL: http://www.joycemeyer.org⟩.

Yes, it *is* Christ's Holy Spirit – who he promised he would give to *all* who come to him[30] in spirit and in truth[31] – it is *He* who reveals himself to the weakest, lowliest, and most rejected of us – what this world would deem as unimportant, unworthy, "unrighteous"... mere infants from the viewpoint of the rest of mankind. And to those who are willing to accept him, they gain a friend who truly *does* bear all their sins and griefs when this world has turned its back on them. For as the classic hymn rightly states:

---

[30] As Christ stated: "I will ask the Father, and He will give you another Helper [Comforter, Advocate, Intercessor], that He may be with you forever; that is the Spirit of truth, whom the world cannot receive, because it does not see Him or know Him, but you know Him because He abides with you and will be in you. I will not leave you as orphans; I will come to you." [John 14:18];

as well as:

"When the Spirit of truth comes, he will guide you into *all* the truth. . . He will glorify me, because He will take what is mine and declare it to you." [John 16:13-14]

[31] See Chapter 6 on page 89 for a full explanation of what Christ meant by "in spirit and in truth".

What a friend we have in Jesus
All our sins and griefs to bear!
What a privilege to carry
Everything to God in prayer!
O what peace we often forfeit
O what needless pain we bear
All because we do not carry
Everything to God in prayer

Are we weak and heavy laden
Cumbered with a load of care?
Precious Savior, still our refuge
Take it to the Lord in prayer
Do thy friends despise, forsake thee?
Take it to the Lord in prayer!
In His arms he'll take and shield thee
Thou wilt find a solace there [32]

For he is *greater* than our sins, so that we must not let our past mistakes and present faults grieve us any longer when he has taken over. For as it is said:

> I, even I, am He who blots out your transgressions for *My* own sake, and remembers your sins no more.
>
> ISAIAH 43:25

---

[32] *What a Friend We Have in Jesus* – Lyrics by Joseph M. Scriven, 1820-1886; score by Charles C. Converse, 1832-1918.

When you turn to Christ, you are *forgiven* –
and are *continuously* forgiven as He continuously
works in your heart and mind – until the day you
go to be with Him. So if God has forgiven you,
do you forgive yourself? No need to confess to a
priest. For *Christ* is your High Priest. You can go
*directly to* him, and skip the middleman. For as
it has been rightly said:

> Since, then, we have a Great High Priest
> who has passed through the heavens, Je-
> sus, the Son of God, let us hold firmly to
> the faith we profess. For we do not have a
> High Priest who is unable to sympathize
> with our weaknesses, but we have one
> who in every respect has been tempted
> as we are, yet he did not sin. Let us
> therefore approach God's throne of grace
> *with confidence*, so that we may receive
> mercy and find grace to help us in our time
> of need.
>
> HEBREWS 4:14-16

No need for religion. For *He* is your confidence,
your faith. And if you *really* want to use the term,
than yes – your 'religion'. No need to *repetitively*
ask Him to forgive you of something over and
over and over again when you have *already* done
it once. That is guilt, and is *not* of God. When you
have been forgiven, you must *move on*! Remorse

– or regret if you will – on the other hand, is used by God to nudge you into improving the self. But stale guilt only chokes you – preventing you from bearing the fruit that He wants you to bear – such as growing, being the salt of the earth and a light to the world, loving, and *being* loved. You *can* forgive yourself and let go when you *know* He has already said:

> OK, so you screwed up. Get back up, get out of that ditch, and just *keep following me*. And remember... I *still* love you, and *always* will.

Yes, through the blood of Christ, you *are* allowed to finally let go. Will you allow yourself at least *that*? He has chosen you out of the world to be His child, has he not? So get up! Shake the dust away – and follow! *Please* allow yourself *at least* that.

And what a friend he *truly* is. For *all* authority in heaven and on earth has *indeed* been given to him,[33] *once and for all*. Can one find a friend

---

[33] As Christ said to his followers before he was taken up to Heaven after his resurrection:

> All authority in heaven and on earth has been given to me. Go therefore and make disciples of all nations, baptizing them in the name of

more powerful, more faithful, more loving, or more gently?  Again, he does not call us to be 'religious'...to be *"like* them."  No.  He calls us to be *his* kids.  To love and to hold...forever.  And all *you* have to do is say *yes* to Christ.  Nothing more.  Nothing less.  And you are his – *forever*.

For that *is* the Gospel according to Christ.

the Father and of the Son and of the Holy Spirit, and teaching them to obey everything that I have commanded you.  And remember, I am with you always, to the end of the age. [Matthew 28:18-20]

Chapter Eleven

# *Love is the Only Command*

Christ stated that we are to adhere to two commandments on which everything else that God would expect of us are *all* summed up in – these being to love God, and to love our neighbor as ourselves. For as he stated in response to how one obtains eternal life, and which is the primary commandment from God, it is said:

> One of the scribes came and... asked him, 'What commandment is the *foremost* of all?' Jesus answered, 'The foremost is... you shall love the Lord your God with all your heart, and with all your soul, and with all your mind, and with all your strength. The second is this: you shall love your neighbor as yourself. There is no other commandment greater than these.'

> MARK 12:28-31

To the believer – one needs to interpret how such love is to become manifest on an individual basis, as God's Spirit guides us. Furthermore, it is God Himself who enables us, through His Spirit, to love in the ways that one ought to love. For *me* personally, the following are the ways in which *I* would read it, as you may very well get your own interpretations out of these commandments for yourself:

# Loving God...

As C.S. Lewis has said:

> ...a man's spiritual health is exactly proportional to his love for God. [1]

So therefore, as the first commandment, we are to love God with all our heart, soul, mind, and strength. Thus, I would see loving God with all my heart – that inner man within that consists of who we truly are down to the core – as to love Him above all others, above anything this world would offer us, and even above ourselves. To love Him with all our soul – as the essence and totality

---

[1] As in C.S. Lewis, *The Four Loves*. Houghton Mifflin Harcourt, 1991.

of how we would identity ourselves *to* ourselves
– as to be utterly *in* love with the God who
*Himself* unconditionally loves us as our Creator
and heavenly Father.    To love Him with all
our mind as doing away with negative thinking
that would cause us confusion and inner strife
– those things that would sadden the Father
who loves us so dearly – those things that would
contradict His guidance within us and that would
make us stumble in our faith – and exchanging
such things for a *continual* acknowledgement of
His presence, focusing on Him as the Rock that
brings complete stability of mind – as well as in
exchange for both positive thinking as well as a
*deliberate* love in action towards and for Him,
and therefore towards others, and hence towards
ourselves. And to love God with all our strength
as consciously abiding and remaining with and
*in* a relationship with Him – no matter *what* the
world might throw at us. I know, easier said than
done, but as has been rightly said about the Holy
Spirit as being the Great Enabler:

> ... complete union with God, which is sanc-
> tity, requires a perfect orientation toward
> Him, according to the first and greatest
> commandment of Jesus: 'Thou shalt love

the Lord thy God with thy whole heart, and with thy whole soul, and with thy whole mind' (Mt. 22:37); we have seen that this perfect orientation exceeds our powers, precisely because our knowledge of God and of the way which leads to Him is far too imperfect. 'Must we then renounce sanctity?' Not at all! God, who wants our sanctification, has provided us with the means of attaining it: He has given us the Holy Spirit.[2]

As Fr. Gabriel of St. Mary Magdalen, the writer of the above quote, states throughout: "Persevere, and the rewards will be great". Yes, it is indeed God's Holy Spirit who is the Great Enabler. All we need is a willing heart, perseverance, and the recognition that we will *never* be perfect, though Christ is always with us, and that he loves us *consistently* – no matter what.

---

[2] As in Father Gabriel of St. Mary Magdalene, *Divine Intimacy: Meditations on the Interior Life for Every Day of the Liturgical Year*. Tan Books, 1996.

# With All Your Heart

To love God with all of one's heart is to follow Christ's teaching in regards to placing our unshifting trust on God as we come to Him in spirit and in truth[3] – in other words, by our inner and sincere spirit that cannot be lied to (not even by ourselves) and that cannot lie, and this without ritual or religious tradition – naked in spirit, just as we are. With all the good and bad. Just as we are. For, as we have seen, and as Christ said:

> But the hour is coming, and is now here, when the true worshipers will worship the Father in spirit and truth, for the Father seeks such as these to worship him. God is spirit, and those who worship him must worship in spirit and truth.
>
> JOHN 23-24

And though no one is ever fully capable of adoring God with all of one's heart – for we are human – God does not look on the quantity, intensity, or strength of our reverence for Him, but merely that we love Him enough to acknowledge Him as who He is, and – with patient endurance – to *continue* and never cease to follow. It is no

---

[3] See Chapter 6 on page 89.

use attempting to be 'religious' in order to please God, for He is not about religion, but rather about a trusting, child-like *relationship* to Him as our heavenly Father. As such, we can communicate and adore Him even in our silence – knowing that we will never be able to fully love as He loves us. For:

> In the presence of the unspeakable mystery of the Trinity, the highest praise is silence, the silence of the soul that adores, knowing that it is incapable of praising or glorifying the divine Majesty worthily.[4]

## With All Your Soul

To love God with all one's soul is to surrender our inner man within to the source that gives all life, and *is* Himself life – to let go, and let God. Do *you* have the courage to let go, and trust Him enough to make it all work? As has aptly been said:

> Courage is fear that has said its prayers and decided to go forward anyway. [5]

---

[4] As per Magdalene (as in n. 2 on page 234).

[5] As in Joyce Meyer, *I Dare You: Embrace Life with Passion*. FaithWords, 2007.

Why do we always feel like it is *we* who must figure it all out by tossing and turning, mulling over that potential solution over and over again in our minds, and getting heart disease, strokes, and heart attacks as a result when we can just, well, chill out, and let God? And why do we need to always try and have every single theological idea figured out in our heads first, or have our conscious clear first, or attempt to become 'perfect' first – before we come to God? God *is* love. For, as it is well written:

> Whoever does not love does not know God, for God is love... God *is* love, and those who abide in love abide in God, and God abides in them.
> I JOHN 4:8 & 16

Yes. God *is* love. He's *true* love. So why do we not come to Him naked, just as we are, without having to clean everything up in our lives before we can *allow* ourselves to do so? God wants our souls – *just as we are*. And *that* is what loving God is. Letting go and – with the simple faith of a child – letting *Him* take over. Can you do that? *Anybody* can. For that is the nature of God. He welcomes anybody. Yes ... *anybody*. Can you let go and allow Him to start doing *His* work in

you – because He loves you and wants what's best
for you? He knows you better than you will ever
know yourself – better than anyone in this earth
will *ever* know you. As is said,

> For it was You who formed my inward
> parts; You knit me together in my mother's
> womb. I praise You, for I am fearfully and
> wonderfully made. Wonderful are Your
> works; that I know very well. My frame
> was not hidden from You, when I was
> being made in secret, intricately woven in
> the depths of the earth. Your eyes beheld
> my unformed substance.
>
> PSALM 139:13-16

His love for you is deeper than anyone else's on
this planet. Can you put your trust in Him and
just let go? Let *Him* guide you? Let *Him* direct
your paths? Let *Him* handle it? He knows what's
best for you better than you know yourself, and
He will never – *ever* – let you down. *Never*. It
*could* seem like He might at some time in your
life, but one day – whether in this life or the next
– you will realize just *why* it happened as it did –
and that, *even then*, He never left you, but *carried*
you.

For,

> We know that God makes *all things* work
> together for good for those who love God,
> who are called according to his purpose.
> For those whom he foreknew he also pre-
> destined to be conformed to the image of
> his Son, in order that he might be the
> firstborn within a large family. And those
> whom he predestined he also called; and
> those whom he called he also justified; and
> those whom he justified he also glorified.
>
> ROMANS 8:28-30

Yes, as the classic poem *Footsteps in the Sand*[6] il-
lustrates, when you look back at the troubles you
have faced, and notice but one set of footprints
in the sand, you may realize that you were never
alone. For you had placed your faith on Christ,
and were carried *by* him through it all to the very
end – even when you could not walk further by
yourself. Similarly, as was preached in London,
England in 1880:

> ...And did you ever walk out upon that
> lonely desert island upon which you were
> wrecked and say, 'I am alone— alone—
> *alone*— nobody was ever here before me'?
> And did you suddenly pull up short as

---

[6] See also Gail Giorgio, *Footprints in the Sand - The Life
Story of Mary Stevenson*. Gold Leaf Press, 1995.

you noticed, in the sand, the footprints
of a man?  I remember right well passing through that experience—and when I
looked, lo, it was not merely the footprints
of a man that I saw, but I thought I
knew whose feet had left those imprints.
They were the marks of One who had
been crucified, for there was the print of
the nails.  So I thought to myself, 'If He
has been here, it is no longer a desert
island.   As His blessed feet once trod
this wilderness-way, it blossoms now like
the rose and it becomes to my troubled
spirit as a very garden of the Lord!'  My
objective, in this discourse, will be to try
to point out the footprints of Jesus in the
sands of sorrow. . . [7]

Yes, when you look back at the troubles in your
life, you might well conclude, as I did even though
I had turned away from God for a decade-and-a-
half – yes, *even* then – that though I had left Him,
He *never* left me.  Thank *God* for that!  Thank
God for His mercy, long-suffering patience, and
everlasting love – even for a rebel and black
sheep such as I! And now, whenever I face any
challenges, I *know* that He will *always* get me
through. For His grace truly *is* sufficient for me –
as our good friend Paul himself states:

---

[7] From C. H. Spurgeon, *The Education of Sons of
God*. Sermon by Spurgeon as delivered at the Metropolitan
Tabernacle, London, June 1880.

But he said to me, 'My grace is sufficient for you, for my power is made *perfect* in weakness.' Therefore I will boast all the more gladly about my weaknesses, so that the power of Christ may dwell *in* me. That is why, for Christ's sake, I delight in weaknesses, in insults, in hardships, in persecutions, in difficulties. For when I am weak, then I am strong. [II CORINTHIANS 12:9-10]

# With All Your Mind

To love God with all one's mind is to freely *allow* Him to be the authority over your mind. For an empty mind just wanders and always winds up missing out on life – as well as on what amazing things God has to offer us, and *freely* gives us without precondition. And if the running of one's mind is not given to its Creator – the One who genuinely knows best how it should function in all of its varied and seemingly limitless ways – it *will* eventually wind up being filled with inferior and less adequate *replacements* instead.

Will *your* mind be given to God in order to *let* Him modify, improve upon, and optimize in all of the capabilities that it was *designed* to – or will it be given to the things of this world that never fully satisfy, never fully embrace you as the worthy and dignified human being that you truly are, and that often break? Will you deliberately *choose* (through the authoritative use of your mind) to let your Creator take over – or will you always have to find someone or something to follow and that eventually just disappointingly lets you down in more ways than one?

Will your mind be a refined, finely-tuned instrument that seeks to please its Creator who truly loves it – or will it be used and abused by those who think they *know* better?[8] If you don't give your mind to God, you can be sure someone, something, some theory, some form of theological fanaticism, or some party-pooper *will* hijack it

---

[8] Even many of the Jewish religious leaders in Christ's time decided to keep their minds and focus on religious tradition in order to *please* man rather than God – and this by not accepting that Christ was their promised Messiah, in order that they might not be kicked out of their synagogues, their traditions, and their group. For as it is said in the Gospels:

> Nevertheless many, even of the authorities, believed in him. But because of the Pharisees they did not confess it, for fear that they would be put out of the synagogue; for they loved human glory more than the glory that comes from God. [John 12:42-43]

instead. Ultimately, the choice is always up to you, and you alone. For as has rightly been said:

> How much better to get wisdom than gold! To get understanding is to be chosen rather than silver.
>
> PROVERBS 16:16

and,

> The fear of the Lord is the *beginning* of wisdom, and the knowledge of the Holy One is insight. For by me your days will be multiplied, and years will be added to your life. If you are wise, you are wise for yourself; if you scoff, you alone will bear it.
>
> PROVERBS 9:10-12

Furthermore, it is imperative to keep in mind that:

> My people are *destroyed* for lack of knowledge;
>
> HOSEA 4:6

In order for the mind to function at its optimum – and to thus love Him with *all* of our mind – it is imperative that one consciously *chooses* to lean more on positive, rather than on negative thinking. For we all have the conscious, *deliberate* choice to either look at a half-filled glass as *half-full* rather than as *half-empty*. Looking at it as half-full allows us the freedom to enjoy the water that we have, and gives us the motivation to fill it even more. Looking at it as half-empty might lead to unsatisfaction when we already have the important things in life, to take the water that we *do* have for granted, and possibly to despair at how empty it truly is. For the mind was *made* for positive thinking. When one considers the myriad of diagnosable conditions of the mind, and the negative cognitive processes that either catalyze, or directly cause emotional and mental imbalances of all kinds, it is plain to see just how powerful negative thinking can be in its long-term affects in our lives, behaviors, and attitudes.

Loving God with all of one's mind also means to be *appreciative* of life, content with what we *do* have, accepting of how He has created us to be, hopeful of all that He has in store for us, in love with who we are as *His* own children, and faithful to His voice. So, therefore, *give* yourself a break, and *allow* yourself to consciously choose to look at the glass as half-full whenever you can, and you will excel at being all that you were always meant to be – and all that you have the *potential* to be –

for *His* honor and glory. And you can facilitate it by adhering to good advice tainted by tried-and-true wisdom – such as how you *chooses* to think.

For, like a computer, if you allow garbage to come in, you will get garbage out. If you allow for stable, balanced, positive, truthful, organized, and realistic thought-processes to come in – you'll get a super-brain-fueled fruition of all that is good, stable, and positive out. Yes, advice such as:

> Finally, beloved, whatever is true, whatever is honorable, whatever is just, whatever is pure, whatever is pleasing, whatever is commendable, if there is any excellence and if there is anything worthy of praise, *think* about these things.
>
> PHILIPPIANS 4:8

# With All Your Strength

To love God with all of one's strength is to start developing power-strength muscles for Him – to be unshifting while the rest of mankind shifts and staggers; and this because you know *where* your foundation and strength comes from; to be as strong as a stone house built upon the Rock of

Christ, so that when the waves crash against it, you can confidently say "I'm still standing!";[9] to continue and persevere even when doubt or fear might unwittingly enter your mind due to false teachers, fanciful philosophies, and the latest "religious craze" to hit your neck of the woods[10]... and *to stand*.[11] It is to, with *patient endurance*, persevere and not let the worries of this world, the deceitfulness of money,[12] nor the desire for

---

[9] See Luke 6:46-49.

[10] See both Chapter 14 on page 307 in relation to cults that destroy the mind; as well as Appendix A on page 357, which continues the discussion with a look at global waves of religions that, though appearing positive on the outside, entrap and confuse those that adhere to their whims.

[11] As Paul rightly said:
"Finally, be strong in the Lord and in the strength of his power... Therefore take up the whole armor of God, so that you may be able to withstand on that evil day, and having done everything, *to stand* firm." [Ephesians 6:10 & 13]

[12] Yes, money, which will make one think they do not need God when they have much, or that they have "other things to worry about" besides God if they have very little. Is money your life's thermometer? What an ever-changing reference-point in life to build one's confidence, happiness, and security on indeed! As Christ said,

> No one can serve two masters; for a slave will either hate the one and love the other, or be devoted to the one and despise the other. You cannot serve God and wealth. [Matthew 6:24]

Yes, neither riches, nor prestige, ever fully satisfy. And there is no shame in recognizing this and turning to God

other things choke your faith, your happiness,
your devotion to your First Love and Creator, and
the quality of fruits that you can bear – as Christ
said in the parable of the Sower and the Seed.[13]
For while Christ was explaining this parable, he
said:

> Now the parable is this: The seed is
> the word of God. The ones on the path
> are those who have heard; then the devil
> comes and takes away the word from their

---

when one realizes there really is *nothing* else that can
completely satisfy. It's not a hypocritical act to turn to Him
after such a realization. No. Rather, it is an act of *wisdom*
to be willing to do so. For He will *always* welcome us unto
Himself, regardless of how we have lived before. As it is
said:

"Let me implore the reader to try to believe, if only for a
moment, that God, who made these deserving people, may
really be right when He thinks that their modest prosperity
and the happiness of their children are not enough to make
them blessed: that all this must fall from them in the end,
and if they have not learned to know Him they will be
wretched. And therefore He troubles them, warning them
in advance of an insufficiency that one day they will have
to discover. The life to themselves and their families stands
between them and the recognition of their need; He makes
that life less sweet to them... If God were proud He would
hardly have us on such terms: but He is not proud, He
stoops to conquer, He will have us even though we have
shown that we prefer everything else to Him, and come to
Him because there is 'nothing better' now to be had." [As
per Lewis, *The Problem of Pain* (as in n. 2 on page 106).]

[13] As in Matthew 13:1-23; Mark 4:1-20; and Luke 8:4-15.

hearts, so that they may not believe and be saved. The ones on the rock are those who, when they hear the word, receive it with joy. But these have no root; they believe only for a while and in a time of testing fall away. As for what fell among the thorns, these are the ones who hear; but as they go on their way, they are choked by the cares [*anxieties, worries*] and riches [or, *deceitfulness of wealth*] and pleasures of life, and their fruit does not mature. But as for that in the good soil, these are the ones who, when they hear the word, hold it fast [or, *accept it*] in an honest and good heart, and bear fruit with *patient endurance* [or, *perseverance*].

LUKE 8:8-15

Yes, it is to *accept* God's Word with an honest heart, and to bear fruit with patient endurance and perseverance. It's to *not quit* when things get hot. It's to keep going when everyone else has stopped trying. It's to not lose heart, nor your joy and peace, when everyone else is in panic-mode. It's to take Christ at *his word* when he tells those of us in times of despair:

Do not fear, only believe.

MARK 5:36

It's to be joyful in a world that has lost much of its joy. It's to be loving in a world where "most of man's hearts have grown cold", as Christ said would happen before his return.[14] It's to be frank – but to also be wise and without haste. It's to be mentally *sharp* – and to wait upon God without panic. It's to be at peace – and to enjoy life as God meant for us to enjoy it. It is to persevere. It is to go on. It is to be happy. It is to live. As has been aptly said:

> If you have run with footmen and they have tired you out, how can you compete with horses? If you fall down in a land of peace, How will you do in the thicket of the Jordan?
>
> JEREMIAH 12:5

# Loving Your Neighbor...

And the second commandment was this: to love your neighbor as yourself. Not necessarily a *sentimental* – touchy-feely – sort of love. No, but rather a love *in action*. As Paul aptly describes it:

> Bless those who persecute you; bless and do not curse them. Rejoice with those who

---

[14] See Appendix A on page 357.

rejoice, weep with those who weep. Live
in harmony with one another; do not be
haughty, but *associate* with the lowly; do
not claim to be wiser than you are.  Do
not repay anyone evil for evil, but take
thought for what is noble in the sight of
all.  If it is possible, so far as it depends
on you, live peaceably with all.  Beloved,
never avenge yourselves, but leave room
for the wrath of God; for it is written,
'Vengeance is mine, I will repay, says the
Lord.'  No, 'if your enemies are hungry,
feed them; if they are thirsty, give them
something to drink; for by doing this you
will heap burning coals on their heads.'  Do
not be overcome by evil, but overcome evil
with good.

ROMANS 12:14-21

Yes, to love one's neighbor is to treat him or
her with dignity as one of God's creations –
with respect and without put-downs nor cold-
shoulders. *That* is what Christ meant by loving
your neighbor as yourself.  Not *feeling* love, but
rather – *being* love. For,

If I speak in the tongues of mortals and
of angels, but do not have love, I am a
noisy gong or a clanging cymbal.  And if
I have prophetic powers, and understand
all mysteries and all knowledge, and if I
have all faith, so as to remove mountains,

but do not have love, I am nothing. If
I give away all my possessions, and if I
hand over my body to be burned, but do
not have love, I gain nothing. Love is
patient; love is kind; love is not envious
or boastful or arrogant or rude. It does
not insist on its own way; it is not irri-
table or resentful; it does not rejoice in
wrongdoing, but rejoices in the truth. It
bears all things, believes all things, hopes
all things, endures all things. *Love never
fails*.

I CORINTHIANS 13:1-8

For as has been aptly said:

The litmus test of our love for God is our
love of neighbor.[15]

Loving your neighbor as yourself does not, of
course, mean that you become a doormat. For
doormats are too busy being trampled on under
foot by man, and by the random subjugations to
this world, to where they cannot be free to bear
the genuine and affective fruit that God would
have them bear. For a follower of Christ cannot
get bogged down with little complications as a
result of having given *exceedingly* too much to

---

[15] As in Manning, *Brennan Manning, The Wisdom
of Tenderness: What Happens When God's Fierce Mercy
Transforms Our Lives* (as in n. 2 on page xviii).

those who would take advantage of one's generosity and in return use the good that they have been given to then turn around and use it *against* them. For as Christ stated:

> Do not give what is holy to dogs; and do not throw your pearls before swine, or they will trample them under foot and turn and tear you to pieces.
>
> MATTHEW 7:6

As such, it is imperative that one learn to set *healthy* boundaries. If we want to bear fruit, and to be there for those who *genuinely* need us, we *must* set boundaries when appropriate – lest we become exhausted, frustrated, and angry with those who have not done anything to us, as well as angry with ourselves, to consequently become muddled and trapped in situations that eat away at our time and energy. We must therefore take great care not to do anything out of guilt – but rather because it is the right and Christ-like thing to do when we have decided to follow Jesus. For,

> Guilt can prevent us from setting the boundaries that would be in our best interests, and in other people's best interests. Guilt can stop us from taking healthy

care of ourselves. . . We can trust ourselves
to know when our boundaries are being
violated.[16]

And that is why it is so important to be *dependent*
on God and His Holy Spirit, rather than to be
*codependent* on individuals or whatever it may
be – such as on things as varying addictions
that control and take over our lives and free
will, career accomplishments as a barometer for
our self-esteem, other's approvals both in society
as well as in our workplaces, or even on religious extremisms that *neither* glorify God nor
exemplify Christ as the equitable stability and
unwaveringly-balanced rock that he always was;
as well as on pleasing others above pleasing God,
which ultimately entraps and curtails our lives
and our potential to better mankind – hence,
having the independence and courage to be a
God-pleaser rather than a man-pleaser.[17]   For,
to be codependent is to live life *reacting* to what
others say, think, or do – whereas to depend upon
God is to be set free and to *willingly* let Him mold

---

[16] As in Melody Beattie, *The Language of Letting Go*.
Hazelden, 1990.

[17] As likened to the song *Godpleaser*, as per Petra, *Not
of This World album*. Star Song Music, 1983.

our minds through wisdom, liberty, and balanced stability. As has been said:

> Codependents are reactionaries. They over-react. They under-react. But rarely do they act. They react to the problems, pains, lives, and behaviors of others. They react to their own problems, pains, and behaviors.[18]

On the other hand, one must not have an *un-healthy* form of independence for the mere sake of trying to *not* be dependent on the basic relation-ships, values, and faith that makes for a complete human being. For,

> People with unhealthy independence pre-tend to be in control, independent and *not* in need of help or assistance from others. But underneath this veneer they have the basic feelings and dynamics of any co-dependent person. They may just mani-fest their co-dependence differently than the more stereotyped overly dependent co-dependent. Certainly, they have difficulty asking for help and accepting it. So they have difficulty being dependent, and often end up feeling isolated and alone... they

---

[18] As in Melody Beattie, *Codependent No More: How to Stop Controlling Others and Start Caring for Yourself* . Hazelden, 1986.

often deny important aspects of their inner life, and are closed to its empowering experiences. They may have difficulty supporting others and may be critical or rejecting. Being so 'independent', they often feel 'better than' others. People who have healthy independence have clear and healthy boundaries. They can be either firm or flexible, as needed and appropriate. They tend not to control, manipulate, exploit or abuse others. They have a healthy sense of self, and care for themselves by getting their needs met without hurting others... they are compassionate with themselves and with others... they have a loving and constructive relationship with their Higher Power, and are free and growing.[19]

Furthermore, to love one's neighbor means that one be there for others, and do what one can do for them when they may be in need – whether that be in need of a listener, of food and shelter, of clothing, of encouragement, of a visit – whatever the case might be. But this does *not* mean that one need to become a close 'friend' to just anyone one meets to the point of *confiding* in them unreservedly with one's personal, private life. It is imperative that one *chooses* one's friends

---

[19] As in Charles L. Whitfield, *Co-Dependence - Healing the Human Condition*. Health Communications Inc., 1991.

wisely, so that, again, one does not become a doormat to those who would bog one down and prevent one from bearing the fruits that Christ has called us to bear. For, as is wisely stated:

> Pleasant speech multiplies friends, and a gracious tongue multiplies courtesies. Let those who are friendly with you be many, but let your advisers be one in a thousand. When you gain friends, gain them through testing, and do not trust them hastily. For there are friends who are such when it suits them, but they will not stand by you in time of trouble. And there are friends who change into enemies, and tell of the quarrel to your disgrace. And there are friends who sit at your table, but they will not stand by you in time of trouble. When you are prosperous, they become your second self, and lord it over your servants; but if you are brought low, they turn against you, and hide themselves from you. Keep away from your enemies, and be on guard with your friends.
>
> SIRACH 6:5-13

Therefore, do good to all – even your enemies – for that *is* what loving one's neighbor as oneself is about. But don't *blindly* make just everyone you meet your "new best friend" without having known them well enough to get a grasp as to where they are coming from in relation to you. For true friends are faithful, loyal, and do not use those things that you have confided them with against you.   Yes, balance, and well-set boundaries, are everything! For,

> Faithful friends are a sturdy shelter: whoever finds one has found a treasure. Faithful friends are *beyond price*; no amount can balance their worth. Faithful friends are life-saving medicine; and those who fear the Lord will find them. Those who fear the Lord direct their friendship aright, for as they are, so are their neighbors also.
> SIRACH 6:14-17

... and,

> Do not consult the one who regards you with suspicion; hide your intentions from those who are jealous of you... But associate with a godly person whom you know to be a keeper of the commandments, who is like-minded with yourself, and who will grieve with you if you fail.   And heed the counsel of *your own heart*, for no one is more faithful to you than *it* is.   For our own mind sometimes keeps us better informed than seven sentinels sitting high on a watchtower. But above all pray to the Most High that He may *direct* your way in truth.
> SIRACH 37:10 & 12-15

Furthermore, when you have had enough – don't
panic, don't throw a tantrum, don't despair; but
genuinely *trust* in God, His guidance, and the
fact that He indeed *does* hold both you and your
future in His hands – for:

> One who is *slow* to anger is better than
> the mighty, and one whose temper is *con-*
> *trolled* than one who captures a city. The
> lot is cast into the lap, but the decision is
> the Lord's *alone*.
>
> PROVERBS 16:32-33

A true friend is able to *keep secrets*, and again,
will not use the confidentiality that you have
entrusted to them *against* you in any way. As
such, be wise, and do not let just anybody know
your thoughts – for when you give your thoughts
and intentions to just about anyone you meet on
the street, at work, or at play, you may soon feel
a slight insecurity within you that says "should
I have said that", or "what if..." – and as a
result, your slip-of-the-tongue might very well
drive away your inner confidence, peace, and
happiness for a time. Not worth it!

So, therefore, *choose* your friends wisely and
deliberately – but also love your neighbor as
yourself. Follow this advice, and you will have the

stamina to love all in action, while at the same time not *becoming* a doormat:

> Do not let the insolent bring you to your feet, or they may lie in ambush against your words... Do not go traveling with the reckless, or they will be burdensome to you; for they will act as they please, and through their folly you will perish with them. Do not pick a fight with the quick-tempered, and do not journey with them through lonely country, because bloodshed means nothing to them, and where no help is at hand, they will strike you down. Do not consult with fools, for they *cannot* keep a secret. In the presence of strangers do *nothing* that is to be kept secret, for you do not *know* what they will divulge. Do not *reveal* your thoughts to anyone, or you may *drive away* your happiness.
>
> SIRACH 8:11, & 15-19

This being said, love your neighbor – those in your life, or accessible to you, that you are able to be a friend, confidant, servant, or merely kind to in your actions as a genuine follower of Christ – for he himself was such to all, including the lowly, the desperate-hearted, the sick, the weak, and the sinner – *regardless of* who they might be, and this do with *wisdom* as your companion. As Christ said:

If you love those who love you, what credit
is that to you? For even sinners love those
who love them. If you do good to those who
do good to you, what credit is that to you?
For even sinners do the same. If you lend
to those from whom you hope to receive,
what credit is that to you? Even sinners
lend to sinners, to receive as much again.
But love your enemies, do good, and lend,
expecting nothing in return. Your reward
will be great, and you will be children
of the Most High; for he is kind to the
ungrateful and the wicked. Be merciful,
just as your Father *is* merciful.

LUKE 6:32-36

# As You Love *Yourself*

Furthermore, to love one's neighbor as oneself
implies that one must *also* love oneself. As it is
rightly said:

God assumed love of self when He said,
"Love thy neighbor as thyself." [20]

Do *you* love yourself? You should, you know. It's
part of the commandment, is it not? Or have you

---

[20] As in Robert Hemfelt, Frank Minirth and Paul
Meier, *Love is a Choice: Breaking the Cycle of Addictive
Relationships*. Monarch Publications, 1990.

been hurt by others long enough to start believing their many abusive or devious words against who you are – who you *truly* are – on the *inside* – and as God sees you. It is vitally important that one not take every word that is said *too* seriously, for:

> Do not pay attention to every word people say, or you may hear your servant cursing you – for you know in your heart that many times you yourself have cursed others.
>
> ECCLESIASTES 7:21-22

And it is important that one not take every insult, threat, or put-down to heart when such things rise up against you – for God Himself, in *His* unconditional Agape love for you, truly *is* your shelter. For,

> O how abundant is your goodness that you have laid up for those who fear you, and accomplished for those who take refuge in you, in the sight of everyone! In the shelter of your presence you hide them from human plots; you hold them safe under your shelter from contentious tongues.
>
> PSALMS 31:19-20

So, therefore:

> Be strong, and let your heart take courage,
> all you who wait for the Lord.
> PSALMS 31:24

So love your neighbor as you love yourself. Do to them as you would have them do to you, and you will not go wrong. Yes, the "Golden Rule" that Christ gave those who would follow, and that sums up God's law in a mere sentence as Christ spoke it:

> In everything do to others as you would have them do to you; for this is the law and the prophets.
> MATTHEW 7:12

So have a *genuine, merciful* love for yourself – in order that you may *likewise* know how you can love and do the same for others. Do you really believe God would create you as someone who is inwardly rotten to the core? Only *He* can change your mind about yourself ... if you'll just *let* Him. Will you let Him? He loves you, and wants to bless you, and be there *for* you. Always and forever. Will you let Him love you like nobody else can? Like *nothing* else can? The 'religious' might not like you. The wealthy might "look down" on you. Society may not understand you. But God does. And He loves you – oh so very, very much.

You're his precious kid! Yes, you're so precious to Him indeed! Can you accept that – even if everybody else might say it's not true? Well, who cares about "everybody else" anyway. It's *your* life, not theirs, after all. Who *cares* what they think. But do *you* care about what your Heavenly Father thinks? Do you care about what you think of *yourself*? He *can* heal you, you know, and make you fall in love with yourself *all over again*. Ready?

So love God, who loved you first; love your neighbor in action (don't worry, you don't have to feel the love – just *be* it) – and in so doing, don't forget to love yourself. For you *are* God's precious child, His precious and dear creation.

For to love is to be blessed (to be *happy*). How can you be blessed? Only through love. And what can you do to be blessed? Love God, your neighbor, and yourself.

The Son of Man stated that the love of many would grow cold before he returned, when he said:

> And because of the increase of lawless-
> ness, the love of many will grow cold. But
> the one who endures to the end will be
> saved. [MATTHEW 24:12]

Nevertheless, God's love for you will *never* grow cold – no matter *who* you are, or *what* you have done. So mine as well *embrace it* – and live it to the full – and this simply by letting *Him* love you, reflecting His love onto *others*, allowing *yourself* to be loved; as well as allowing yourself to love who you are as a child of Almighty God. You don't *have* to be the 'many' who's love grows cold. No. You *can* be the exception. So, if you're willing –


*Be* the exception!

Beloved, let us love one another, because love is from God; everyone who loves is born of God and knows God. Whoever does not love does not know God, for God is love. God's love was revealed among us in this way: God sent his only Son into the world so that we might live through him. In this is love, not that we loved God but that he loved us and sent his Son to be the atoning sacrifice for our sins. Beloved, since God loved us so much, we also ought to love one another. No one has ever seen God; if we love one another, God lives in us, and his love is perfected in us.

By this we know that we abide in him and he in us, because he has given us of his Spirit. And we have seen and do testify that the Father has sent his Son as the Savior of the world. God abides in those who confess that Jesus is the Son of God, and they abide in God. So we have known and believe the love that God has for us.

God is love, and those who abide in love abide in God, and God abides in them ... There is no fear in love, but perfect love casts out fear ... We love because he first loved us.

I JOHN 4:7-19

Yes, love *is* bold indeed!

Chapter Twelve

# *When You Lose... You Win*

> Then Jesus told his disciples, 'If any want to become my followers, let them deny themselves and take up their cross and follow me. For those who want to save their life will lose it, and those who lose their life for *my* sake will find it. For what will it profit them if they gain the whole world but forfeit their life? Or what will they give in return for their life?
>
> MATTHEW 16:24-26

*Losing* one's life for the sake of following Christ means to give up trying to fit the status quo of what society, friends, and family might 'expect' one to be when it may contradict Christ's teachings; giving up the rat-race pursuit of riches at any and all costs – especially if one has to step on other people to do so; giving up one's

time and energy in order to do good to those
who need assistance, attention, or just a hand
to hold when they are sick, friendless, lonely,
grieving, in despair, or overwhelmed with confusion; standing up for Christ (no, *not* being
annoying for the sake of religious dogma nor
'moral' agendas, but rather fighting for justice,
mercy, and compassion for the *sake* of Christ)
without shame on occasions where this may be
called for in the world around us; being a peace-
maker rather than a rebel-rouser when one has
the clear power and ability to be; keeping one's
opinions to oneself when this may be called for
(irrespective of what religious 'leaders' might
demand); being *willing* to be persecuted and
humiliated for the sake of doing the right thing
when one needs to do so – such as looking like
a 'non-team-player', 'disloyal', or 'heretical' to
one's work colleagues, friends, or fellow Christians for standing up for (or at the very least,
being a *friend* and confidant to) the bullied co-
worker, the homeless woman on the street, or the
homosexual teen or straight and sexually-active
young adult being unfairly treated at church, at
work, or in the school; giving up the cycle of
constantly freezing oneself with the anxieties of

this world and with the overriding preoccupation on please everyone else above God Himself; being willing to get out of one's "comfort zone" and risk ridicule from other believers in order to go where those who might not want to hear about Christ may be at if one is so led (whether bars, clubs, social events, or whatever it might be)[1] and to thus be as Christ-like to those one meets as he was both in friendship and mercy to the religiously-ostracized, the prostitutes, and tax collectors – and thereby, by such as as these examples above, *choosing* to follow Christ as one's counselor, teacher, and Lord in life, and following

---

[1] For, as Christ said as he was praying to the Father:

> But now I am coming to you, and I speak these things in the world so that they may have my joy made complete in themselves. I have given them your word, and the world has hated them because they do not belong to the world, just as I do not belong to the world. I am not asking you to take them *out* of the world, but I ask you to protect them from evil. They do not belong to the world, just as I do not belong to the world. Sanctify them in the truth; your word is truth. As you have sent me into the world, so *I* have sent them *into* the world. And for their sakes I sanctify myself, so that they also may be sanctified in truth. [John 17:13-19]

*his* example and *his* commands to love God with all of one's heart, and one's neighbor as oneself. As Christ said, when one is *willing* to lose one's life for the sake of following Christ and doing the right thing, one *finds* life – and will indeed find it *abundantly*. One finds oneself. As Christ said:

> For to all those who have, more will be given, and they will have an abundance; but from those who have nothing, even what they have will be taken away.
>
> MATTHEW 25:29

One finds purpose and meaning to life. And one finds that subtle joy and consistent peace within that will never be taken away – neither by man, nor by the schemes that he might invent, nor by the world that might try to object, and nor by some – but certainly not all – who are too busy being 'religious' to take the time to care for, befriend, support, assist, love, and visit the ones around them who Christ died for and loves totally and without shame. But the objections of the few – whether in the world, or in religiosity itself – will *never* overtake a Seeker of Truth and follower of Jesus; for Christ has *indeed* conquered this world. For, as Jesus has said:

> I have said this to you, so that in me you
> may have peace. In the world you face
> persecution. But take courage; I have
> conquered the world!
>
> JOHN 16:33

Losing one's life for the sake of following Christ
means to place our trust on him above even
ourselves and what we think we can figure out
on our own. For God *is* the perfect love[2] that
will *never* let you down, and – if you allow Him
– a wall of fire of protection around you and your
family when He is allowed to be thus, and the
glory within it, who will *never* fail, nor ever falter.
Again, as previously quoted:

> ... I will be a wall of fire all around it, says
> the Lord, and I will be the glory *within* it.
>
> ZECHARIAH 2:5

Real faith gets you to the very much achievable
level where you are securely comfortable *not*
knowing... *not* knowing what you are going to
do or how you are going to do it... *not* having to
have all the answers to every challenge life might
throw at you, and to simply, and consciously,

---

[2] See Chapter 11 on page 231.

choosing to *put away* insecurity and worry,[3] to "cast your cares on God".[4] As Peter rightly said:

> Humble yourselves therefore under the mighty hand of God, so that He may exalt you in due time [*in His perfect timing*]. Cast *all* your anxiety on Him, because He cares for you.
>
> I PETER 5:6-7

True faith means to stop thinking that one is "smart enough" to figure out every problem one might have, and to stop always trying to figure out the future.[5] For your *present* time as it stands and as it concerns you – God is not in the future, but right here, right now. And yet, the future is solely under *His* authority. And though He *holds* the future, He also holds your life in His hands – and He will *always* give you the answers in *His* perfect timing. Are you willing to *lose* some of

---

[3] As has been aptly stated:

"Do not give yourself over to sorrow, and do not distress yourself deliberately. A joyful heart is life itself, and rejoicing lengthens one's life span. Indulge yourself and take comfort, and remove sorrow far from you, for sorrow has destroyed many, and no advantage ever comes from it. Jealousy and anger shorten life, and anxiety brings on premature old age." [Sirach 30:21-24]

[4] This paragraph as paraphrased by Meyer, *Enjoying Everyday Life broadcasts* (as in n. 29 on page 225).

[5] Ibid..

your obsessing about the future, in order to *gain* His perfect peace, serenity, and timely guidance? For as it is said:

> Trust in the Lord with *all* your heart, and lean not on your own understanding. In all your ways acknowledge him, and He *will* direct your path.
> PROVERBS 3:5-6

One can alleviate *so much* of life's stresses by simply allowing the self to *not* be wise in one's own eyes, to where you slowly kill yourself struggling to figure everything out all at once – as the above states. To the believer, this does not in the least mean that one should hide one's head in the sand, so-to-speak. It simply means to *allow* God to lead the way, and to allow Him to take control of a tricky situation – and of your own future – or whatever the case might be. It is to face your problems boldly and head-on when you know through prayer and consulting with God that it's the godly thing to do – knowing and *trusting* that God is always in control, and that He will make a way out where you don't see a way out, that He will raise you up onto a level path, turn your sorrows right-side up, give you indescribable peace through your storms, cover you with His joy and the inner rush of Living water that is the Spirit of Truth, and move those seemingly insurmountable mountains out of your path.[6] For,

> Now to Him who by the power at work *within us* is able to accomplish abundantly *far more* than all we can ask or imagine, to Him be glory in the church and in Christ Jesus to all generations, forever and ever.
>
> EPHESIANS 3:20

It is what it is, so deal with it wisely and prudently, without haste, without panic, and in full confidence that He is right there at your side, covering you with the shadow of His hand –

> I have put My words in your mouth and have covered you with the shadow of My hand.
>
> ISAIAH 51:16

– that He is surrounding you on *every* side, as we have seen above, and has not given us a spirit of fear, but of power:

---

[6] As paraphrased from the song *Preacher Man* in the live concert version as per Rance Allen, *The Live Experience*. Tyscot Records, 2004; the viewing of which is highly recommended.

... for God did not give us a spirit of cowardice, but rather a spirit of power and of love and of self-discipline.

II TIMOTHY 1:7

– and that nothing will touch you so long as you're in His care –

I will say of the Lord, 'He is my refuge and my fortress, my God, in whom I trust.'... He will cover you with His feathers, and under His wings you will find refuge... You will not fear the terror of night, nor the arrow that flies by day, nor the pestilence that stalks in the darkness, nor the plague that destroys at midday. A thousand may fall at your side, ten thousand at your right hand, but it will not come near you ... If you say, 'The Lord is my refuge,' and you make the Most High your dwelling, no harm will overtake you, no disaster will come near your tent. For he will command his angels concerning you to guard you in all your ways; they will lift you up in their hands... 'Because he loves me,' says the Lord, 'I will rescue him; I will protect him, for he acknowledges my name. He will call on me, and I will answer him; I will be with him in trouble, I will deliver him and honor him. With long life I will satisfy him and show him my salvation.'

PSALM 91:2-16

To those who have chosen to place their trust on Christ rather than on the delicate fragilities and ever-swaying opinions and demands of this world – rest assured that He will *always* help you, and He will *always* fight for you. For,

> No evil will befall the one who fears the Lord, but in trials such a one will be rescued again and again.
>
> SIRACH 33:1

Yes, He *will* fight for you, and He will not keep you waiting long, so wait upon the Lord – be still, and know that He *is* God. For,

> Have you not known? Have you not heard? The Lord is the everlasting God, the Creator of the ends of the earth. He does not faint or grow weary; his understanding is unsearchable. He gives power to the faint, and strengthens the powerless. Even youths will faint and be weary, and the young will fall exhausted; but those who wait for the Lord shall renew their strength, they shall mount up with wings like eagles, they shall run and not be weary, they shall walk and not faint.
>
> ISAIAH 40:28-31

To the believer – if you have placed your trust on Christ while at the same time not allowing the daily anxieties of this world to overwhelm you as you focus on his Spirit alone – know that you are *self-sufficient* in Christ's sufficiency. Keep going. Keep placing your trust on him. Just *keep going*. Don't waiver, lest you may fall. Believe on Christ, and believe in yourself – that's all you need to do you some good. And when he gives you a way out, a solution to a problem, or the *responsibility* to pro-actively face up to your troubles head-on and with the great confidence of being a follower of the Almighty God and Creator of the Universe – do so with the knowledge that He Himself is fighting *with* you, and *for* you. And never forget:

> ... all things work together for good for those who love God, who are called according to his purpose.
>
> ROMANS 8:28

Therefore, the simple solution to many of the challenges that we encounter in this life, to how we might be feeling in any particular moment or circumstance, and to self-doubt itself, may very well be:

> Faith in God... *always* forward. [7]

---

[7] M.W. Sphero

In other words, always have your faith and trust in Christ, and *always* be moving forward – not backwards by allowing yourself to get into depression and despair; nor letting yourself be frozen from bearing fruit because of self-imposed and *consciously-adopted* fear; nor getting stuck with some of the many conflicting voices that we hear from society, religious institutions, and government actors every day – no. *Always* forward. Never faltering. Are you willing to let go – to *lose* – that sense of control in your life in order to *gain* some inner peace, mental stability, and ultimately the power to move forward and re-take control of this or that situation when it is again time to pick up where you left off after having slept on it – as led by God's timing and will? Are you wiling to stand up for Christ through your actions, examples, servitude, and sometimes even words – so that others might truly *see* his Light shine forth from your life *both* in theory *and* in practice? For as Christ said:

> ...let your light shine before others, so that they may see your good works and give glory to your Father in heaven.
>
> MATTHEW 5:16

And when you are willing to 'lose' like this and let *him* guide you, what you gain is life, the bearing of much fruit that those around you will benefit from, and the incomprehensible peace and *genuine* inner joy that this world just *cannot* give – no matter how hard it might try – *nor* take away, as clearly stated by Christ, and as previously seen and *re-quoted* herein:

> Peace I leave with you; my peace I give to you. I do not give to you as the world gives. Do not let your hearts be troubled, and do not let them be afraid.
>
> JOHN 14:27

– and mental balance and tranquility that many have lost in this day and age. For as Christ said,

> Very truly, I tell you, I am the gate for the sheep. All who came before me are thieves and bandits; but the sheep did not listen to them. I am the gate. Whoever enters by me will be saved, and will come in and go out and find pasture. The thief comes only to steal and kill and destroy. I came that they may have *life*, and have it *abundantly*.
>
> JOHN 10:7-10

And if you need to make tough decisions to where you might have to lose more than what you may want to for the sake of Christ, be sure that he *will* give you abundantly more in this present life, even if you are persecuted for it. Besides, your inheritance is *not* in nor of this world, and will not come *from* this world. For it is *he* who is the worthwhile and lasting inheritance. For,

> But in the land of the people he has no inheritance, and he has no portion among the people; for the Lord *Himself* is his portion and inheritance.
> SIRACH 45:22.

In addition – to the believer – when you hold on and persevere in your walk with Christ, you will *always* be given more of his wisdom, strength, power, and confidence. Yes, you get to the point where you *recognize* God's voice as He leads and directs you – when you consciously *let* Him – as He does so from within your heart, your *core* being – to where you oftentimes *"just know"* to do something, to be somewhere, to make that phone call, to go after that job, to speak to that person about whatever, to keep silent no matter what, to take a break, or to make that choice. Some might call it intuition – but for those who follow Christ – I call it the *Holy Spirit* of Jesus, who he promised would teach us *all* things, and bring to our remembrance *all* that he had taught us, and all that would occur:

> But the Advocate, the Holy Spirit, whom the Father will send in my name, will teach you *all things*, and bring to your remembrance all that I have said to you.
>
> JOHN 14:26

It's not some sort of mystic "New Age" thing – that newly-revived ancient form of religion being, in many ways, nothing but a counterfeit of the things of God.[8] But *no one* can counterfeit Christ's voice. For as he stated, "my sheep *know* my voice and will *not listen* to a stranger's voice".[9] Yes, Christ promised those who place their faith and reliance on him that he would *freely* give them of his Holy Spirit – the great Comforter, Helper, Advocate, Intercessor, and Counselor to those who believe.[10] For, again, as Christ said:

> I will ask the Father, and He will give you another Helper [or *Comforter, Advocate, Intercessor*], that He may be with you

---

[8] See also Appendix A on page 357, in regards to false religions and false prophets whom Christ warned us about as appearing in the end times.

[9] John 10:5 & 27.

[10] See also Walvoord, *The Holy Spirit* (as in n. 4 on page 199).

> forever; that is the Spirit of truth, whom the world *cannot* receive, because it does not see Him or know Him, but you know Him because He abides *with* you and will be *in* you. I will not leave you as orphans; *I will come to you...* Peace I leave with you; My peace I give to you; not as the world gives do I give to you. Do not let your heart be troubled, nor let it be fearful... I have said these things to you while I am still with you. But the Advocate, the Holy Spirit, whom the Father will send in my name, will teach you *everything*, and *remind you* of all that I have said to you.

JOHN 14:16-18, & 25-27

and Christ also said,

> I have much more to say to you, more than you can now bear. But when He, the Spirit of Truth, comes, he will guide you into *all* truth. He will not speak on His own; He will speak only what He hears, and He will tell you what is *yet* to come. He will glorify me because it is *from me* that He will receive what He will make known to you. All that belongs to the Father is mine. That is why I said the Spirit will receive from me what He will make known to you."

JOHN 16:12-15

But to persevere in Christ means *to gain*. To persevere means to win when others lose – the *many* on the wide path[11] who will prefer to listen to the many voices bombarding the world today instead of on the voice of the Incarnate Truth. For as Christ states, on referring to the religious leaders who placed their trust on pleasing man, and on man's traditions – while at the same time referring to those who do not produce fruit towards God – that though they considered themselves as having *much* – the respect of their colleagues and community, lifestyles of comfort but without caring for the less fortunate, and the like – they nonetheless had *nothing* without Christ; while those who bore fruit for God by loving others in action and loving their Creator who they honored above the fallacies of man, and who likewise placed their trust on Him indeed had very, *very* much. For, again he stated elsewhere:

> For there is nothing hidden that will not be disclosed, and nothing concealed that will not be known or brought out into the

_____

[11]As Christ said: "Enter through the narrow gate; for the gate is wide and the road is easy that leads to destruction, and there are many who take it. For the gate is narrow and the road is hard that leads to life, and there are few who find it". [Matthew 7:13-14]

> open. Therefore consider carefully *how*
> you listen. For whoever *has* will be given
> more; whoever does not have, even what
> he *thinks* he has will be taken from him.
>
> Luke 8:17-18

And when one is *willing* to listen to this Incarnate Truth that dwells within us – to Christ's Holy Spirit – the Counselor – one will *know* the truth that seems to just be ignored by the many who may *not* want to listen – or else they would have a very different change of heart and mind as to who Christ truly *is*. For as Christ explained:

> My teaching is not mine but His who sent
> me. Anyone who resolves to do the will
> of God will *know* whether my teaching is
> from God or whether I am speaking on my
> own. Those who speak on their own seek
> their *own* glory; but the one who *seeks the*
> *glory of Him who sent him* is true, and
> there is *nothing false* in him.
>
> JOHN 7:16-18

Those who cling to their present life above *all else* will lose it, and those who lose their life *will* find it. God never reneges on a promise. *Rest* on His word. As Christ has said,

> Truly I tell you, there is no one who has
> left house or brothers or sisters or mother

> or father or children or fields, for my sake
> and for the sake of the good news [or, *the*
> *Gospel*], who will not receive a hundred-
> fold now in this age—houses, brothers and
> sisters, mothers and children, and fields,
> *with* persecutions—and in the age to come
> eternal life. But many who are first will
> be last, and the last will be first.

MARK 10:29-31

Yes, it is so *very* true. When you have *God* on your side:

When you lose – you win![12]

To the weary: please *know* that you have hope in Christ, who redeems from the myriad of enchainments, schemes, and oppressions of this world. The key is to be willing to apply *patient endurance* – perseverance – when you are doing the right thing and still suffering for it. Don't be a doormat – for a doormat cannot sustainably bear fruit because he is stuck in time-wasting and oftentimes meaningless affairs that weary and dampen his energy, to where he is prevented from

---

[12] As per the song *Love Comes Down*; from Rez Band [a.k.a. Resurrection Band], *REZ: Compact Favorites album.* Sparrow Records, 2008; the listening of which is very much highly recommended!

doing the important things that God might have him do. *Value* your time, your energy, and your health – both spiritually, as well as physically. For what good is works without the healthy body to do them? But bear the fruit that is called for as a genuine and *true* follower of Christ – such as love in action, sensibility, the inner joy that only God can give even when one is surrounded by darkness, and steadfast stability of the mind and body with God's help and guidance. Yes, even in your times of trial – rejoice in the Lord *always*, for your vindication *will* come.

Listen to me, you who know righteousness, you people who have my teaching in your hearts; *do not fear* the reproach of others, and do not be *dismayed* when they revile you. For the moth will eat them up like a garment, and the worm will eat them like wool; but my deliverance will be forever, and my salvation to all generations. . . I, even I, am He who comforts you; *why then* are you *afraid* of a mere mortal who must die, a human being who fades like grass? You have forgotten the Lord, your Maker, who stretched out the heavens and laid the foundations of the earth. You fear *continually* all day long because of the fury of the oppressor, who is bent on destruction. But *where is* the fury of the oppressor?. . . I have put my words in your mouth, and have *covered you* with the shadow of my hand.

ISAIAH 51:7-8,12-13, & 16

# Chapter Thirteen

# So Banish Anxiety from Your Mind

Put simply, life is too short. We have a choice every day. Do we let our emotions overwhelm us to the point where *they* are in control, or do we use the mind that God has given us in order to apply the concept to *trust* in God – and to always move forward? For,

> It is evident that reason rules even the more violent emotions: lust for power, vain glory, boasting, arrogance, and malice. For the temperate mind repels all these malicious emotions, just as it repels anger—for it is sovereign over even this. When Moses was angry with Dathan and Abiram, he did nothing against them in anger, but controlled his anger by reason. For, as I have said, the temperate mind is able to get *the better* of the emotions, to correct some, and to render

others powerless[1]...Now when God fashioned human beings, He planted in them emotions and inclinations, but at the same time He *enthroned the mind* among the senses as a sacred *governor* over them all. To the mind He gave the law; and one who lives subject to this will rule a kingdom that is temperate, just, good, and courageous[2]...No one of us can eradicate anger from the mind, but reason can help to *deal with anger*. No one of us can eradicate malice, but reason can fight at our side so that we are *not overcome* by malice. For reason does not uproot the emotions but is their antagonist[3]...For the temperate mind can conquer the drives of the emotions and quench the flames of frenzied desires;[4] it can overthrow bodily agonies even when they are extreme, and by nobility of reason spurn all domination by the emotions[5]...You too must have the same faith in God and *not be grieved*.[6]

---

[1] IV Maccabees 2:15-18

[2] IV Maccabees 2:21-23

[3] IV Maccabees 3:3-5

[4] These *desires* being in reference to such things as letting anger control one's reason, to hate, to be unforgiving, to be anxious and to worry perpetually, to be vindictive, to allow oneself to become jealous, to hold grudges, being power-hungry, to be arrogant, to covet what belongs to another, to be vindictive... essentially, these and related sorts of negative emotional desires that only serve to destroy us from within.

[5] IV Maccabees 3:17-18

[6] IV Maccabees 16:22

Will we deliberately *choose* to be in control of our emotions and let Christ take care of us as he promised...will we put our trust in him on a daily basis to guide us into *all* truth (both heavenly as well as earth-bound), take care of our needs, and as a result rest in *his* peace – or will we panic, and let the world take over? As is rightly stated in the Old Testament book of Ecclesiastes:

> Banish anxiety from your mind, and put away pain from your body; for youth and the dawn of life are vanity.

> ECCLESIASTES 11:10

Therefore, one can *choose* to – consciously and deliberately – banish anxiety from the mind. Yes, we can *choose* to do so – isn't that what the above essentially says?  Like the words of Christ, we don't really need to look too deeply into what a phrase means. We must use the *common sense* that God has given us – and *accept* His word – and this *by faith*.  God wants to get through to us in *simple* terms without all the 'religiousness' getting in the way. So take *His* word for it, let go, and just *keep moving forward*!

Take what He has so many times said to you,
and *rest* in His care. When you speak to God, and
He speaks to you, you're not visiting a lawyer,
while needing yet *another* lawyer to interpret for
you what the first lawyer says. No. If God says
it, just believe it – take Him at *His* word. He
*never* fails, and never will. You don't *need* any
sort of secondary interpretations. You don't *need*
theology. You don't *need* some New Age guru or
yogi telling you how simple it is, while in the
background twisting a godly statement or piece of
Biblical scripture to his or her own benefit while
trying to pass it off as his or her own. No. If God
is telling you to let go, than just... let go. For as
Christ clearly said,

> I thank you, Father, Lord of heaven and
> earth, because you have hidden these things
> from the wise and the intelligent and have
> revealed them to infants; yes, Father, for
> such was your gracious will.
>
> MATTHEW 11:25-26

If God has revealed His word to you – probably
without you even having to have consulted a
church, preacher, or theologian for reassurance
– than *rest* in what He has given you. For it
is *His* Holy Spirit that teaches you all things,

and who brings to your remembrance all that Christ said.[7] As such, if Christ says such anti-"politically correct" statements such as this:

> Therefore I tell you, do not worry about your life, what you will eat or drink; or about your body, what you will wear. Is not life more than food, and the body more than clothes?... So do not worry, saying, 'What shall we eat?' or 'What shall we drink?' or 'What shall we wear?' For the pagans run after all these things, and your heavenly Father knows that you need them. But seek first *His* kingdom and *His* righteousness, and *all* these things will be given to you as well. Therefore do not worry about tomorrow, for tomorrow will worry about itself. Each day has enough trouble of its own.
>
> MATTHEW 6:25-34 NIV

...than you can rest assured that He's got your back – He's got *you* – covered; *if* by the faith of a child you accept Him at His word. Therefore,

> Do not give your heart to grief; drive it away, and remember your own end.
>
> SIRACH 38:20

---

[7] As Jesus said: "But the Advocate, the Holy Spirit, whom the Father will send in my name, will teach you *all* things, and bring to your remembrance all that I have said to you." [John 14:26]

Again, life is *way* too short. But with Christ, it can become – to you *irrevocably and specifically* – lengthy, peaceful, full, enjoyable, and fruitful... regardless of what boat you might be in at the present time. For,

> It is I who answer and look after you. I am like a luxuriant cypress; your fruit comes from Me.
>
> HOSEA 14:8

Furthermore, always speak to God – your Heavenly Father and Creator of the Universe – in much the same way that you would speak to anyone else on this earth. Tell Him your problems, doubts, and fears. And let Him *guide you* without reservation or fear. Pray – and *leave it*. By faith, leave it *with Him* to take care of, and to guide you on how you should approach it once more at the proper time. Leave it, sleep on it, and wake up rejoicing that God has given you a new day, and don't waste it away by carrying loads that only God can sort out. If there is anything for you to do, He *will* let you know – in *His* perfect timing, and in *His* faultless way. Let God take care of the rest. And pay attention to signs that He may reveal to you. For, as is rightly said:

> Rejoice in the Lord always; again I will
> say, Rejoice. Let your gentleness be known
> to everyone. The Lord is near. Do not
> worry about anything, but in everything
> by prayer and supplication with thanks-
> giving let your requests be made known
> to God. And the peace of God, which
> surpasses all understanding, will guard
> your hearts and your minds in Christ
> Jesus.
>
> PHILIPPIANS 4:4-7

For Christ is *indeed* the voice in the silence who consistently – if you listen by faith and an open soul – reminds you that He's *always* there, so that you need not worry when you are going through rough times, because as long as your trust is in Him, He will *always* guide and see you through to the end.[8]

Christ warned us of how the world would become before his return: How mankind would be deceived and follow after false teachers;[9] how the love of many would grow cold;[10] how some of his followers would be put to death by murderers and

---

[8] From the song *He's the Hand on My Shoulder,* B.J. Thomas, *Happy Man album*. Myrrh Records, 1978.

[9] See Appendix A on page 357.

[10] As Jesus stated:

And because of the increase of lawlessness, the love of many will grow cold. But the one who

terrorists who would *think* they were doing God's will;[11] and how many imitators of Christ – *false christs* – would appear to mislead, if possible, *even* the elect.[12] Yet he was clear in letting us know that he was warning us of how such times would transpire, in order that we not lose heart nor be afraid. For as Jesus himself told us:

> These things I have spoken to you so that you may be kept from stumbling... These things they will do because they have not known the Father or Me. But these things I have spoken to you, so that when their hour comes, you may remember that I told you of them... These things I have spoken to you, so that in Me you may have peace. In the world you have tribulation, but take courage; I have *overcome* the world.
>
> JOHN 16:1-4 & 33

---

> endures to the end will be saved. [Matthew 24:12]

[11] As Christ said:

> Indeed, an hour is coming when those who kill you will think that by doing so they are offering worship to God. [John 16:2]

[12] Again, Appendix A on page 357 goes into greater detail in regards to false teachers and false christs whom Christ warned us would appear before his return.

After all, if you know what's around the corner, you'll be prepared, will you not? You won't suddenly be "taken by surprise". And you will certainly *not* lose faith in the one who warned you of *precisely* what would transpire before his return, so that we must not lose heart, nor be fearful, when we see such things taking place against followers of Christ throughout the world.

In the same way, if so many have been deceived into getting turned off to Christ because of *some* – but certainly not all – who claim to 'know' him even when what they really place their trust on and live by is in fact a modernized version of some so-called 'Christianity' but without the Christ being involved; because they have been drawn down an endless rabbit-hole by false christs and false prophets of this day and age who mimic Jesus' teachings while adamantly denying who he was; or because they simply feel that they *don't* need God because they have everything they want – until it comes knocking at their back door – do you allow them to affect *your* personal faith in Christ? Again, he *did* warn us of these present times, and he *did* say:

> However, when the Son of Man comes, will
> He find *the* faith on the earth?

LUKE 18:8

As the author of this title, let me just digress for a second and say that I don't know what the future has in store for me. I've gone through a lot of oppression by those who claim to be religious in one way or another, though I have also been loved and cared for by genuine followers of Christ. I have been both loved and hated by those from varying religions, as well as those who adamantly admit to hating God. As many of you have as well – no denying it! But he has *never* left me – even though the religious, the *non*-religious, the believers in Christ, the believers in totally opposite things, the very very rich, the poverty-stricken poor, the very well educated, the totally clueless, the utterly clean, the joyfully waisted, the good, the bad, and the ugly... yes, even while all of these good, amazing, very intriguing and interesting types of people have at many points in *my* personal life either condemned or abandoned me in one way or another – yet I can say, without a shadow of a doubt nor a fallacy of the mind, that the Jesus Christ – *not,* mind you, the one politicized and *used* by many churches, *not* the one demeaned in society through their inventive new religions of "political correctness" and "bully for survival", and *not* the one put down and vilified on the big screen while preachers of hate are not – no, but rather *the* Jesus Christ who is God's Son, God the incarnate who loved me enough to say –

> Hey, forget about *them*...see, I'm here *with* you. I have never left you, and *never* will – no matter *what* they say, no matter *who* they are or claim to be. You're *mine*. My precious child. Always and forever.

– yes, *that* guy – he's never, *ever* left me, even though *I* left *him* for years because I had stopped looking at Him, and instead had begun to wrongly place my focus on organized religion, and all the grief that often comes with it instead... to where I had simply gotten turned off. But *despite it all*, He never let go of His prodigal child, His black sheep...His child. No, my First Love never left me, though I had left *him*. And *that* is Christ's Gospel; yes, His *good* news. Though the world may forsake you, He never, *ever* will. Not for a trillion bucks. For as it is said:

> But as for me, I will watch expectantly for the Lord; I will wait for the God of my salvation. My God will hear me. Do not rejoice over me, O my enemy. Though I fall I will rise; though I dwell in darkness, the Lord is a light for me. I will bear the indignation of the Lord because I have sinned against Him, until He pleads my case and executes justice for me. He will bring me out to the light, and I will see His righteousness. Then my enemy will see, and shame will cover her who said to me, "Where is the Lord your God?" My eyes will look on her; At that time she will be trampled down like mire of the streets.
>
> MICAH 7:7-10

But it should be of no surprise when people treat the followers of Christ like this. For, again, he *did* clearly warn us that such things would happen to those who belong *not* to the world and its ways of interacting with itself, but to *him*. As Christ told his apostles:

> If the world hates you, be aware that it hated me before it hated you. If you belonged to the world, the world would love you as its own. Because you do *not* belong to the world, but I have chosen you *out* of the world—therefore the world hates you. Remember the word that I said to you, 'Servants are not greater than

their master.' If they persecuted me, they
will persecute you; if they kept my word,
they will keep yours also. But they will do
all these things to you on account of my
name, because they do not know Him who
sent me. If I had not come and spoken to
them, they would not have sin; but now
they have no excuse for their sin. Whoever
hates me hates my Father also. If I had
not done among them the works that no
one else did, they would not have sin. But
now they have seen and hated both me
and my Father. It was to fulfill the word
that is written in their law, 'They hated
me without a cause.'

JOHN 15:18-25

No, those who follow Christ are indeed *not* of
this world. To paraphrase a song that hits
the nail on the head[13] – we indeed are only
passing through as pilgrims and strangers who
don't belong here – for our home is being well
prepared for our arrival someday, and we will not
miss that appointed arrival – for he *will* carry
those who love him all the way to eternity, and
will never surrender. For he has indeed *already*

---

[13] This being the revealing song *Not of This World* by
Petra, *Not of This World album* (as in n. 17 on page 253).

conquered the world,[14] and the gates of hell will *never* prevail against his children.[15]

Yes, *that* is the Gospel of Christ. The Good News of Christ. That the God of this Universe cared so much for the weaker, the rejected, and the ostracized of society – to take as *His* own. As such, the Gospel according to Christ is not *only* the written Gospel in accordance to Christ's words, but the Living Gospel within those who have personally *experienced* it, and have *lived* it – not through religion, but by the Spirit of the Living God. Sometimes one cannot understand such a Gospel, no matter how much might be written about it, until one actually experiences it for themselves – *personally* – outside of everything else. For as the sensational singer Reverend Rance Allen has aptly stated:

> If my dancing looks *strange* to you, you've got to know where I've *been*, in order to know how I *feel*.[16]

To those who will in humility of spirit and boldness of faith consciously *choose* to believe and

---

[14] John 16:33

[15] Matthew 16:18

[16] As stated during the live performance in Rance Allen, *The Live Experience* (as in n. 6 on page 274).

accept: life's too short... take care of it, and rest on the Lord your God, for He *is* One. And of those things you might lose in this life because you might have been rejected by all of the above, just remember where your true inheritance lies. For as has already been said:

> But in the land of the people he has no inheritance, and he has no portion among the people; for the Lord *Himself* is your portion and inheritance.

> SIRACH 45:22

and,

> 'No weapon that is formed against you will prosper; And every tongue that accuses [or, *rises against*] you in judgment you will condemn. This is the *heritage* of the servants of the Lord, And their vindication is from Me,' declares the Lord.

> ISAIAH 54:17

For, to those who have placed their trust in Christ – just as you are, with all your imperfections, doubts, fears, and worries – you don't ever need to be swayed by the schemes of man – for none of mankind's greatest schemes, nor any powers that hell can raise, will ever separate you from the love of God, which is in Christ Jesus. Until then, stand in the power of Christ until he returns or calls you to your inherited home, which was paid in full at the foot of the cross.[17]

... so, therefore, do not let them get you down, but rather:

> ... put away from you mortal thoughts; cast away from you the burdens of humankind, and divest yourself now of your weak nature; lay to one side the thoughts that are most grievous to you, and hurry to escape from these times.
>
> II ESDRAS 14:14-15

... in order that you might put the following advice into daily and deliberate practice, with the help of God:

> Do not give yourself over to sorrow, and do not distress yourself deliberately. A joyful heart is life itself, and rejoicing lengthens one's life span. Indulge yourself and take comfort, and remove sorrow far from you, for sorrow has destroyed many, and no advantage ever comes from it. Jealousy and anger shorten life, and anxiety brings on premature old age.
>
> SIRACH 30:21-24

---

[17] As paraphrased from the song *In Christ Alone*; Stuart Townend and Keith Getty, *In Christ Alone*. Thankyou Music, 2001.

... so that you might finally know what Christ was talking about, when he said:

> Come to me, all you that are weary and are carrying heavy burdens, and I will give you *rest*. Take my yoke upon you, and *learn* from me; for I am gentle and humble in heart, and you will find rest for your souls. For my yoke is *easy,* and my burden is *light*.
>
> MATTHEW 11:28-30

So, therefore:

> Be still, and *know* that I am God!
>
> PSALM 46:10

Chapter Fourteen

# *Cults, Control Freaks, and Christ*

It is better to walk alone with God, I believe, when the *only* other alternative you face is to be amongst a group of worshipers who are stuck on playing games of *organized religion* and mind control, instead of focusing on Christ and his unconditional love – and who dominate, judge, condemn, and attempt with all their might to change you and who you are – particularly when they load unnecessary mental burdens, doubts, and false guilt on your mind and spirit – to where the spiritual satisfaction and joy you once had gets into danger of becoming dulled and lukewarm, to eventually get ripped away from you altogether by the very people who claim to be doing "God's work".

It is not worth wasting your time arguing with these people about matters of doctrine when they themselves have become dead to Christ and the simple faith that he taught. For their focus is on *religion* instead of on God. Their goal is submission instead of acting on love. They have exalted themselves above God Himself, as they hang on to misquoted scripture in order to keep their pride and earthly 'reputations' at the expense of the poor in spirit. So... no, don't waste your time getting into arguments with them. Trust in God, and keep going forward! For, as the Book of Proverbs rightly says:

> Whoever corrects a scoffer wins abuse; whoever rebukes the wicked gets hurt. A scoffer who is rebuked will only hate you; the wise, when rebuked, will love you. Give instruction to the wise, and they will become wiser still; teach the righteous and they will gain in learning.
>
> PROVERBS 9:7-9

Furthermore, Proverbs also states:

> Do not answer a fool *according* to his folly, Or you will also be like him. Answer a fool as his folly *deserves*, that he not be wise in his own eyes.
>
> PROVERBS 26:4-5 NASB

If you conduct that highly recommended experiment of sorts at some point, and look only at what Christ said in the Gospels – I'm sure you will find many examples on how he oftentimes answered those who were hypocritical and self-righteous as their folly *deserved,* while they sought to trap him – at times answering them with another question, sometimes with a parable, and sometimes even with silence. You don't have to enter into someone else's mind games. Trust in God – always forward!

This being said, it must be emphasized that most – yes, *most* – churches, religious groups, and faithful Christians are *not* at all like this, but are genuine and true followers of Christ who by observable actions put their faith into practice through humility, the love of justice – loving those in desperate circumstances and those living in despair by their compassionate, attentive actions. They indeed are real reflections of Christ's non-judgemental, non-condemnatory welcome to all who will receive them. In addition to this, we must remember that, whatever church one might choose to attend – if one chooses to do so of course on one's own prerogative – one *will* always find imperfect people.   For we are *all* imperfect in many ways. This does *not* mean that this chapter automatically applies to either said church, group, or persons within it. This chapter is merely included here in order to make the reader aware of *what* is out their, and is not speaking of the *majority* of churches, religious groups, or faith-loving individuals in general. We are all imperfect in one way or another. Christ only commands that we love and support one another in action, as having been quoted in this work's Preface, and again re-quoted herein:

> I give you a new commandment, that you *love* one another. Just as I have loved you, you also should love one another. By this *everyone* will know that you are my disciples, if you have love for one another.
>
> JOHN 13:34-35

Therefore, if you, on your own free will, and with attentive prayer and wise discernment, decide to attend a particular church or faith-based group, and observe *for yourself* that such a group is following this clear command as given by Christ, and is specifically following Christ's teachings in the Gospels of MATTHEW, MARK, LUKE, and JOHN as you see them – than you probably have yourself a winner! On the *other* hand, if people's

'imperfections' turn out to be oppressive man-
dates, clear-cut condemnations, and judgements
on who you are; and if they seem to *supersede*
Christ's own words with something else, whatever that might be – it would be wise to go ahead
and directly *ask* your Heavenly Father for some
advice, listening carefully to His Holy Spirit,
and possibly *consider* finding another place that
genuinely follows the Christ that we know so well
from the Gospels. For as has rightly been said:

> The ragamuffin gospel reveals that Jesus
> forgives sins, including the sins of the
> flesh; that He is comfortable with sinners
> who remember how to show compassion;
> but that He cannot and will not have a re-
> lationship with pretenders in the Spirit.[1]

Pray for wisdom, and use the discernment that
God has given to all who will listen to His voice.
For you do not want your faith to get trampled
under foot by those who, though claiming to
follow Christ, behave no better than the Pharisee and Sadducee religious leaders that Christ

---

[1] As in Manning, *The Ragamuffin Gospel: Good News
for the Bedraggled, Beat-Up, and Burnt Out* (as in n. 13 on
page 209).

called vipers, snakes, and hypocrites[2] because of
their self-righteous arrogance and condemnation
of those not like themselves. As has been rightly
said:

> The fierce words of Jesus addressed to the
> Pharisees of His day stretch across the
> bands of time. Today they are directed not
> only to fallen televangelists but to each of
> us. We miss Jesus' point entirely when
> we use His words as weapons against
> others. They are to be taken personally
> by each of us. This is the form and
> shape of Christian Pharisaism in our time.
> Hypocrisy is not the prerogative of people
> in high places. The most impoverished
> among us is capable of it. Hypocrisy is the
> natural expression of what is meanest in
> us all.[3]

A good way to discern if the church you might
want to get involved in is following Christ's command to love God, one's neighbor, and His very
own followers themselves, is to observe what it
does for its congregation, and what it does for its
community. Again, as Christ has said:

---

[2] As in Matthew 12:34, 15:7, 22:18, 23:13, 15, 23, 25,
27, 29, & 33; Mark 7:6; and Luke 13:15.

[3] As per Manning, *The Ragamuffin Gospel: Good News
for the Bedraggled, Beat-Up, and Burnt Out* (as in n. 13 on
page 209).

> By their *fruits* you will know them.
> MATTHEW 7:16

And, as is said:

> Love one another with mutual affection;
> outdo one another in showing honor. Do
> not lag in zeal, be ardent in spirit, serve
> the Lord. Rejoice in hope, be patient in
> suffering, persevere in prayer. Contribute
> to the needs of the saints; extend hospital-
> ity to strangers...Rejoice with those who
> rejoice, weep with those who weep. Live
> in harmony with one another; do not be
> haughty, but associate with the lowly...
> [ROMANS 12:10-16]

Furthermore, as James rightly states in the New
Testament:

> What good is it, my brothers and sisters,
> if you say you have faith but do not have
> works? Can faith save you? If a brother or
> sister is naked and lacks daily food, and
> one of you says to them, 'Go in peace; keep
> warm and eat your fill,' and yet you do
> not supply their bodily needs, what is the
> good of that? So faith by itself, if it has no
> works, is dead. [JAMES 2:14-17]

In addition, observe how a group or church you
may be interested in – if you so choose to even
*attend* a church – treats its own people, the
strangers that might walk in, and those in despair. Do they take the time to speak to you if
you approach them? Do they show favoritism to a

certain 'type' of person – such as its more wealthy members, or do they treat everyone with equal respect and dignity? Do they vocally condemn or give a cold shoulder to certain groups of people – such as homosexuals, the young, singles who may be sexually (but responsibly) active? Well, Christ *did* allow for homosexuality.[4]  He never explicitly stated that premarital sex was in any way against His teachings,[5] and he associated – yes, even *welcomed* – the outcast of society, such as tax collectors and prostitutes. For as he asked the religious leaders of his day who were constantly condemning those that he associated with:

> What do you think? A man had two sons; he went to the first and said, 'Son, go and work in the vineyard today.' He answered,

---

[4] Please see Appendix C on page 433 for a full discussion on how Christ *allowed for* homosexuality, and how it is *not* in any way against the Bible – to where condemning homosexuals, who have been *born* that way – as Christ acknowledged – goes against the teachings of Christ. Yes, churches who *aggressively* condemn gay people are but stumbling blocks no better than the Pharisees and Sadducees – religious leaders of Christ's time – and have absolutely no Biblical excuse for their overt and verbally violent prejudices.  By condemning the homosexual, they condemn Christ, who created them to be who they are.

[5] See Appendix B on page 397 for a full discussion on premarital sex.

'I will not'; but later he changed his mind and went. The father went to the second and said the same; and he answered, 'I go, sir'; but he did not go. Which of the two did the will of his father? They [*the religious leaders whom he was speaking to*] said, 'The first.' Jesus said to them, 'Truly I tell you, the tax collectors and the prostitutes are going into the kingdom of God ahead of you. For John came to you in the way of righteousness and you did not believe him, but the tax collectors and the prostitutes believed him; and even after you saw it, you did not change your minds and believe him'.

MATTHEW 21:28-32

So, does the church that you attend, or that you are considering attending, follow the teachings of Christ, or the enslavements of regulatory religiosity – while looking down on those whom Christ most loved and cared for?

As James rightly states in regards to a church's treatment of others – and remember, James was one of Christ's brothers[6] while on earth, to where he knew very well what Christ taught, and who

---

[6] See Douglas J. Moo, *The Letter of James (Pillar New Testament Commentary)*. Wm. B. Eerdmans Publishing Co., 2000.

he fought for and defended as against religious hypocrisy and self-righteousness:

> My brothers and sisters, do you with your acts of favoritism *really* believe in our glorious Lord Jesus Christ? For if a person with gold rings and in fine clothes comes into your assembly, and if a poor person in dirty clothes also comes in, and if you take notice of the one wearing the fine clothes and say, 'Have a seat here, please,' while to the one who is poor you say, 'Stand there,' or, 'Sit under my footstool,' have you not made *distinctions* among yourselves, and become judges with evil thoughts? Listen, my beloved brothers and sisters. Has not God *chosen* the poor in the world to be rich in faith and to be *heirs* of the kingdom that He has promised to those who love Him? But you have *dishonored* the poor. Is it not the rich who oppress you? Is it not *they* who drag you into court? Is it not *they* who blaspheme the excellent name that was invoked over you? You do well if you really fulfill the royal law according to the scripture, 'You shall love your neighbor as yourself.' But if you show partiality, you commit sin and are convicted by the law as transgressors.
>
> JAMES 2:1-9

So how *does* your church treat the outcast, the homosexual, the single youth, the atheist, the agnostic, the poor, the mentally challenged... and *particularly* the so-called 'underdogs' of society? It is interesting to note that Christ said:

> Not everyone who says to me, 'Lord, Lord,' will enter the kingdom of heaven, but only the one who does the will of my Father in heaven. On that day many will say to me, 'Lord, Lord, did we not prophesy in your name, and cast out demons in your name, and do many deeds of power in your name?' Then I will declare to them, 'I never knew you; go away from me, you evildoers.'
>
> MATTHEW 7:21-23

It is also interesting to note that Christ taught that, to receive one genuine follower of Christ such as the above, is to receive him! This will mean to you whatever it is *meant* to mean to you, but Christ has said that:

> Whoever welcomes you welcomes me, and whoever welcomes me welcomes the one who sent me. Whoever welcomes a prophet in the name of a prophet will receive a prophet's reward; and whoever welcomes a righteous person in the name of a righteous person will receive the reward of the righteous; and whoever gives *even* a cup of cold water to *one* of these little ones in the

name of a disciple—truly I tell you, *none*
of these will lose their reward.

MATTHEW 10:40-42

Likewise, Christ said, during the Passover Supper immediately before he was arrested to be
crucified, that:

Very truly, I tell you, whoever receives one
whom I send receives *me*; and whoever
receives *me* receives *Him* who sent me.

JOHN 13:20

But to look back at those who were mentioned
at the very beginning of this chapter – those who
oppress any and all that get in their path through
religious control and condemnation against even
their very own members, and who seek to do
the same to anyone else that they can get a
hold of and manipulate – including good Christian people who trustingly hold the same in
too high and lofty of an unwarranted esteem,
and to soon after fall into their trap, only to
realize what they have gotten into when it is
too late – it is those who seek to "win over
souls" at any cost, to *then* simply draw them
away from their new-found relationship with God
as they make His very children stumble with

unnecessary confusion, guilt, self-doubt, and fear brought on by the firm grasp of man's traditions, the desire to appear 'righteous' before others, and by oftentimes using meaningless, repetitive rites and rituals as a form of mind control. But in regards to such things, Christ instructed that we *not* be like them, nor give into them, nor give ourselves to them – while also stating such things as:

> Beware of practicing your piety before others in order to be *seen* by them; for then you have no reward from your Father in heaven.
>
> MATTHEW 6:1

and, in regards to praying, Christ said:

> And whenever you pray, do not be like the hypocrites; for they love to stand and pray in the synagogues and at the street corners, so that they may be seen by others. Truly I tell you, they have received their reward... And when you are praying, do not use meaningless repetition as the Gentiles do, for they suppose that they will be heard for their *many* words. So do not be like them; for your Father knows what you need *before* you ask Him.
>
> MATTHEW 6:5 & 7-8

Furthermore, in regards to giving to the poor, he said:

> So whenever you give alms, do not sound a
> trumpet before you, as the hypocrites do in
> the synagogues and in the streets, so that
> they may be *praised* by others. Truly I tell
> you, they have received their reward. But
> when you give alms, do not let your left
> hand know what your right hand is doing,
> so that your alms may be done in secret;
> and your Father who sees what is done in
> secret will reward you.
>
> MATTHEW 6:2-4

Even in regards to fasting as a religious practice, Christ states:

> And whenever you fast, do not look *dis-
> mal*, like the hypocrites, for they disfigure
> their faces so as to *show others* that they
> are fasting. Truly I tell you, they have
> received their reward. But when you fast,
> put oil on your head and wash your face,
> so that your fasting may be seen *not* by
> others but by your Father who is in secret;
> and your Father who sees what is done in
> secret will reward you. [MATTHEW 6:16-18]

Yes, many seemingly 'religious' people have indeed forgotten who they are meant to represent – and will oftentimes become the very stumbling blocks to those who yearn for a personal relationship with God. For Christ is *not* a God of fear

– but of love, peace, and mental and spiritual tranquility and balance. And as he has said,

> ... I came that they may have life, and have it abundantly.
>
> JOHN 10:10

As a result of their forced-upon control, they make the world stumble as a consequence of their pious, self-righteous, and religiously-judgmental words.  And even worse, as a result of their actions, they make even believers in Christ *themselves* stumble with self-doubt, confusion, despair, and isolation. As Christ has clearly stated:

> They [*the religious leaders that he was speaking of*] tie up heavy burdens and lay them on men's shoulders, but they themselves are *unwilling* to move them with so much as a finger. But they do all their deeds to be *noticed* by men.
>
> MATTHEW 23:4-5

and,

> But woe to you, scribes and Pharisees, hypocrites, because you *shut off* the kingdom of heaven from people; for you do not enter in yourselves, *nor do you allow* those who are entering to go in.
>
> MATTHEW 23:13

And in regards to the result of such heavy-handed, controlling religiosity – which again does not make for the majority of good, moderate churches within Christianity (though it is the former who seem to get more media coverage than the over-whelmingly *moderate* majority within Christendom) – the words of Christ against similar religious leaders certainly applies, when he said:

> Woe to you, scribes and Pharisees, hypocrites! For you cross sea and land to make a single convert, and you make the new convert twice as much a child of hell as yourselves.
>
> MATTHEW 23:15

Additionally, Christ stated that religious leaders such as these are extremely *particular* about religious law, tradition, and regulatory oppression in the likes of "straining out a gnat"; but that by these very acts totally miss – and likewise make their very listeners gloss over or completely disregard – those things that are *most important* to God: these being justice, mercy, and faith – when he says:

> Woe to you, scribes and Pharisees, hypocrites! For you tithe mint, dill, and cummin, and have neglected the weightier

> matters of the law: *justice and mercy and faith*. It is these you ought to have practiced without neglecting the others. You blind guides! You strain out a gnat but swallow a camel!
>
> MATTHEW 23:23-24

And in the same context, Christ gives us the meaning of *true* piety, or religious practice, when he states:

> The greatest among you will be your servant. For all who exalt themselves will be humbled, and all who humble themselves will be exalted.
>
> MATTHEW 23:11-12

As such, Christ teaches us *not* to follow religion, nor religious leaders and organizations – but rather to place our trust on him, and him *alone* – as our teacher and Lord – when he likewise states that:

> They love to have the place of honor at banquets and the best seats in the synagogues, and to be greeted with respect in the marketplaces, and to have people call them rabbi [*a religious teacher or leader*]. But you are *not* to be called rabbi, for you have *one* teacher, and you are all brothers. And call no one your father [*spiritual father*] on earth, for you have

> *one* Father—the one in heaven. Nor are
> you to be called instructors, for you have
> one instructor, the Messiah.
>
> MATTHEW 23:6-10

It must also be noted that many of these same minority of peoples and organizations that they belong to are oftentimes likewise known for separating families, making sincere believers in Christ stumble in their faith, and destroying individual lives. It is very much encouraged that the reader, especially the Christian-based reader, take a look at the ever eye-opening and very much revealing site CULTWATCH.COM,[7] which speaks in detail about the damage these and other groups have caused innocent and trusting Christians worldwide. In fact, the site sums this up excellently in the following quote that, though speaking about a particular cult, nonetheless applies to most:

> ... The spiritual dynamics of Mind Control result in the Christian having the Holy Spirit replaced in their life by the counterfeit of an earthly middleman. The Super Apostle and his leaders insert themselves between the Christian and God. Instead of the Christian being convicted by the Holy

---

[7] CultWatch, ⟨URL: http://www.cultwatch.com⟩

Spirit the Christian receives false conviction from men. Christians are told by men what they have done wrong according to the rules those men have invented. This leads to a spiritual dependency on those men rather than a dependency on the Holy Spirit. Christians, who should become strong, instead become weaker as their dependency on their leaders and the church organization grows. Of course this is what the leaders desire since it makes these Christians more controllable. However this spiritual counterfeit is a slow poison that crushes the spirit of the Christian. After the 'Honeymoon' period with the church is over, the Christian emerges to find they are struggling to meet the standards of the group. They are told that life should be perfect, but it is not. The constant meetings, the controlling pressure, the stress, and the condemnation from the leadership, takes its toll.t The Christian tries harder. But fails again and again. Finally the Christian burns out. Too long they have been running on man-made power rather than God's. 'If this is Christianity', they say, 'then I don't want to have anything to do with it!' So they reject Jesus and turn to the world. Convinced that the counterfeit they experienced was Christianity they never again consider following our

> Lord. Not all reject Christianity, but those who return to biblical churches struggle to cope. They suffer depression and feelings of guilt. The preaching of their false apostle is still in their head. Those who have wasted years in the counterfeit group feel a tremendous sense of loss. They take much time to recover. This is the fruit of Mind Control, numerous shipwrecked Christians.[8]

I could not have described it better myself! And this is usually the outcome from being involved in any cult from whatever relevant church, political movement, corporation, or marketing strategy it may take the form of. The likes of these are but wolves in sheep's clothing. Generally speaking, any church, group, or organization that attempts to *separate* families on its own accord; that shuns the *entirety* of television, music, or the arts as a whole; and that feels its group is the *only* sect that is following God – and that all others are going to burn, are heretical, or deceived – should *probably* be avoided. I know I would. For, why should *I* suffer needlessly... and why should *you*?

---

[8] As in CultWatch, *Attack of the Super Apostles!* ⟨URL: http://www.cultwatch.com/superapostles.html⟩.

This having been said, it would be of great benefit to the reader, especially to one who may be looking for a church to attend (though again, this is not in the least required in order to follow Christ, as one follows him *individually*, and *not* through any form of earthly representation; though it could prove to be of benefit to spiritual growth, maturity, and strength when one finds a group or church that *indeed* follows Christ's teachings and loves in action and in truth) – but it would be of great benefit that the reader be made aware of certain tell-tale signs of what has so far been described herein in regards to the less favorable congregations, groups, or leaders... these being, the signs that one might be dealing with a cult. And so, the bullet-points that follow are provided for your perusal, enjoyment, and avoidance of future grief:

# A Cult's Red Flags

The following list of points are paraphrased summations from the site WWW.HOWCULTSWORK.COM. It is greatly encouraged that the reader look through it in detail.

Tell-tale signs that a church – as well as some political movements, "self-help"-styled groups, certain introductory "yoga classes", many New Age-related organizations,[9] and few corporate environments and similar organized schemes – may in fact be a form of cult include the following:

- *deception*: It uses deception in order to hide the truth of what it is really about, or what it truly represents, so that others are initially *willing* to join.

- *controlling member's time:* By *constantly* involving them in meetings, lectures, conferences, classes, and so forth – while limiting the time that a member is able to spend with his or her own family, personal friends, leisure activities, and work responsibilities.

- *using fear, intimidation, condemnation, guilt, and personal character assassination:*
  Through attacking one's motives, character, and sincerity – or by getting very aggressive, hostile, or angry when someone displays any form of disagreement with the group's key concepts, philosophies, or leadership; often quoting from the disagreeing person's own faith and scriptures to use *against* him or her – much like Satan did when tempting Christ in the wilderness (see Matthew 4:1-11).

---

[9] See Appendix A on page 357 for details.

- *contribution-pressure:* Using guilt, fear, and other manipulative techniques to acquire your money.

- *lack of confidentiality:* To where members are *instructed* to report on confidential conversations between themselves and target recruits to a designated leader.

- *exclusivity*: To where non-members are seen as "in the wrong" – or on their way to hell-fire – if they are not part of, or in agreement with, that particular church – or whatever group or organization it might be.[10]

---

[10] Even some who militantly preach evolution seem to oftentimes behave in this form of exclusivity, as they frequently consider creationists as either idiots or religious freaks, while treating evolution as a religion in its own right. Yet many prominent scientists now conclude that it is statistically much more probable that the over six million individual parts of a disassembled Boeing 747 aircraft strewn throughout a junk yard would by sheer chance be put back together again to perfectly re-build the original aircraft through a passing tornado – than for evolution to have taken place without an intelligent designer being involved...whatever our earth's age may be. See the highly analytical works of Fred Hoyle, *Mathematics of Evolution.* Acorn Enterprises Llc., 1999; Lee M. Spetner, *Not by Chance.* Judaica Press, 1997; Michael J. Behe, *Darwin's Black Box: The Biochemical Challenge to Evolution.* 2nd edition. Free Press, 2006; and Idem, *The Edge of Evolution: The Search for the Limits of Darwinism.* Free Press, 2007.

If you are interested in this subject, it is greatly encouraged that you look into the references cited above, as many scientists bent on proving evolution have as a

- *"love bombing":* Displaying an instant and seemingly "intimate" friendship with someone they have just met; while attempting to control the private lives and relationships of its members in regards to existing family and friends.

- *controlling information:* Such as restricting what one can and cannot read, watch, and research; while claiming that only *their* literature (their own books, magazines, tapes, DVD's, and so forth) hold the truth.

- *pressure selling:* Through *overly-enthusiastic* meetings and *intensive* – at times to the point of even being aggressively "in-your-face" – one-on-one conversations where one is asked to reveal one's personal life, thoughts, and intentions;

---

result come to a personal belief in a Creator due to the widespread factual inaccuracies of the theory that, though proven untrue in recent decades, are still being taught in our schools and universities as facts. Many now feel that it would take much more faith in believing we came from apes than to accept God's involvement in our creation. Consequently, the theory of evolution has unnecessarily had a major negative affect on our present global societies and governments – even Hitler used the theory to argue that the Nazis were part of a superior race, as he hoped to induce the "continued" evolutionary development of a perfect and superior Aryan race on earth. Consequently, due to the widespread belief that there is no Creator, and that we are here purely by chance without anyone to account to – it's every man for himself, survival-of-the-fittest takes precedence over social responsibility, and both money and power over "the weaker" have now for some become the prime motivators of societal progression and individual aspirations above personal accountability.

or where one is coercively made to feel inferior, weak, or guilty if one does not agree, show mutual enthusiasm. . . and eventually obey whatever non-sense they are demanding of their members.

- *using "herd mentality" as a weapon:* In order to make one feel inferior or excluded because they are not "fitting in" to the group's philosophies or beliefs – no matter how irrationally-sounding their principles might be.[11]

---

[11] The concept of "herd mentality" refers to the way in which a mass population so easily accepts as truth whatever is popularly or widely accepted to be such without questioning its validity on a personal level or by individual investigation and free-will. It is the status quo of the majority, the "acceptable norm" of the masses – to where whoever does not prescribe to it may at times be deemed by a dominant societal group to be an outcast, rebel, blasphemer, heretic, infidel, or otherwise "confused" or "misled". An example of this would be Nazi Germany in WWII and the accepted popular assumption that the long-suffering Jewish people, the homosexual, and the mentally and physically disabled were inferior simply because the Third Reich had claimed them as such, and because "everyone else" (many of those living in Germany at that time who considered themselves as "Aryan", for instance) seemed to accept such a claim as truth, so that it "must be true" – at least in the eyes of the majority acquiescing to herd mentality. See also Michael Berenbaum, *A Mosaic of Victims: Non-Jews Persecuted and Murdered by the Nazis*. I.B. Tauris, December 1990; as well as Malcolm Gladwell, *The Tipping Point: How Little Things Can Make a Big Difference*. Back Bay Books, 2002.

As is rightly said:

> Remember, people are not perfect, but if
> they employ them constantly you are most
> likely dealing with a cult.[12]

God never intended that we should live separate
from the rest of the world, but that we should
be a light in the darkness, and this without
being subjected to all the enchainments that
come with organized religion. God intended that
we have a personal and intimate relationship
with *Him*... without being 'religious' in any way.
Religion is for those that need to be led, and
for such as these, that can oftentimes become
a dangerous thing to depend on indeed. For
when dependence on religion takes the place of
a dependence on God and His guidance; when dependence on hard text and legalistic approaches
to doctrinal interpretation take the place of being
led by the Spirit of Truth (or Holy Spirit) that
was promised to all who would receive Him;
all bets are off... *anything* can happen. And
it usually does. Be *in* the world, but not *of*
the world. This does *not* mean believers should

---

[12] As per HowCultsWork, ⟨URL: http:
//howcultswork.com⟩.

isolate themselves in religion. And as Jesus also stated in JOHN 17:15 when he was praying,

> I do not ask You to take them *out* of the world, but that You protect them from the evil one.

JOHN 17:15

Yet *again*, it must be *emphasized* that not every church or religious organization is like the few bad apples that fit such tell-tail signs – in fact, most are not. There are *many* fine, sincere, and genuinely loving and balanced churches out there that are *not* radical or manipulative; and that – from the Christian perspective – teach Christ's love, mercy, and grace as *he* taught it.

Therefore, it is obviously imperative that you always use that rational brain and intuition that God has given you. And if you *do* choose to visit or join a church, it is suggested that you do so through prayer, shrewd observation, a balanced degree of common sense without initially being either too open nor too suspicious, cool rationality, patience, and an independent mind. And above all else, always keep in mind that *nobody* is perfect.

So if you *do* find a group that encourages and acknowledges you as a *genuine* child of God without judging your personal life and intentions – when you know that you have in fact come to Him in sincerity and truth – than more power to you! Again, one does not *need* religion to have a personal one-on-one relationship with Christ – but fellowship is always important and beneficial when done with the *right* people. So long as this remains *consistent*, and they do not come between you and how God is leading your life on a *personal* level – than stick with them unless God tells you otherwise.

Again, it is Christ's promised Spirit of Truth (or Holy Spirit) that personally and directly reveals *all things* to us – as Christ clearly explained,[13] and as has been previously mentioned. If you have sincerely opened your door to God with the *simplest* of faith – simply by putting your trust in Him and saying "Father, I'm yours, come into my life", He *has* now become part of your life, and *will* guide you into *all* truth if you just stop and listen to His voice within. Talk to Him as you would a loving friend, and He *will* re-

---

[13] See Chapter 2 on page 23; as well as Chapter 12 on page 267.

veal Himself to you, and will show you the abundant purpose He has for your life...guaranteed! All you have to do is ask.

Don't let them take your faith away, nor prevent you from *continuing* to speak to your Father – who loves, understands, and cares for you so much more than anyone else on earth *ever* will...no matter *who* you are, what battles you've fought, or where you presently find yourself in life's journey.

So if the sort of *religious* group you find yourself in consists only of those who have long forgotten about coming to God as a child, and who have replaced Him with the worship of church bureaucracy, attempted control of members' personal lives, memorized verses to judge and implement fear onto attendees who do not obey, and religious-borne piety and self-righteousness – than get out of their, and don't look back – and know that God is *with you*, and that if it is *His* will for you to find a place that worships Him in spirit and in truth, than He *will* lead you to it. And *if* it is God's will that you take some months – or even years — off from any involvement with organized religion, than He will make this clear to you as well. As is stated:

> *Trust* in the Lord with *all* your heart, and
> lean not on your *own* understandings. In
> all your ways *acknowledge Him*, and He
> *will* direct your path. [PROVERBS 3:5-6 NIV]

You don't *need* organized religion. No one does...
no one *ever* did. Christ *himself* made this clear.
You are flesh and spirit – so worship Him *not*
in temples built by man, but "*in* spirit and in
truth",[14] as he so clearly said.  Not to say you
should not associate with others who are worshiping Him in this way as well and who treat
you as a responsible and intelligent human being
who is led by God as He sees fit.  They *are* out
there. And again, fellowship – with the *right* people – *is* of utmost importance for encouragement,
support, and friendship. But if you presently find
yourself in the 'wrong' *religious* crowd – who's
god *is* religiosity itself – detach from them before
they do you and your family – and especially your
mind and soul – any *more* damage.

Detach from those – the overly-religious, the
controlling, and the fanatical – that would hinder
your mind and soul – and find people who respect
*you*, *your* choices... and *most* of all, the teachings
of Christ.

---

[14] See Chapter 6 on page 89.

# Chapter Fifteen

# *Abide in Me*

And will not God grant justice to his chosen ones who cry to Him day and night?
Will He delay long in helping them? I tell
you, He *will* quickly grant justice to them.
And yet, when the Son of Man comes, will
he find *The Faith* on earth?

JESUS CHRIST, AS PER LUKE 18:7-8

To those who have placed your trust on Christ,
and Christ alone, can you respond to what Jesus
is saying in the above verse, and with confidence
state, "Yes Lord, you *will* find faith on earth when
you come back. You will find it in *me*"? For as he
also stated,

I am the true vine, and My Father is the
vine-dresser.  Every branch in Me that
does not bear fruit, He takes away; and
every branch that bears fruit, He prunes
it so that it may bear more fruit. You are
*already* clean because of the word which

> I have spoken to you. Abide in Me, and I in you. As the branch cannot bear fruit of itself unless it abides in the vine, so neither can you unless you abide in Me. I am the vine, you are the branches; he who abides in Me and I in him, he bears much fruit, for apart from Me you can do nothing.
>
> JOHN 15:1-5

The Greek word for *abide* as per the above is *meno*, which means to "rest in", to "remain in", to *stand*, and to "persevere in".[1] For,

> Blessed are those who trust in the Lord, whose trust *is* the Lord. They shall be like a tree planted by water, sending out its roots by the stream. It shall not fear when heat comes, and its leaves shall stay green; in the year of drought it is *not* anxious, and it *does not cease* to bear fruit.
>
> JEREMIAH 17:7-8

Furthermore, *abiding in* has also aptly been described as follows:

> Because I was constantly worrying about something, I never enjoyed the peace that

---

[1] See Lockman Foundation, editor, *Greek Dictionary of the New American Standard Exhaustive Concordance*. Zondervan, 2000.

Jesus died for me to have. It is absolutely impossible to worry and live in peace at the same time. Peace is not something that can be put on a person; it is a fruit of the Spirit (Galatians 5:22), and fruit is the result of abiding in the vine (John 15:4 kjv). Abiding relates to entering the 'rest of God' spoken of in the fourth chapter of Hebrews as well as other places in the Word of God.[2]

Yes, bearing fruit means not letting life get you down, not letting anxiety nor the fragile and uncertain futures and promises of this world phase you. It is, as Christ put it in the parable of the Sower and the Seed,[3] *accepting* his words with and honest heart, and with *patient endurance*[4] – or perseverance – bearing much fruit through keeping your eyes on him – through a deliberate but very simple childlike faith. It is to be happy

---

[2] As in Joyce Meyer, *Battlefield of the Mind: Winning the Battle in Your Mind.* Hodder & Stoughton, 2007.

[3] As found in Matthew 13:1-23; Mark 4:1-20; and Luke 8:4-15.

[4] As Christ stated,

But as for that [*the seed*] in the good soil, these are the ones who, when they hear the word, hold it fast in an honest and good heart, and bear fruit with *patient endurance*. [Luke 8:15]

within yourself even when the world is agitated and insecure. It is to be at peace even when the nightly news states otherwise. It is to be friendly even when the rest of mankind can't be bothered. It is to be a light, even when all you see all around you may be darkness. For you can light even a huge, darkened arena with a single match of light, to where everyone can – and *will* – see it, no matter where or who they are.

Christ taught us to follow the commandments of God – to love Him, and to love our neighbor as we live by faith and apply the clear teachings of His Son and *His* Word – rather than striving to follow organized religion, man-made tradition, and the choking deceptions of pleasing mankind for the sake of our own perceived and ever-changeable 'reputations' – as other religions do because they feel they *have* to in order to please God. For either we follow a Paulinian-style of modern-day religion – though it did not come from Paul but rather through those who substitute Christ for religiosity and man-made tradition – or the simple and freeing faith taught to the world by Christ. So do not fear, and *rest* in his love, for God does *not* make mistakes.

To abide in Christ is to have faith in God, and to *consistently* move forward – even in times of doubt, challenges, difficulties, humiliations, and rejection. As is rightly said:

> My child, when you come to serve the Lord, prepare yourself for testing. Set your heart right and be steadfast, and do not be impetuous in time of calamity. *Cling to Him* and do not depart, so that your last days may be prosperous. Accept whatever befalls you, and in times of humiliation *be patient*. For *gold* is tested in the fire, and those found acceptable, in the furnace of *humiliation*. Trust in Him, and He *will* help you; make your ways straight, and hope in Him. You who fear the Lord, *wait* for his mercy; *do not stray*, or else you may fall. You who fear the Lord, *trust* in Him, and your reward will not be lost. You who fear the Lord, hope for *good* things, for lasting *joy* and *mercy*...has anyone trusted in the Lord and been disappointed? Or has anyone *persevered* in the fear of the Lord and been forsaken? Or has anyone called upon Him and been *neglected*? For the Lord is compassionate and merciful; He *forgives* sins and *saves* in time of distress.

SIRACH 2:1-11

Yes, gold *is* indeed tested in fire! Therefore, *never* give up, but *always* – with boldness and confidence – rely on Christ to carry you through. You may stumble, you may fall, you may fail a thousand times. But don't quit. *Never* quit. No matter what the world might say, object to, or crumble under. Don't let it phase you. For you stand on the Rock – the Rock of Jesus Christ of Nazareth, who is the same yesterday, today, and forever.[5] For he *is* with you – and *in* you. And he *never* fails, nor ever will. *Abide* in his love so that you may bear the fruits of faith, confidence, mental stability, and a peaceful existence where your light reflects The Light of the world.

Therefore, *never* give up. *Never* panic. As Christ *constantly* said, never be afraid, nor let your heart ever be troubled. Trust in him, and go out and bear some fruit! For God, for your community, for your family, for the world to see by example that they might follow, and for *yourself*. And though it has been quoted throughout this work, it is worth a final look, where Christ lovingly reminds those who will follow:

---

[5] Hebrews 13:8

> Do not let your heart be troubled, nor let
> it be fearful.
>
> JOHN 14:27

... and again, Christ states:

> These things I have spoken to you, so that
> in Me you may have peace. In the world
> you have tribulation, but take courage; I
> have overcome the world.
>
> JOHN 16:33

So *trust* in Him. With *all* things. Even when you fall. Even when you might be at fault. Recognize it, turn, *accept* his forgiveness – and *move on* – always trusting, never faltering in The Faith. *Always*.

*Rest* in his love, and abide *in* him – as *he* abides with you, and is *in* you – forever. In this you will bear much fruit indeed.

For you are no use to anyone if you are constantly overcome by worry, fears, insecurities about tomorrow, and obsessing about the opinions of others as they pertain to you. It is only on *abiding* in Christ as the ultimate representation of what *true* love is – as he having been referred to as the believer's *First Love,* and as the Light of the world – that one can *than* be able to bear such fruits as described in this famous prayer:

Lord, make me an *instrument*
of your peace.
Where there is hatred, let me sow love
where there is injury, pardon
where there is doubt, faith
where there is despair, hope
where there is darkness, light
and where there is sadness, joy [6]

For as has rightly been said:

> ...we have not ceased praying for you
> and asking that you may be filled with
> the knowledge of God's will in all spiri-
> tual *wisdom* and understanding, so that
> you may lead lives worthy of the Lord,
> fully pleasing to Him, as you *bear fruit*
> in every good work and as you *grow in
> the knowledge of God.* May you be made
> *strong* with all the strength that comes
> from his glorious power, and may you
> be prepared to endure everything with
> *patience*, while joyfully *giving thanks* to
> the Father, who has enabled you to share
> in the inheritance of the saints in the
> light.
> COLOSSIANS 1:9-12

*Abide* in Christ, and all else will soon fall into
place around you.

---

[6]Saint Francis of Assisi, *Prayer of Saint Francis of Assisi*. La Clochette, 1912.

Chapter Sixteen

# *Where Do We Go from Here?*

Christ calls *all* of mankind to Himself so that, should you *answer* His call, you will find that you do not have to become *like* some who turn out to be modern-day religious zealots to be His child. Seek Him from within the sacred privacy of your heart and you *will* find Him – seek Him from an organized and religiosity-tainted platform and you will more often than not find contradiction, confusion, and manipulations. But again, it must be said that *not* all religious organizations, *nor* all religious *people*, are thus. For it is not religion in and of itself that oftentimes turns negative, but rather the hearts of its participants when driven by self-righteousness, judgemental-ism, hypocrisy, and fanaticisms of every sort.

Christ taught us to be *like* his Father – a God of unconditional love, limitless mercy, and undeserved grace. It is when we turn our focus *away* from Christ and his Gospel that we soon go the way of the Pharisees and Sadducees of Christ's time, and make religion into a god in and of itself – which is idolatry as it then takes *the place of* God – while transforming ourselves into religious obsessives hungering for the temporal approvals of mankind, rather than seeking the approval that comes from the One and only God.

Thus, for those that seek Him – find Him by beginning to speak to Him *directly* and on your own initiative and free will – talk to Him in faith, knowing that He *will* listen and *will* reveal Himself to those that come to Him with a willing and open heart and spirit – to those who sincerely seek for Truth in a world where love is all but lost.

Enter into His presence in *whatever* way He leads you. Enjoy it! And don't over-analyze and complicate. If you wish, open a Bible and read the four gospels of MATTHEW, MARK, LUKE, and JOHN. And pay especially-close attention to the words of Christ. Much of what he has to say will certainly surprise you in that there are *countless* hidden and eye-opening a-ha moment treasures in his words and deeds that many would not expect coming from him – hence the importance of taking such a personal and private experiment on and looking at the Gospels – and *his* words in particular – *for yourself.* You *will* be enriched – particularly when you are willing to stretch forth your faith.[1] Don't delve any deeper than is necessary, just take these four books in on this initial experiment.

Maybe later – much, much, later on – *if* it so suits you, you might decide to find a church[2] or group that *accepts you* for who you are as God has Himself created you to be – and who will not desecrate your relationship with Him through misinformation, rule, ambiguity, slan-

---

[1] See Chapter 7 on page 97.

[2] One that reflects on Christ's teachings rather than unduly emphasizing ritual, ceremony, and controlling its members – which lead to religiosity, and on the extreme scale, can be signs of a cult [see also Chapter 14 on page 307]. But there *are* many good, balanced and sensible churches out there that make all feel welcome, that enrich the lives of those who attend, and that proclaim the Gospel of Christ rather than religious rule. Nothing wrong with attending a few to see which ones actually fit into the teachings of Christ as you might have picked up from the aforementioned experiment. Not the teachings of a church leader, nor of Paul as they might see it, nor of a church-released book of rules – but the teachings of *Christ*.

der, hypocrisy, misplaced guilt, shame, and fear. This is totally up to you – and is a decision made *exclusively* by yourself and with the guidance of God's Holy Spirit. Let *Him* lead you to the right church (or to *no* church at all), and no one else.[3]

And if and when you *do* decide to delve into the remainder of the Old or New Testament – *if* you so desire – do so with the awareness that it must be taken in context, with balanced common sense, and by the leadership of the Holy Spirit – considering the time of writing, who was writing, and to whom was being written. Christ's words in the aforementioned Gospels are far weightier, more powerful, and more revealing than probably anything you will *ever* read on earth – and I am personally content with that. For his words, much as the Kingdom of Heaven itself, are like fine pearls – or *the* fine pearl – worthy in exchange of all that one has.

For as Christ stated:

> Again, the kingdom of heaven is like a
> merchant in search of fine pearls; on find-
> ing one pearl of great value, he went

---

[3] See also Chapter 14 on page 307 for suggestions on how to approach finding a good church. . . if you ever wish to do so.

and sold all that he had and bought it.
[MATTHEW 13:45-47]

For as a faithful and worthy follower of Christ
has himself rightly said in regards to such a
priceless pearl:

> ... the kingdom of heaven is worth all you
> have. The way to that pearl will cost
> you nothing, because you get the pearl by
> following the Gospel. By living the Ten
> Commandments... So there you have it,
> a message sent from God. The symbol
> of the pearl. They say on earth dia-
> monds are forever... The Gospel message
> is forever. No matter where life occurs
> in the universe, the message, the word
> exists, it will always exist because it is
> the truth. Christ's words once spoken
> last forever because he has spoken the
> truth about human behavior, his words
> sparkle from the diamonds and spread
> light everywhere, the light are his words
> and they last forever, and all those who
> listen and believe will follow him into
> eternal life forever. They have chosen
> eternal life for themselves because they
> have *chosen* to follow Christ.[4]

As having been previously explained, Christ has
promised us that *His* Spirit of Truth would per-

---

[4] As in Henry Thomas Grosse, *Thomas De Thomas*.
Henry Grosse Publications, 1996.

sonally and individually reveal to us *all things* as we sincerely listen to His voice, and as we continually and straightforwardly ask God for guidance – so don't supersede what the Spirit of God tells you with the external words, doctrines, and traditions of man. And never, *ever*, lose the God-given fearless confidence[5] that He has *already* given to you (all you have to do is *use* it) – and which He wants you to always live by. For He is within *all* who open their door to Him *without* preconditions or exceptions – and He will *never* let you go. For as Christ clearly stated:

> My sheep listen to my voice; I know them, and they follow me. I give them eternal life, and they shall *never* perish; and *no one* can snatch them out of my hand. My Father, who has given them to me, is *greater than all*; and *no one* is able to snatch them out of my Father's hand. I and the Father are one.
> JOHN 10:27-30

Lastly, neither let the trials and tribulations of life, nor the religious, snatch your faith away

---

[5] As Christ rightly said: "These things I have spoken to you, so that in Me you may have peace. In the world you have tribulation, but *take courage*; I have overcome the world." [John 16:33] ... and, "Do not let your heart be troubled, nor let it be fearful." [John 14:27]

from your heart – remember Christ's parable of the Sower and the Seed?[6] Don't deprive yourself the joy, peace, enjoyment, and clarity of talking to and *knowing* Christ; of knowing *for yourself* of His perfect and rewarding guidance for your life; and of *personally* experiencing His unconditional and eternal love for you – not on *anyone's* account – for the kingdom of God, that fine pearl, *belongs* to you for the taking, *just as you are*. As Jesus says:

> Very truly, I tell you, everyone who commits sin is a slave to sin. Now a slave has no permanent place in the family, but a son *belongs* to it forever. So if the Son sets you free, you *will* be free indeed. [JOHN 8:34-36]

And with this, I bid you, my dear reader, that the peace of Christ always be *with* you, and *in* you:

> Finally, beloved, whatever is true, whatever is honorable, whatever is just, whatever is pure, whatever is pleasing, whatever is commendable, if there is any excellence and if there is anything worthy of praise, think about these things. Keep on doing the things that you have learned and received and heard and seen in me, and the God of peace will be with you *always*. [PHILIPPIANS 4:8-9]

---

[6] As discussed in Chapter 11 on page 231; and as found in Matthew 13:1-23; Mark 4:1-20; and Luke 8:4-15.

# Appendices

# What Christ Said of the End Times

Christ warned the world that, before his return, there would appear false christs, false teachers, and false prophets who would mislead many, and who would lead those who put their trust in them astray. He warned us that these false teachers would perform signs and deceptive illusions that would appear to most people as being miraculous acts, to where even some followers of Christ would *themselves* get fooled by these deceptions. As Christ stated:

> Beware that no one leads you astray. For many will come in my name, saying, 'I am the Messiah!' [or, *the Christ*] and they will lead many astray...Then they will hand you over to be tortured and will put you to death, and you will be hated by all nations because of my name. Then many will fall away, and they will betray one another and hate one

another. And many false prophets will arise
and lead many astray... Then if anyone says
to you, 'Look! Here is the Messiah!' [or *the
Christ*] or 'There he is!'—do not believe it. For
false messiahs and false prophets will appear
and produce great signs and omens, to lead
astray, if possible, even the elect [*those who
had previously turned to Christ*]. Take note, I
have told you beforehand. So, if they say to
you, 'Look! He is in the wilderness,' do not
go out. If they say, 'Look! He is in the inner
rooms,' do not believe it. For as the lightning
comes from the east and flashes as far as the
west, so will be the coming of the Son of Man.
Wherever the corpse is, there the vultures will
gather... Then the sign of the Son of Man will
appear in the sky, and then all the tribes of the
earth will mourn, and they will see the Son
of Man coming on the clouds of the sky with
power and great glory. And he will send out
his angels with a loud trumpet call, and they
will gather his elect from the four winds, from
one end of heaven to the other.

MATTHEW 24:4-5, 9-11, 23-28, & 30-31

Many false teachers, false prophets, and self-proclaimed
'christs' have indeed been appearing throughout the
world through to modern times – and continue to do so
in ever-increasing frequency. We see them in various
forms of "cults of personality", where they explicitly
state that they are the modern embodiment of Christ[1]
– while misleading millions of very good, honest, and
exceptional people with sincere intentions to better

---

[1] See also H. Wayne House, *The Jesus Who Never
Lived: Exposing False Christs and Finding the Real Jesus*.
Harvest House Publishers, 2008.

themselves physically, mentally, and spiritually – and making a very wealthy living off of their follower's backs.[2]

Oftentimes, many of these false spiritual leaders will prefer Western populations to convert as their followers in order to massively increase their personal multi-million dollar annual income by which their mansions, private planes, and luxuries are financed through what are now *multi-billion*-dollar-a-year industries.[3] They will oftentimes teach their listeners to exalt the self as a god, or to invoke ancient pagan deities – while often implying a universal "creator" – but which to them means to ultimately refer to the creator *within*, or the god of self – or rather, the self *as* god[4] because "*all* is God, and God is *in* all" as per many of their now modernized and sanitized root form of the ancient pagan religion of *One-ism* (or, *monism*)– while at the same time denying the One *true* God and Creator of all. Thus they teach that the earth, that all of mankind, beasts, nature, and the Universe itself all constitute, and are *themselves* God – being explicit in stating that we don't *need* a monotheistic God because God is in everything, that everything is God – and that God *is* everything.

But what *is* One-ism? One-ism has been around for thousands of years, and it is the essential element on which pagan religions have always been based on,

---

[2] See also Chapter 14 on page 307.

[3] See Caryl Matrisciana, *Out of India: A True Story about the New Age Movement*. Lighthouse Trails Publishing, 2008.

[4] See also Dave Hunt, *Yoga and the Body of Christ: What Position Should Christians Hold?* The Berean Call, 2006.

and what the world seems to be heading towards today as a unified belief system on a massively globalized scale. It worships creation, and false deities that are attributed to characteristics of nature, rather than on the Creator *Himself*.

One-ism teaches that there is *no* contrast between God and His creation, and thereby claims that, because God created everything, that He is *in* everything, is a part of everything, and that everything is a part of God. Many of its followers now use terms such as "Mother Earth" to deify planet earth, and to worship it – and all things in it – as being one with its Creator. It teaches that one does not *need* to humbly look to God for salvation, because it is *the self* that saves by the pursuit of self-enlightenment. This of course rings of the sin of arrogant pride, which is one of the greatest, if not *the* greatest of all sins, and the bases on which the most heinous crimes and negative behaviors of humanity have always been based on.

One-ism teaches that there is *no* difference between good or evil – that evil is what you decide to make of it, and is dependent on one's *perspective*, culture, and personal *opinion* – to where universal moral truths do not exist, or don't matter – because it is all up to individual choice and how one looks at it. It teaches that there is no difference between mankind and the rest of creation, again, because all are one – to where every individual is a god in his or her own right, and therefore does not *need* to fear the One true God as the Creator of the Universe – who Himself does not exist as a separate entity from mankind and nature in the first place. . . again, because all are one, and one is all.

In the same manner, One-ism teaches that *all* religions are essentially the same, that they *all* pretty much teach the same things, and that they *all* lead to the same goals and destination – to where many from a diverse and *wide* variety of One-ism's followers – whether or not they even realize that what they are following is rooted in this Old Religion of paganism – themselves often prefer to be deemed as 'spiritual' rather than as followers of God. One-ism, in its wide and varied manifestations, teaches that the answer to mankind's (and earth's) problems lies in a vague pagan-inspired kind of "universal spirituality", and that global peace will only be accomplished when *all* religions unify and worship together as one. Because of this, it also teaches that there is *no difference* between angels and demons, Jesus and Satan, or good and evil – and see *anyone* claiming otherwise as a threat to what it hopes is a coming world Utopia where global peace and love are the results of a "Universal Consciousness" of oneness. As has been said,

> The "new synthesis" is made up of spiritually hungry secular humanists converting to Neo-paganism.[5]

Thus One-ism, though having the guise of a spirituality that is non-religious and disconnected from an organized system of religiosity, is nonetheless *in itself* and by its own definition a major world *religion* made up of quasi-denominations that include modernized forms of ancient Greek and Roman polytheism, most

---

[5] As in Peter R. Jones, *One or Two: Seeing a World of Difference*. Main Entry Editions, 2010.

flavors of Hinduism that involve the worship of thousands of different gods, the foundational philosophies
of Yoga in theory if not (in many circles) in practice,
Wicca in its more polytheistic varieties, and Santeria
and Voodoo in their worship of spirit-based elements,
among others.  It is essentially Neopaganism – or
literally *New-paganism* – but which is firmly rooted
in Old Religion – and in the West tailor-made to fit
humanism with its often subtly-injected philosophy
that we are all "little gods", so to speak.

One-ism allows for no moral absolutes; and when
wider society begins to believe that nothing is necessarily right or wrong, that the concept of "survival of
the fittest" rules the earth, and that the conviction
that we will not have a God to answer to when it's
all said and done and – by proxy – that God did not
create anything because everything has 'evolved' from
nothingness, to where it is "every man for himself";
things can start to go rather pear-shaped indeed –
both globally, as well as in the lives of very innocent
and good-hearted people. For even Hitler used evolution to justify the violent progression of what he saw
as a 'superior' Aryan race, to where it has likewise
now for *some* become the ultimate justification for
societal progress at *any* cost to whomever is seen to
be 'weaker', as well as (again, for *some*) a rationality
to the fulfillment of individual aspiration *irrespective
of* personal accountability.

It is certainly not that we *need* religion for mankind
to 'behave' itself in order for the world to not run
amok. For it is true that organized religion has *oftentimes* caused some of the greatest trouble throughout
earth's history.  But I would humbly propose that we
do *need* God – the Creator of all who knows each and

every one of us *infinitely* better than we will ever know ourselves. But one does not *need* religion to have the type of relationship with God that He Himself seeks to have with mankind on a *personal* one-on-one level, as having been shown throughout this book, correct? And as has been said in regards to one of the most long-surviving, long-term goals of the Old Religion of One-ism:

> Global unity will *not* overcome egotism and greed... The urgency to create a Utopian planet is driven by prophecies of cataclysmic natural disasters such as global warming, which, in light of an embarrassing cooling trend, has been renamed "climate change."... With its added power and planetary reach, global utopia will doubtless be history's most terrifying experiment, a mixture of Golding's *Lord of the Flies* and Orwell's *Animal Farm*. I see the specter of a future world community melting into a mixture of anything-goes-selfishness of the ruling elite, which justifies all its actions as acts of benevolence for the common good. It all ends in ruthless totalitarianism, controlled by an elite class of occult shamans... The answer to Utopian hopes is found in the complex and unique person of Jesus....[6]

Yes, One-ism has indeed been around for *thousands* of years. Some would even say that it has been around from Day One when the serpent told Eve that "you will be like gods" in Genesis 3:5. Furthermore, One-ism is now being widely and radically revived today – even within some well-intending Christian circles – and this in full force and on a massively *global*

---

[6] As in Jones (as in n. 5 on page 361).

scale. For example, yoga – strictly as a philosophy and *apart from* its physically-beneficial exercises – which is sometimes translated as meaning either "to yoke" or "yoked to God" – is oftentimes just one of One-ism's many, *many* vehicles. For, as has been said of yoga, *specifically* in regards to it as a current-day, exponentially-growing industry:

> Everybody loves yoga; sixteen and a half million Americans practice it regularly, and twenty-five million more say they will try it this year. If you've been awake and breathing air in the twenty- first century, you already know that this Hindu practice of health and spirituality has long ago moved on from the toe-ring set... Yoga has now ascended to the category of "platform agnostic," the highest praise marketers can conjure for any kind of content, trend, or person. Translation? Consumers drop $3 billion every year on yoga classes, books, videos, CDs, DVDs, mats, clothing, and other necessities.[7]

But with such mass consumerism of yoga also comes its One-ism-based philosophies alongside it. For instance, many modern-day churches and Christian circles – for the most part innocently and with good intent – encourage what boils down to the roots of what are oftentimes pagan-based forms of Eastern practices, sincerely believing that such mystic philosophies are merely a part of harmless yoga exercises for physical fitness, while being unaware of One-ism principles that they are unknowingly marketing as

---

[7] Robert Love, *Fear of Yoga*. Columbia Journalism Review, November 2006.

per its pagan-based, ancient teachings behind its core One-ism-rooted ideologies. As has been explained,

> Yoga is derived from the Sanskrit word yug, which means "to yoke." This is a term [most Christians are] familiar with from the Bible (Phil. 4:2; Matt. 11:9). A yoke is a crossbar that joins two draft animals at the neck so they can work together; the term, therefore, is applied metaphorically to people being joined together or united in a cause. In Hinduism, as in many religions, union is desired with nothing less than God or the Absolute, and yoga is the system that Hindus have developed to achieve that end.

> The historic purpose behind yoga, therefore, is to achieve union with the Hindu concept of God. This is the purpose behind virtually all of the Eastern varieties of yoga, including those we encounter in the West. This does not mean it is the purpose of every practitioner of yoga, for many people clearly are not practicing it for spiritual reasons but merely to enhance their physical appearance, ability, or health.[8]

Yes, yoga is indeed a vehicle for Hindu-based teachings, which in turn is deeply rooted in pagan-based philosophy and the worship of many gods. But, in comparison to the Gospel of Christ, calling oneself a god is idolatry;[9] calling everything as *part of* God is denying the One and *only* God while worshiping

---

[8] See Elliot Miller, *The Yoga Boom: A Call for Christian Discernment – Part I: Yoga in its original Eastern Context* . 31th edition. Christian Research Journal, 2008, 2.

[9] See Dave Hunt et al., *The Lie of The Serpent: The New Age and the End Times*. Adullam Films, 2008.

His creation instead;[10] and "emptying the mind" for purposes of ultimately reaching 'self-enlightenment' during meditation practices only serve to bring participants to the point at which they will deliberately *allow* themselves to become open to influences[11] other than those of their own individual cognitive judgement and reasoning,[12] and that of God's guidance *through* His Holy Spirit[13] – which in itself can be very dangerous in that, when the purpose is to *separate* the mind from the body, from reality, and from one's own mental aptitude and reasoning by 'emptying' it; one *can* oftentimes lose control of *whatever* might come through, and *will* often become open to suicidal thoughts, depression – some have even suggested demonic attacks – and the heightened inability to discern truth from fiction, and illusion from reality – such situations having already been well-documented

---

[10] See Caryl Matrisciana, *Yoga Uncoiled From East to West*. Caryl Productions, 2009.

[11] Much of said influences being satanic in form. See also Johanna Michaelsen, *The Beautiful Side of Evil*. Harvest House Publishers.

[12] For our mind is also a gift from God that must be used for such things as discernment, wisdom, emotional balance, and the peace that comes from God's promises in His word. See also J. P. Moreland et al., *Love Your God with All Your Mind: The Role of Reason in the Life of the Soul*. NavPress, 1997.

[13]Again, as Christ told his followers:

> When the Spirit of truth comes, he will guide you into all the truth...He will glorify me, because He will take what is mine and declare it to you. [John 16:13-14]

with heartbreakingly tragic results.[14] Meditation in and of itself is not wrong – rather it is the *manner* and *approach* in which meditation is performed that can either be beneficial or harmful to one's psychology.

And it is in such meditative practices like these where otherwise physically-beneficial exercises are tainted by religious philosophies and rituals involving repetitive mantras of adoration either to pagan gods or to the god of the self and the "god *within*" others – these sayings that yoga participants oftentimes do not even know the meaning of but will nevertheless agree to repeat – as they are generally not said in their own native tongue. Yet ironically, the vast *majority* of physical exercises as taught today and labeled as 'yoga' have absolutely *nothing* at all to do with original practices of the same in the first place – as genuine yoga has always been a *religious act* rather than a means for improving one's physical health and fitness. As has been said,

> In spite of the immense popularity of postural yoga worldwide, there is little or no evidence that āsana [posture] (excepting certain seated postures of meditation) has ever been the primary aspect of any Indian yoga practice tradition—including the medieval, body-oriented haṭha yoga—in spite of the self-authenticating claims of many modern yoga schools. The primacy of āsana performance in transnational yoga today is a new phenomenon that has no parallel in premodern times.[15]

---

[14] See also Armin Weidle, *Bowing to Yoga? The truth about the roots and fruits of yoga*. Xulon Press, 2010.

[15] As in Mark Singleton, *Yoga Body: The Origins of Modern Posture Practice*. Oxford University Press, 2010.

Furthermore, on speaking of One-ism, and the various pagan cults that adopted and put into practice its philosophies in the Roman times in which he lived in,[16] Paul states:

> For what can be known about God is plain to them, because God has shown it to them. Ever since the creation of the world His eternal power and divine nature, invisible though they are, have been understood and seen through the things He has made. So they are without excuse; for though they knew God, they did not honor Him *as* God or give thanks to Him, but they became futile in their thinking, and their senseless minds were darkened. Claiming to be wise, they became fools; and they exchanged the glory of the immortal God for images resembling a mortal human being or birds or four-footed animals or reptiles ... they exchanged the truth about God for a lie and worshiped and served the creature rather than the Creator.
>
> ROMANS 1:18:31

As is rightly said regarding the above passage:

> Here Paul identifies only two possible kinds of worship: worship of creation or worship of the Creator.[17]

Could the ancient pagan religion and philosophy of One-ism, as it has always existed as the worship of false gods, and as the exaltation of creation and self *above* God Himself – either be a significant *part of*, or become the most consequential *facilitator*

---

[16] See also C on page 433.

[17] As in Jones (as in n. 5 on page 361).

for the eventual "powerful delusion" that will make many "believe what is false" at the time when the prophesied-about Anti-Christ – possibly a global political figure but who Christ himself specifically referred to as the "abomination that causes desolation"[18] – takes *his* place on the world stage? For if mankind eagerly continues to buy into the belief that we are self-sufficient *without* God because we (along with everything else) are *all* gods, it will make for a very easy transition for mankind to eventually – and wholeheartedly – *accept* such a figure with open arms – he who will initially *appear* to unite the world with a false sense of peace and security, and with his enforced declaration of a unified one-world religion[19] – but who will soon after betray mankind with his own brutal theocracy on which he will set himself up as the deified head of when he will claim to the world that he is either God Himself, or the Messiah; he who will control nations with unimaginable global oppression for a short time; and who will perform holocausts against *all* faiths that get in his way – and all of this before Christ returns to take back what is His, and to prevent mankind from being totally destroyed.[20] For, as has been written of that time that is yet to come:

---

[18] As in Matthew 24:15 and Mark 13:14.

[19] See Revelations 17, especially in regards to its discussion relating to what it calls "the great harlot who sits on many waters". See also Jim Simmons, *The Last Generation: Prophecy, Current World Events, and the End Times*. Focal Point Publications, 2008; as well as Mark Hitchcock and John F. Walvoord, *Armageddon, Oil, and Terror*. Tyndale Momentum, 2007.

[20] See also John F. Walvoord, *Every Prophecy of the Bible: Clear Explanations for Uncertain Times*. David C.

As to the coming of our Lord Jesus Christ and our being gathered together to him, we beg you, brothers and sisters, not to be quickly shaken in mind or alarmed, either by spirit or by word or by letter, as though from us, to the effect that the day of the Lord is already here. Let no one deceive you in any way; for that day will not come unless the rebellion comes first and the lawless one [*the Anti-Christ*] is revealed, the one destined for destruction. He opposes and exalts himself above every so-called god or object of worship, so that he takes his seat in the temple of God, declaring himself to *be* God. Do you not remember that I told you these things when I was still with you? And you know what is now restraining him, so that he may be revealed when his time comes. For the mystery of lawlessness is already at work, but only until the one who now restrains it is removed. And then the lawless one will be revealed, whom the Lord Jesus will destroy with the breath of his mouth, annihilating him by the manifestation of his coming. The coming of the lawless one is apparent in the working of Satan, who uses all power, signs, lying wonders, and every kind of wicked deception for those who are perishing, because they refused to love the truth and so be saved. For this reason God sends them a powerful delusion, leading them to believe what is false...

2 Thessalonians 2:1-11

And so it is of *great* concern when many in modern Christendom are focusing on what in comparison

---

Cook, 2011; as well as Randall Price, *The Coming Last Day's Temple*. 1999.

should be *non-issues*, such as homosexuality,[21] pre-marital sex,[22] pornography,[23] inter-denominational animosities, and the straining out of gnats which result in religious atrophy; while unquestioningly submitting their lives to various denominations and self-appointed leaders of intolerant aggression; showing a tolerant approval for certain televangelists who claim to follow Christ but who are not much different than slick care salesmen who thrive on poisoning listeners with illegitimate guilt-trips in order to get their wealth-promoting lifestyles continuously fed; being virtually silent in regards to global religious acts of hate, the beheading of both Christians as well as countless other innocents, terrors, and other diabolical forms of injustices as performed by others in the name of God; adhering to various church traditions that are not founded on Christ's own teachings in any way whatsoever; and needlessly being grieved by doubt and a weakened faith because of the many voices they listen to when they should be listening to their Lord instead – as many modern Christians focus and live by such diversions rather than on Christ's very words and command to love in action, while not being willing to get out of their comfort zones in order to mix with the lost in the ways that Christ socialized with the outcasts of society – to where it was by *his* attentive, accepting love *in action*, and through his lived-out example that his listeners opened their hearts and lives to God. Shameful. Can we *truly* be so easily fooled enough to drop the ball and

---

[21] See also Appendix C on page 433.

[22] See also Appendix B on page 397.

[23] See also Appendix B on page 397.

vilify the innocent, while at the same time making the rest of the world believe we're just a bunch of prude, inflexible, ambivalent, judgemental, and self-righteous fanatics of religion rather than the *genuine* followers of Christ that he called us to be? Where has the Great Commission gone?[24]

That is why it will be *so easy*, as Christ warned, for many who follow him to *themselves* become deceived – and this because, to loosely paraphrase the song *Witch hunt*[25] – many in current-day Christianity make it a habit to do nothing but spent God's time and resources executing their own condemnatory witch hunts while deliberately misusing the name of Christ, as they attempt to find evil where there isn't any – while forgetting about preaching the gospel and being the light to the world that they were *commanded* to be – and all of this while assuming that Christ will not mind such anti-Christian actions that only make

---

[24] The Great Commission having been when Christ told his disciples before ascending back to the Father: "All authority in heaven and on earth has been given to me. Go therefore and make disciples of all nations, baptizing them in the name of the Father and of the Son and of the Holy Spirit, and teaching them to obey everything that I have commanded you. And remember, I am with you always, even to the end of the age." [Matthew 28:18-20]

[25] The song *Witchhunt*, which does *not* touch on any mentioned issues herein, but which very much *accurately* describes how many in Christianity forget about Christ in order to conduct their own witch-hunt styles of condemnation – thus going against Christ's very teachings – as found in the exceptional Petra, *Beat the System album* (as in n. 15 on page 133); the listening of which is *highly* recommended.

the world stumble over what results as globally ill-perceived and misrepresented teachings of Christ.

It is interesting to note that, it is oftentimes best to stick to the basic principles of Christianity as Christ taught it, and as the believer saw it from the beginning of his or her acceptance of Christ; as opposed to allowing the self to get bogged down, discouraged, perplexed, and ultimately lose sight of the guidance of the Holy Spirit due to the many voices that attempt to "raise issues" on questions of faith in this day and age where there is no 'issue' to justifiably be raised. For as has been aptly said:

> We should be on our guard against the seductive arts of false teachers. They are often plausible; they can urge arguments which we may not be able to answer; they may have much more learning than we have; and they may put on the appearance of great humility and of real piety; Colossians 2:3-4.3. It is, in general, a safe rule for a Christian to abide by the views which he had on the great subjects of religion when he became converted; Colossians 2:6. Then the heart was tender and soft - like wax - and received the impression which the Spirit made on it. There are some things in which the heart judges better than the head; and in which we are quite as likely to go right if we follow the former as we are the latter. In relation to the performance of many of the duties of life - the duties of kindness and charity - the heart is often a more safe guide than the head; and so in many things pertaining more immediately to religion, a man is more likely to judge right if he follows the promptings of his feelings in the happiest moments of piety, than he is to wait for the

more cool and cautious course of argument.
The same thing may be true even of many of
the doctrines of religion. When a poor sinner
trembles on the verge of hell, he feels that
none but an Almighty Saviour can deliver him,
and he goes and commits himself to Jesus as
God - and he is not in much danger of erring in
that. He will be more likely to be drawn aside
from the truth by the artful reasonings of the
advocates of error, than he will by his feelings
at that moment.[26]

But the final judge of mankind will not be made
by human hands, and *neither* is He "one with the
Universe", that which is *His* creation and solely to His
credit *alone*, but is – and will *eternally* remain – King
of kings and Lord of lords.[27] For, as Paul respectfully
spoke to pagan idol worshipers in Athens, he rightly
explained that:

The God who made the world and everything
in it, He who is Lord of heaven and earth,
does not live in shrines made by human hands,
nor is He served by human hands, as though
He needed anything, since He Himself gives
to all mortals life and breath and all things.
From one blood He made all nations to inhabit
the whole earth, and He allotted the times
of their existence and the boundaries of the
places where they would live, so that they
would search for God and perhaps reach out
for Him and find Him—though indeed He is
not far from each one of us. For 'In Him
we live and move and have our being'... Since
we are God's offspring, we ought not to think

---

[26] As per Barnes (as in n. 1 on page xviii).
[27] Revelations 19:16

that the deity is like gold, or silver, or stone, an image formed by the art and imagination of mortals. While God has overlooked the times of human ignorance, now He commands all people everywhere to repent, because He has fixed a day on which He will have the world judged in righteousness by a man whom He has appointed, and of this He has given assurance to all by raising him from the dead.

ACTS 17:24-31

This is what it all boils down to: If one looks at the world today – as it has pretty much always been – one either views a belief in God as *Two-ism*, where one acknowledges *one* God and Creator of all that is, and who is a *separate entity* from His creation; or *One-ism*, where God is in everything, and everything *is* God (or similarly, that there is *no* God at all *because* we are all 'gods' from a philosophical perspective and thereby part of a kind of "Universal force"). Everyone falls into either one of these two camps. As is aptly explained:

> The truth is what we will call *two-ism*. Two-ism is the biblical doctrine that the Creator and creation are separate and that creation is subject to the Creator... The lie is what we will call *One-ism*. One-ism is the pagan and idolatrous doctrine that there is no distinction between Creator and creation, and/or a denial that there is a Creator. The popular word for this notion is *monism*. Practically, One-ism is the eradication of boundaries and differences to bring opposites together as one. The materialistic form of One-ism is atheism. Spiritual One-ism is also often called New Age, New Spirituality, or Integrative Spirituality. According to spiritual One-ism, the universe is a living organism with a spiritual force

> present within everything. Thus, everything
> is interconnected by the life force or the world
> soul.[28]

Furthermore, another explanation rightly states that:

> Two-ism (God is outside His creation). One-
> ism (God is the creation)...In One-ism, every-
> thing shares the same essence. In a word,
> everything is a piece of the divine...Two-ism
> believes that God placed distinctions in the
> natural world, whereas One-ism rejects those
> distinctions. Two-ism believes that the main
> distinction is the one between the Creator and
> this creatures, whereas pagan One-ism con-
> fuses the two, making nature divine. Two-ist
> spirituality worships and serves God by honor-
> ing Him and giving him thanks, whereas pa-
> gan One-ism worships creation and the self.[29]

And as for these very foundational teachings of One-
ism which state that "God is in everything", and that
we are all a "part of" God, and that we ourselves are
gods in our own right – has this not been said before
by Satan in the Garden of Eden, as previously noted?
For as the story goes:

> But the serpent said to the woman, "You will
> not die; for God knows that when you eat of it
> your eyes will be opened, and *you will be like
> gods*, knowing good and evil."
>
> GENESIS 3:4-5

But in regards to One-ism – and all the varied and different religions, philosophies, and humanism-oriented

---

[28] As in Mark Driscoll and Gerry Breshears, *Doctrine:
What Christians Should Believe*. Crossway, 2011.

[29] As in Jones (as in n. 5 on page 361).

views that make up the myriad number of its parts throughout the world and in practically every culture – is Satan (or Lucifer, the so-called "Angel of Light") – *still* telling mankind to forget about following its Creator, and to instead turn to the *self* for "enlightenment" because we are *all* gods – and that we have the self-manifesting ability within *ourselves* to ultimately become *as* God – this being one of the cornerstone teachings of most varieties of "New Age" off-shoots? As has been rightly said:

> For such boasters are false apostles, deceitful workers, disguising themselves as apostles of Christ. And no wonder! Even Satan disguises himself as an angel of light. So it is not strange if his ministers also disguise themselves as ministers of righteousness. Their end will match their deeds.
>
> II CORINTHIANS 11:13-15.

Yes, Satan is truly cloaked as an "Angel of Light", and will promise mankind everything and anything to keep it from placing its core heart-felt trust on God, and God alone – even promising it Utopia much as he did in the Garden of Eden in exchange for the great deception that man is, or one day can *become*, God. As has been rightly put,

> Satan proposes the unrealistic dream that human beings, once they sense their own divinity, can bring about the end of the garden probation and realize that final, Utopian state, using their own wisdom.[30]

---

[30] As in Jones (as in n. 5 on page 361)

Yet does Satan even *exist* in the first place? Well, to those who believe – one of the most affective ways in which Satan uses to deceive mankind is to convince it through varying philosophies, religions, and trains of thought, that in fact he does not exist. When mankind begins to accept this as fact, Satan is empowered to continue to deceive on a massive scale, and to essentially do whatever he likes with those who follow the traditions of man – even if they are traditions rooted in ancient pagan practices – rather than the commandments of God.[31] But is there even any modern-day evidence of Satan's existence? Just look around at what you see in this day and age in regards to how mankind treats itself, and the excuses it uses to try and justify – to license – how it treats its own kind – whether it be in the workplace, in communities, within nations, or throughout the world.[32]

Many false christs that Christ warned us about – but certainly not exclusively – have Hindu roots, and are commonly known as gurus – self-proclaimed "enlightened god-men", yogi masters, or just plain "messiahs";[33] while others surprisingly have Christian roots and are quick to explain why in fact they are the Christ who has already returned[34] – and they

---

[31] See also Hal Lindsey, *Satan Is Alive and Well on Planet Earth*. Zondervan, 1972.

[32] See also M.W. Sphero, *Escaping the Shithole: How and Why to Leave a Bad Neighborhood Once and for All*. Herms Press, 2009.

[33] See Rabi R. Maharaj, *The Death of a Guru*. Harvest House Publishers, 1984; as well as various, *Gods of the New Age*. Jeremiah Films, 1984.

[34] See the documentary as per The National Geographic Channel, *The Second Coming*. National Geographic, 2010.

have misled many – yes, "even the elect", as Christ clearly warned – in the process. But than again, is that not why he clearly told us that, when he *does* return, that it will be as lightning flashing from east to west[35] – to where all of mankind will see his return at the same time and therefore know that it is he? He *did* explain that all tribes of the earth would see his sign (could it be the cross)[36] in the sky (could it be from the upper layers of our stratosphere), to where all the tribes (or nations, races, and cultures) of the earth would mourn, as they in unison witness his return from above[37] – or as again Christ himself put it:

> Then the sign of the Son of Man will appear in the sky, and then all the tribes of the earth will mourn, and they will see the Son of Man coming on the clouds of the sky with power and great glory.
>
> MATTHEW 24:30

As such, there is absolutely no reason to mistake anyone proclaiming himself (or herself) as the returned Christ anywhere on earth for the real deal, because when Christ *does* return, all of mankind will know –

---

[35] Matthew 24:27

[36] ...and is it possible that this sign of the cross could be armies of angels robed in brilliant white light who will be following the returned King of kings and Lord of lords as they descend through the upper stratospheres in such a formation that takes the globally-familiar shape of the empty cross in order to provide all of mankind with a very distinctive and unmistakable symbol of who is arriving and is at the center of it all? Who knows. But on reading Christ's own description of his coming, it certainly seems like a possibility.

[37] See Matthew 24:27-30.

both believers as well as unbelievers – that Christ has indeed come back for those who have turned to and followed him in spirit and in truth ... with the faith of a child. *Everyone* alive at the time will witness his return and descent towards planet earth. Everyone will know.

And this is indeed possible in modern times, what with the ability to globally broadcast live news coverage throughout the entire world in an instant, and where media technology has now reached virtually every corner of the world. And this is why Christ warned us that "many false prophets will arise and lead many astray",[38] and that we are not to believe it when people state that Christ is here or there[39] – for at that time, *all* of mankind will see him coming back with their own eyes[40] – and there will be no mistaking who it might be, to where "all of the tribes of the earth will mourn"[41] on the realization that they have been denying the loving and ever faithful God of the Universe in order to follow false christs, false prophets, reckless politicians, unfulfilling and unsatisfying world religions, and oppressive world systems and regimes – as well as one another in the place of God as man-pleasers rather than as God-pleasers[42] – and now He has returned.

Now, again, there is nothing wrong with meditating – such as meditating on God's word, being silent and meditating on your God-given cognitive thoughts,

---

[38] Matthew 24:11

[39] Matthew 24:23-26

[40] Matthew 24:27

[41] Matthew 24:30

[42] See also the song *Godpleaser* as by Petra, *Not of This World album* (as in n. 17 on page 253).

and meditating through prayer – but when such 'meditations' are utilized to either focus on oneself as a sort of 'god' – thus denying God while essentially elevating or even worshiping the self *as* god and therefore worshiping the *creation* while denying the *Creator* – or when one repeats mantras one does not even know the translated meaning of – that is when such forms of 'meditation' become facilitators and vehicles for the occult[43] rather than tools for genuine spiritual growth.

At the same time, there is nothing wrong with exercise for the benefits of improving one's health, flexibility, joints, and breathing. God has generously *given* us the ability to do such exercises – and much more – as the awesome creation that He has made us to be.[44] Furthermore, it is the *responsibility* of every individual to *stay active* and to exercise in whatever manner that suits the person best – for what good is a weakened body that cannot put into action that which is good for the self, for others, and for the well-being of mankind? For God has indeed created us in such a way that we are to *take the initiative* to do so, and our bodies will see amazing rewards in strength, endurance, mental stability, and optimum performance of mind, body, and soul as a result. But when such exercises are tainted by spiritual roots and practices that, in addition to it all, are being marketed more and more to overtly *hide* their true origins in order to be more easily accepted by the West – practitioners place themselves

---

[43] See also Chapter 14 on page 307.

[44] See also Weidle (as in n. 14 on page 367) – for alternative physical exercises that do not involve yoga-based indoctrinations.

in danger of becoming psychologically conditioned to more comfortably accepting New Age doctrine, false teachings, and the oftentimes tragic psychological and spiritual outcomes that come with it all.

But what is so 'wrong' with New Age teachings, if what is being taught is love for the self, for the planet, for living things, and for the world? That *right there* is the major trap that allows many good and well-meaning people – especially those who would otherwise "know better" or be more discerning than the average bear – to fall away from a faith in Christ, or to not be willing to enter it at all – and instead turn to false prophets and false teachers. For, just because a teaching or philosophy markets itself as having such positive principles does not necessarily mean that it is good, wholesome, or right – as we all know. Furthermore, such teachings often go well *beyond* philosophy, and into matters of cult-based control and obsession when one digs deep enough to observe what is *really* going on in the background.[45] In addition to this, as having been well put:

> Any guru who demands your obedience is a false prophet.[46]

It is not merely enough to look at the superficial bullet-points of a belief system and claim it is all well and good. One must not only look at the highlights,

---

[45]See also *from* sub-section on cults in Chapter 14 on page 327; where the signs that one may be dealing with a cult are listed and explained in depth.

[46] From the excellent article Mike Adams, *How to spot a sociopath - 10 red flags that could save you from being swept under the influence of a charismatic nut job*. Natural News, 2013.

but on its fruits (what its leadership as well as self-confessed followers *do*) as well. As Christ himself said,

> Beware of false prophets, who come to you in sheep's clothing but inwardly are ravenous wolves. You will know them by their fruits. Are grapes gathered from thorns, or figs from thistles? In the same way, every good tree bears good fruit, but the bad tree bears bad fruit. A good tree cannot bear bad fruit, nor can a bad tree bear good fruit. Every tree that does not bear good fruit is cut down and thrown into the fire. Thus you will know them by their fruits.
>
> MATTHEW 7:15-20

Therefore, if certain sects of a religion preach for the murder of a human being – or for the genocide of certain *types, races,* or *religions* of human beings – its fruits will be the very obvious flashing red flag that testify against it.[47] If they preach peace, but control the lives of their members – including prohibiting them from seeing family and friends, scheduling every single hour of their day while denying them any free personal time, demanding that they give all of their income to an organization, and the like – their fruits will be evident to anyone who is willing to take the time and examine things just that bit further than what is seen superficially.[48] If they advocate for violence against homosexuals while holding up placards stating such things as "God hates fags",

---

[47] See Wafa Sultan, *A God Who Hates*. St. Martin's Griffin, 2011; Robert Spencer et al., *What the West Needs to Know*. DVD edition. Quixotic Media, 2007; as well as Jihad Watch, ⟨URL: http://www.jihadwatch.org⟩.

[48] See also Weidle (as in n. 14 on page 367).

and rejoice at the funerals of both gay victims of an epidemic as well as soldiers who died in battle while genuinely intending to defend freedom and democracy – and to add insult to injury hold up signs at said funerals that say such things as "Thank God for dead soldiers",[49] their fruits should tell you they are certainly *not* genuine followers of Christ even though they may claim to be.

In like manner, one can oftentimes see this in many self-proclaimed 'peaceful' and 'loving' New Age groups that turn out to be oppressive and overbearing cults that indoctrinate their followers by controlling almost every aspect of their personal lives including who they can associate with, how their time needs to be spent, where their money should go, and what self-proclaimed guru they should follow and in many instances worship as a human deity. Many of these cults have now successfully flourished in the West while hiding under the guise of introductory yoga classes that slowly indoctrinate participants into Hindu-originating Eastern philosophies and pagan-based religions once they have a commitment from their well-intended student-participants to willingly immerse themselves further into yoga *as a belief system* rather than as a method for exercise, while at the same time *deceptively* teaching them that Christianity and their own ideologies have similar roots and compliment one another – as they convince unprepared students by quoting the Bible alongside their own so-called "ancient texts", while often going so far as to

---

[49] A cursory search for *Rev. Phelps picket signs*, and selecting *images*, will provide the reader with more than enough evidence of the above.

falsely claiming that Christianity, Judaism, and other world religions were actually founded and built on their own pagan philosophies – which in itself would be laughable if it were not for the fact that so many actually begin to take such nonsense seriously and to heart.

As a result, many accept these claims with blind faith and soon become some of the most vocal 'peace-loving' aggressive attackers of Christianity – often judging and condemning anyone who even *hints* at the notion that the leaders they follow could be false prophets, and that their 'non-religious' New Age form of a very much *organized* religion that markets itself as a global force for "universal love" is in fact a system organized around the rhetoric that is optimized and utilized to win converts by subtle misinformation and deceptive imitations of the real thing.[50] They have exchanged a belief and acknowledgement of God for pulp fiction and the philosophies of mankind which has absolutely no foundational value whatsoever.

That being said, many amongst all of the above extremists (whether so-called 'Christian-based' cults and deified leaders, New Ageism groups, or terrorist organizations) will oftentimes make even children into active participants in their activities, which only compounds the evil that such groups do. It certainly is so *very* true that "by their fruits you *will* know them". For as Christ said:

> Not everyone who says to me, 'Lord, Lord,' will enter the kingdom of heaven, but only the one who does the *will* of my Father in heaven. On that day many will say to me, 'Lord, Lord, did we not prophesy in your name, and cast out

---

[50] See also Chapter 14 on page 307.

> demons in your name, and do many deeds of
> power in your name?' Then I will declare to
> them, 'I never knew you; go away from me, you
> evildoers.' [MATTHEW 7:21-23]

Yes, Christ clearly warned us that we would see things
such as these in ever-increasing frequency before his
return. Even the Old Testament testifies to all of this
in great detail, and in addition states:

> Now therefore, set your house in order, and
> reprove your people; comfort the lowly among
> them, and instruct those that are wise. And
> now renounce the life that is corruptible, and
> put away from you mortal thoughts; cast away
> from you the burdens of humankind, and di-
> vest yourself now of your weak nature; lay to
> one side the thoughts that are most grievous
> to you, and hurry to escape from these times.
> For evils worse than those that you have now
> seen happen shall take place hereafter. For
> the weaker the world becomes through old
> age, the more shall evils be increased upon its
> inhabitants. Truth shall go farther away, and
> falsehood shall come near.
>
> II ESDRAS 14:13-18

Christ warned us about how the last days would be
before his return to earth specifically so that when
we saw tell-tale signs occurring, we would not be
disheartened nor fail in our faith, but rather *recognize*
that he would be coming back for us soon – to where
he clearly stated that we must hold on, *patiently*
persevere, not panic, not be terrified, nor be fearful –
but to be happy, at peace, and content in life *even when*
the rest of mankind may be in turmoil and confusion
– because we know who our Protector is, and hold to

the peace that only *He* can give. For as Christ himself said:

> Beware that you are not led astray; for many will come in my name and say, 'I am he!' and, 'The time is near!' Do not go after them. When you hear of wars and insurrections, *do not be terrified*; for these things must take place first, but the end will not follow immediately... You will be hated by *all* because of my name. But not a hair of your head will perish. By your *endurance* you will gain your lives... Be on guard so that your hearts are not weighed down with dissipation and drunkenness and the worries of this life, and that day does not catch you unexpectedly, like a trap. For it will come upon all who live on the face of the whole earth.
>
> LUKE 21:8-35

Furthermore, Christ stated:

> I have said these things to you to *keep you from stumbling*. They will put you out of the synagogues. Indeed, an hour is coming when those who kill you will think that by doing so they are offering worship to God. And they will do this because they have not known the Father or me. But I have said these things to you so that when their hour comes *you may remember* that I told you about them.... I have said this to you, so that in me you may have peace. In the world you face persecution. But *take courage*; I have overcome the world!
>
> John 16:1-4 & 33

Again, the Old Testament mirrors Christ's many warnings of the signs of the times, such as:

> For in many places and in neighboring cities there shall be a great uprising against those who fear the Lord. They shall be like maniacs, sparing no one, but plundering and destroying those who continue to fear the Lord. For they shall destroy and plunder their goods, and drive them out of house and home. Then the tested quality of my elect shall be manifest, like gold that is tested by fire. Listen, my elect ones, says the Lord; the days of tribulation are at hand, but *I will deliver you* from them. Do *not* fear or doubt, for *God* is your guide. You who keep my commandments and precepts, says the Lord God, must not let your sins *weigh you down*, or your iniquities *prevail* over you. Woe to those who are choked by their sins and overwhelmed by their iniquities! They are like a field choked with underbrush and its paths overwhelmed with thorns, so that no one can pass through.
>
> II Esdras 16:70-77

Furthermore, Christ also told us that we would be sent out "as sheep in the midst of wolves" when he said:

> Behold, I am sending you out like sheep into the midst of wolves; so be *wise* as serpents and *innocent* as doves.
>
> MATTHEW 10:16

As such, when Jesus Christ states that we must be "as shrewd as serpents and innocent as doves", this therefore does *not* mean that we are to behave as *stupid* doves, but rather as wise people who *know* what's going on around them, who can *discern for themselves* the signs of the times, and who can *keep their cool* – as well as their *faith* – during such times of tribulation. For as Christ said:

> When you see a cloud rising in the west, you immediately say, 'It is going to rain'; and so it happens. And when you see the south wind blowing, you say, 'There will be scorching heat'; and it happens. You hypocrites! You know how to interpret the appearance of earth and sky, but why do you not know how to interpret the *present* time? And why do you not judge *for yourselves* what is right?
> LUKE 12:54-57

Furthermore, Christ warned us to be discerning with what we share – but to also not worry beforehand when we do need to share, as it would be *His* Holy Spirit who would give us the words we would need at exactly the right time.[51] Yes – to use our *heads* as well as our hearts. As such, Christ taught us to listen first and not judge (as we ourselves can also be judged for what we do – for we are *all* sinners);[52] to ask God, who would provide for our needs; to do to others as we would want them to do to us ... but again, to be discerning rather than hasty or foolish, remembering that we live in *reality*. For he said:

> Do not judge, or you too will be judged. For in the same way you judge others, you will be

---

[51] As Christ said: "When they bring you to trial and hand you over, do not worry beforehand about what you are to say; but say whatever is given you at that time, for it is not you who speak, but the Holy Spirit." [Mark 13:11]

[52] As it is written: "There is no one who is righteous, not even one." [Romans 3:10]

judged, and with the measure you use, it will be measured to you... Do not give dogs what is sacred; do not throw your pearls to pigs. If you do, they may trample them under their feet, and turn and tear you to pieces... Ask and it will be given to you; seek and you will find; knock and the door will be opened to you. For everyone who asks receives; the one who seeks finds; and to the one who knocks, the door will be opened. Which of you, if your son asks for bread, will give him a stone? Or if he asks for a fish, will give him a snake? If you, then, though you are evil, know how to give good gifts to your children, how much more will your Father in heaven give good gifts to those who ask him! So in everything, do to others what you would have them do to you, for this sums up the Law and the Prophets.

MATTHEW 7:1-2, 6, & 7-12 NIV

So when trouble or persecution comes *because* one may be a follower of Christ, one must consciously *choose* to be balanced, rational, clear-headed; and *not* to be insistent nor 'fanatical', radical, fearful – nor extremist. For, to the believer: *Always* and *continuously* keep in mind who it is that you follow! For *He* is our strength – and *He* is our voice. Thus:

Do not fear the plots against you, and do not be troubled by the unbelief of those who oppose you.

II ESDRAS 15:3

... and likewise,

Behold, I have made your face as hard as their faces and your forehead as hard as their foreheads. Like emery harder than flint I have

> made your forehead. Do *not* be afraid of them
> nor be *dismayed* before them, though they are
> a rebellious house ... But when I speak to
> you, I will open your mouth and you will say
> to them, 'Thus says the Lord God.' He who
> hears, let him hear; and he who refuses, *let*
> him refuse; for they are a rebellious house.
>
> EZEKIEL 3:8-9 & 27 NASB

Lastly, Christ warned us not to be hypocrites – an oftentimes very much *justifiable* common complaint that is rife against many modern Christians of today – but that we are to speak *when prompted* by God's Holy Spirit. To the believer, you will *know* when and how He prompts you in *whatever* circumstance in your life, and not just in regards to the end times – and again, don't *ever* fear nor let anxieties rise in your heart. Trust in Him... *always*. Those against today's sincere followers of Christ have no fear when they malign His kids, and so neither should we fear, for any hidden agenda against us – whether in the workplace, within families, or by a community – will be brought out into the open ... whether it be in *this* life, or in the one to come.

So do not fear them. And when they insult Christ, keep your cool – don't ever "freak out" – as *religious* people – whatever religion it might be – oftentimes do. For blasphemes against Christ *will* be forgiven, but the blasphemy against the Holy Spirit – when one *deliberately*, *consciously*, and *consistently* from one's heart rejects God throughout one's life until the bitter end – will not be forgiven. For as Christ stated,

> Whoever is not with me is against me, and
> whoever does not gather with me scatters.
> Therefore I tell you, people will be forgiven

for every sin and blasphemy, but blasphemy
against the Spirit will not be forgiven. Whoever speaks a word against the Son of Man
will be forgiven, but whoever speaks against
the Holy Spirit will not be forgiven, either in
this age or in the age to come.

MATTHEW 12:30-32

Hence the importance of praying for one's enemies[53]
– at the very least that they one day open their door
to the Father – for God does not desire that *anyone –
whomever* they might be – should perish, [54] but that

---

[53] As Christ taught: "You have heard that it was said,
'You shall love your neighbor and hate your enemy.' But I
say to you, love your enemies [*in action, and not necessarily
in sentiment*], and pray for those who persecute you, so that
you may be children of your Father in heaven; for He makes
his sun rise on the evil and on the good, and sends rain
on the righteous and on the unrighteous. For if you love
those who love you, what reward do you have? Do not even
the tax collectors do the same? And if you greet only your
brothers and sisters, what more are you doing than others?
Do not even the Gentiles do the same? *Be* perfect, therefore,
as your heavenly Father *is* perfect." [Matthew 5:43-48]

[54] As is said: " 'Do I have any pleasure in the death
of the wicked,' declares the Lord God, 'rather than that
he should turn from his ways and live?'... 'Therefore I
will judge you, O house of Israel, each according to his
conduct,' declares the Lord God. 'Repent and turn away
from all your transgressions, so that iniquity may not
become a stumbling block to you. Cast away from you all
your transgressions which you have committed and make
yourselves a new heart and a new spirit! For why will you
die, O house of Israel? For I have no pleasure in the death of
anyone who dies,' declares the Lord God. 'Therefore, repent
and live.' " [Ezekiel 18:23 & 30-32; NASB]

*all* of mankind may come to Him in spirit and in truth. For as Christ stated:

> Be on your guard against the yeast of the Pharisees, which is hypocrisy. There is nothing concealed that will not be disclosed, or hidden that will not be made known. What you have said in the dark will be heard in the daylight, and what you have whispered in the ear in the inner rooms will be proclaimed from the rooftop. I tell you, my friends, do not be afraid of those who kill the body and after that can do no more. But I will show you whom you should fear: Fear Him who, after your body has been killed, has authority to throw you into hell. Yes, I tell you, fear him. Are not five sparrows sold for two pennies? Yet not one of them is forgotten by God. Indeed, the very hairs of your head are all numbered. *Don't be afraid*; you are worth more than *many* sparrows. I tell you, whoever publicly *acknowledges* me before others, the Son of Man will also acknowledge before the angels of God. But whoever *disowns* me before others will be disowned before the angels of God. And everyone who speaks a word against the Son of Man will be forgiven, but anyone who blasphemes against the Holy Spirit will not be forgiven.
>
> LUKE 12:1-10 NIV

Christ *will* come again in order to *prevent* mankind from destroying itself *totally* and utterly – and it seems more and more likely that he will be coming for *all* who have put their trust in him very soon indeed. Are *you* ready? As Jesus said:

> The days are coming when you will long to see one of the days of the Son of Man, and you will not see it...Just as it was in the days of Noah, so too it will be in the days of the Son of Man. They were eating and drinking, and marrying and being given in marriage, until the day Noah entered the ark, and the flood

came and destroyed all of them. Likewise, just as it was in the days of Lot: they were eating and drinking, buying and selling, planting and building, but on the day that Lot left Sodom, it rained fire and sulfur from heaven and destroyed all of them —it will be like that on the day that the Son of Man is revealed. On that day, anyone on the housetop who has belongings in the house must not come down to take them away; and likewise anyone in the field must not turn back. Remember Lot's wife. Those who try to make their life secure will lose it, but those who lose their life will keep it. [LUKE 17:22-34]

For, as the Old Testament prophecy states:

I will display wonders in the sky and on the earth; blood, fire and columns of smoke. The sun will be turned into darkness, and the moon into blood, before the great and awesome day of the Lord comes. And it will come about that *whoever* calls on the name of the Lord *will* be delivered; for on Mount Zion and in Jerusalem there will be those who escape, as the Lord has said, even among the survivors whom the Lord calls.

JOEL 2:30-32 NASB

And as the prophetic book of Daniel speaks in regards to such times:

Many shall be purified, cleansed, and refined, but the wicked will continue to act wickedly. None of the wicked shall understand, but those who have *insight* shall understand.

DANIEL 12:10

But until than,

Let the evildoer still do evil, and the vile still be vile, and the righteous still do right, and the holy still be holy. [REVELATIONS 22:11]

For, as it is rightly and justly said of Jesus Christ, the returning Messiah, who is returning for *His* people:

> See, I am coming soon; my reward is with me, to repay according to everyone's work. I am the Alpha and the Omega, the First and the Last, the Beginning and the End.
>
> REVELATIONS 22:12-13

***

The Spirit and the bride say, "Come."
And let everyone who hears say, "Come."
And let *everyone* who is thirsty come.
Let anyone who *wishes*
take the Water of Life as a *gift*...
The one who testifies to these things says,

"SURELY I AM COMING SOON."

Amen. Come, Lord Jesus!
The grace of the Lord Jesus be with all
the saints.

REVELATIONS
22:17 &
20-21

*

# Christ Came to Give Light, *not* Sexual Celibacy

The Bible *never* prohibits specific sexual acts (such as oral or anal sex, the use of over-priced sex toys, spindles of joy, positions in bed, exotic activities, self-pleasuring, experimentation, and so forth) between consenting individuals – as many non-Christian religions often do ad nauseam in this day and age, while ignoring (or worse... *condemning*) the nature and psychology of God's own creation. No, the Bible does *not* condemn any of this – *anywhere*. Anyone who – whether innocently or not – states otherwise has not looked adequately at what scripture has to say and is unknowingly placing the traditions of man before scripture, common sense, what is natural, and what God has created – to where God's power and sexual design is flat-out ignored and trumped by religious legalisms that cannot even be backed up by biblical exposition whatsoever – such man-made taboos being nothing more than the inventions of puritanical religious leaders throughout church history who exchanged what the Bible actually has to say about one of God's most liberating and life-affirming gifts to us all – for their own oppressive and unscriptural restrictions that cannot be backed up by biblical context.

But if you would like to look further into just how sexually-liberating the Judeo-Christian Bible truly is in regards to all things sex, take a look at the excellently-researched, comprehensive, and detailed books on these and many other related joys as *Divine Sex: Liberating Sex from Religious Tradition*,[1] as well as *Dirt, Greed, and Sex: Sexual Ethics in the New Testament and Their Implications for Today*[2] – both of which further explain in great and clear detail how *none* of these things are *ever* forbidden in the Judeo-Christian scriptures, how *all* sexual positions and methods are natural and God-given, and how our modern sexual hangups have originated *not* from scripture, but from mankind's own self-imposed legalistic restrictions *centuries after* both the times of Christ as well as early followers – such legalistic traditions having nothing whatever to do with either the Jewish or Christian grass-roots origins of faith.

---

[1] Philo Thelos, *Divine Sex: Liberating Sex from Religious Tradition*. Trafford Publishing, 2006.

[2] L. William Countryman, *Dirt, Greed, and Sex: Sexual Ethics in the New Testament and Their Implications for Today*. Fortress Press, 2007.

Sexual restrictions and deprivations first infiltrated the church in the 4th Century AD via the Greco-Roman Platonic philosophy – which had absolutely *nothing* whatsoever to do with either Christ *or* the Bible.[3] For even the early Christians, who lived *long before* such an *externally* hostile influence towards the faith appeared, held to liberal views on sex that today would make many *modern-day* Christians either blush in their church pews, or self-combust with shock and awe.

Sexually-restrictive taboos and puritanical traditions of man that did not even *exist* in the Christian faith until centuries *after* Christ's time on earth not only condemn and repress the innocents amongst us who are both faithful to God and sincerely *accepting* of His gift of life – a gift that is *meant* to be lived and not wasted – they likewise smear the name of Christianity, totally misrepresent its very foundations, and are the modern-day stumbling blocks to both homosexuals *and* heterosexuals... many of whom have a totally *skewed* view about both God and faith in this day and age *precisely because* of such groundless restrictions. Sometimes one might think one is still living during the Dark Ages. And ironically, *true* Christianity does not even have anything to do with it in the first place! And nor does the Gospel *according to* Christ.

For instance, it was not until centuries *after* Christ that church fathers began to restrain sexual behavior amongst the masses for no other valid reason than to comply with and appease what ironically became a more and more sexually-restrictive Roman Empire

---

[3] See Jr. Lawrence Raymond J., *The Poisoning of Eros: Sexual Values in Conflict*. A. Moore Press, 1989.

in comparison to its earlier periods of rule, and to more comfortably fit in with external philosophical ideals. Such restrictions had absolutely nothing to do with anything Christ had taught, had absolutely no scriptural foundations, and set the framework for man-induced dogma that has now been firmly established in many Christian denominations. As has been explained:

> To understand the evolution from the early sex-affirming Hebraic culture to Christianity's persistent discomfort with sex and pleasure, we have to look at three interwoven threads: the dualistic cosmology of Plato [i.e. the soul and mind are at war with the body], the Stoic philosophy of early Greco-Roman culture [i.e., nothing should be done for the sake of pleasure], and the Persian Gnostic tradition [i.e., that demons created the world, sex and your body-in which your soul is trapped, and the key to salvation is to free the spirit from the bondage of the body by denying the flesh]. Within three centuries after Jesus, these influences combined to seduce Christian thinkers into a rampant rejection of human sexuality and sexual pleasure.[4]

For even the concept of 'celibacy' never came from anything Christ ever said, but rather cropped up – yet *again* – centuries *after* Christ; and this *again* as facilitated by the hands of religious men wishing to appear 'righteous' to their observers – rather than from any early Christian teachings whatsoever. For,

> Superstitious zeal for a sanctimonious appearance in the clergy seemed to have prompted

---

[4] As in Robert T. Francoeur et al., *The Religious Suppression of Eros; in The Erotic Impulse*. Tarcher, 1992.

> [celibacy] at first; and crafty policy, armed
> with power, no doubt riveted this clog [celibacy
> being referred to here as a piece of dirt] on
> the sacerdotal order in later periods of the
> Church.[5]

Thus, modern Christian-centric sexual hang-ups have
absolutely, positively, and unquestioningly *nothing*
whatsoever to do with anything Christ *ever* said –
but are rather children of man's traditions, and the
eagerness to appease those in power, those holding to
the philosophies of philosophers, and those willing to
sacrifice the gift of God to His creation – that being
sex – in order to somehow appear 'righteous' towards
their observers. Yes, as has aptly been said:

> What the modern world still understands by
> 'sin' stems *not* from the teaching of Jesus of
> Nazareth, or from the tablets handed down
> from Sinai, but from the early sexual vicis-
> situdes of a *handful of men* who lived in the
> twilight days of imperial Rome.[6]

And indeed sex truly *is* a gift from God. For, when
Adam and Eve where in the Garden of Eden before
having been tempted by Satan, they were absolutely,
positively naked – in *all* respects – and, as scripture
is clear in explaining, they were *not* ashamed.[7] For
they did not even have a *realization* of their physical
nakedness, as they took their nudity as being normal,
without shame, and as a part of how they were *meant*

---

[5] Under the topic *Celibacy*, as in Charles Buck, *Buck's Dictionary*. 1838.

[6] As in Reay Tannahill, *Sex in History*. Scarborough House, 1992; my emphasis.

[7] Genesis 2:25

to be – much as we look at someone's face today and do not see it as being 'naked' – it is normal, unashamed, and as one is *meant* to be. But once Eve was deceived by Satan and was given earthly – rather than divine – knowledge, she was immediately made aware of the concept of *nakedness*; to where she now *irrationally* felt shame for the human body that was *created* by God, and that had been declared as entirely *good* by its Creator.[8]

For Satan *himself*, the "Father of Lies" as Christ called him,[9] lied to mankind – stating that what God had created was not good enough, and that it was *shameful*. Epochs later, we are *still* believing the lie – and taint our religious beliefs *with* that lie – as we look on sex as somehow dirty or evil – even though we know very well that it was God *Himself* who not only *declared* the human body, and sex itself, as good; but who also created our sexual functions to every last, sophisticated, and intricately pleasurable detail to be used and enjoyed as a normal part of life... and of *living* life to the full.

As a result of this, mankind has oftentimes been put through needless confusion, as many see their own body – as well as sex itself – as an object of hate and a source of guilt, while easily forgetting who it is that actually *created* the human body to perfection, and who it is that designed sex *both* as a source of pleasure, *as well as* a means of procreation. As such, too many have wholeheartedly bought into the lie, whether they realize it or not: that sex – God's very own and unique creation – is *somehow* evil, and

---

[8] See Genesis 1:26-31.
[9] John 8:44

that it should be avoided if not adhering to the many restricting and oppressive traditions as invented by mankind, and *not* by God.  For it is *not* God who causes sexual repression.  It is rather the *lie* that has made Christianity look prudish, conservative, and restrictive – such total misconceptions about sex being absolutely opposed to *anything* Christ ever taught – as well as opposed to what God intended when He *generously* gave us the gift of sex. Do *you* believe the lie as well?

No, it is not *God* who represses one's sexuality, but rather the Father of Lies himself who has done so by calling the *good* that God has made as evil – as he *continues* to do so throughout the ages up to this very day. Rightly did Christ state that:

> The thief [*Satan*] comes only to *steal* and kill and destroy.  I came that they may have *life*, and have it *abundantly*.
>
> JOHN 10:10

Has not the deception as first presented to mankind in the Garden of Eden quietly *stolen* sex from many of God's children who, though yearning to follow and love God with all their hearts, have been denied through this lie, and by erroneous church traditions, one of the greatest gifts that God has given humanity from the beginning? But Christ came that they might have life, and have it *abundantly*. Don't let the devil steal your joy.  Don't believe the lie…as many of us have.

To the believer:  who do we follow – church tradition and unscriptural taboos that malign and take one of God's gifts to mankind for granted; or our Creator, and the liberating and abundant life that He has given us – in *all* of its fullness?  Certainly, sex must always be used under Christ's Golden Rule that we are to do to others as we would have them do to us, that we are to love our neighbor as ourselves, and that we are to love God with all our heart[10] – to where sex must never be utilized where it would cause emotional harm to others or to ourselves:  hence the commandments that we are not to commit adultery,[11] nor covet our neighbor's spouse,[12] nor dishonor God by using sex as a method for pagan idol worship as many in the Greco-Roman empire (as well as peoples before it) did[13] – in addition to this being against the first of the Ten Commandments which states that we are to have no other gods before Him.[14]  But besides these Divine commands that God has given for us to follow in order that we might first live our lives out of love for our caring and ever present Creator, for those around us, and for ourselves – rather than out of sheer impulse – what is restricting us from using *and* enjoying our God-given sexual liberty other than what we have heard and learned from the traditions of religion and the philosophies of man?

That being said, each individual must, with the guidance of the Holy Spirit, decide on what is right or wrong for him- or herself.  The discussions herein are based on much research, experience, and long-suffering forethought.  Even so, it is ultimately up to the reader to make his or her *own* choices, and

---

[10] See Chapter 11 on page 231.

[11] Deuteronomy 5:18

[12] Deuteronomy 5:21

[13] See also Appendix C on page 433 regarding how sex was often used in pagan idol worship rituals.

[14] Deuteronomy 5:6-10

to establish personal sexual opinion through *God's* leadership – not mankind's own religious traditions, admonishions, restrictions, prejudices, or even liberties – but rather by the words of Christ as one would read them in the Gospels, by God's guidance, and by what is right for you. And with this, let us begin.

# Premarital sex is *not* adultery

It is understandable why Jesus explicitly mentioned the issue of sexual boundaries *only once* in his ministry – and this strictly within the *context* of adultery – which is defined as having sexual relations with one who is *already* married and who is *not* one's spouse[15] – besides it being against one of the Ten Commandments which Christ taught us to follow. For as the encounter between Christ and a rich young man states:

> Then someone came to him and said, 'Teacher, what good deed must I do to have eternal life?' And he said to him, 'Why do you ask me about what is good?  There is only one who is good.  If you wish to enter into life, keep the commandments.' He said to him, 'Which ones?' And Jesus said, 'You shall not murder; You shall not commit adultery; You shall not steal; You shall not bear false witness; Honor your father and mother; also, You shall love your neighbor as yourself.' The young man said to him, 'I have kept all these; what do I still lack?' Jesus said to him, 'If you wish to be perfect, go, sell your possessions, and give the

---

[15] See Webster, *Webster's New Universal Unabridged Dictionary*. Barnes & Noble Books, 2003.

money to the poor, and you will have treasure
in heaven; then come, follow me.' When the
young man heard this word, he went away
grieving, for he had many possessions.

Matthew 19:16-22

Christ stated that adultery is a legitimate reason
for divorce – as we can see from his referring to
"marital unfaithfulness" when he talked about divorce
in Matthew 5:32[16] – though within the context of
his having referred to adultery on *other* occasions, he
interestingly spoke of the act of adultery as *leaving*
or *abandoning* one's spouse, as opposed to whether or
not extra-marital sex may or may not be involved in
the decision to divorce – so that, in the case of marital
unfaithfulness, it is primarily the act of *abandonment*,
and *not* the subject of sex in and of itself, that may be
the real issue in his looking unfavorably against other

---

[16] As Christ states:

> ...but I say to you that everyone who
> divorces [or *"sends away"*] his wife, except
> for the cause of unchastity [or *"marital
> unfaithfulness"*], makes her commit adultery.
> [Matthew 5:32]

It is interesting to note that the term "sends away" is
used herein. As such, the act of divorce can *in itself*
be considered adultery – even though no sex may be
involved – thus reinforcing the idea that, in Christ's words,
adultery does not *exclusively* refer to one's simply having
had sex with another without one's spouse's consent –
to where adultery can be considered as being the act
of divorcing – or abandoning, or "sending away" – one's
spouse... irrespective of whether or not any extra-marital
sex is involved or not.

reasons for divorcing – as God is in the business of building relationships, not tearing them down.

Of course, that being said, common sense – given to us by God – would state that persistent abuse within a marriage would also be a legitimate reason for divorce – especially as this in itself can be seen as the abuser having already *abandoned* or *separated* from the abused spouse simply by the continuous act of abuse – thus fitting into Christ's own *focused* definition of adultery as being *more so* the act of abandonment, due to his *not* having made any issue about sex in and of itself where none of the participants are already married.

So adultery refers directly to either the *abandonment* of a marriage – which does *not* in itself require any sexual act having been done by anyone involved – or cheating on one's spouse, especially if done *without* mutual consent or agreement between spouses. The reason 'consent' is used herein is because polygamy – being married to multiple spouses at the same time – never seems to have been 'outlawed' in the Judeo-Christian Bible[17] – neither in the Old nor New Testament scriptures. But whatever one's stance may be, the point is – by Christ's very own definition – adultery *always* involves a *marriage* – plain and simple. Whether or not extra-marital sex in and of itself is part of it or not seems only *incidental* to what adultery is conventionally defined as – again, his definition having been focused primarily on the act of abandoning one's spouse – irrespective of whether or not an extra-marital sexual affair exists or not – though it would seem that an extra-marital sexual

---

[17] See note 16 on the facing page.

affair without the consent of one's spouse does indeed constitute adultery.

An important observation to make is that this obviously does *not* include single people having premarital sex in any way whatsoever, and organized religion must stop inferring that it does, lest it continue to turn the world off to the Gospel by its oftentimes obsessively fanatical preaching against a sort of sex that in truth does *not* in fact involve any participant who is married to someone else.

So now that we have clarified what adultery actually *is*, and having noted that premarital sex has nothing whatever to do with it, let us now look into the subject of sex between people who are *not* married to anyone else. So therefore, in regards to sex *outside* of marriage (or premarital sex where no one involved is married to anyone else) – such as gay, lesbian, and premarital heterosexual sex – it would seem that Christ was *completely silent* on these specific issues[18] – to where if sex outside of marriage was such a "big deal" to the God who created sexual desire in the first place, Christ *surely* would have repeatedly and

---

[18] Although Christ *does* seem to state that some people are meant to be born gay from birth, and therefore not meant to marry – thus making it clear that homosexuality (gay or lesbian) is a part of God's plan for some, and must therefore not be condemned – despite what religious tradition and organized religions of most varieties wrongly claim out of either self-righteous hypocrisy, ignorance of what scripture really says about the subject, outright deception when one has been made aware of the true biblical stance on this, or repression-borne homophobia. See section C on page 433 in this appendix for a full explanation.

clearly mentioned this – as he did other issues to do with inter-human relationships.  Furthermore, it is also interesting to note that not even his apostles, nor anybody else in either the Old or New Testaments, ever seem to explicitly and clearly speak *specifically* against premarital sex by name whatsoever.

# Christ welcomes all *regardless of* sexual background

Therefore, in addition to this very vital point – that premarital sex is *not* adultery – please also note that the phrase "sexual immorality" in both MATTHEW 15:19 and MARK 7:21[19] is sometimes *erroneously* translated by modern contemporaries into the word "forni-

---

[19] Furthermore, another word that was used in Mark 7:5-23 was sensuality – the Greek word aselgeia essentially referring to lawless *excess*, such as the squandering love for and dedication to luxuries and wealth before the love of God and one's fellow man; and also translatable as unrestrained lawlessness or *unrestrained* vice, such as in the love of violence or any form of crime against another, as well as *limitless vice* (such as alcoholism or drug abuse – or whatever it might be that is done *excessively* and without moderation – as Christ himself stated that we should not be weighed down with dissipation, drunkenness, and the worries of life in Luke 21:34) – and thus not *exclusively* how this word is commonly thought of today as only referring to sex without *any* boundaries whatsoever in and of itself. Furthermore, Christ also stated herein that it is not what comes into the mouth that makes one 'unclean' – but rather what comes out of the heart.

cation" – the phrase "sexual immorality" having been used therein along with other short-listed terms when Christ was trying to explain things that "defile a man" (such as murder, theft, envy, slander, and arrogance). This phrase, as used in the cited verses, comes from the Greek word *porneia*, which is in turn derived from the word *porneuo* – which by direct translation does in fact mean "sexual immorality" – to where it more often than not refers particularly to how some versions correctly translate it as – that being *whoredom* or *prostitution* – though it must be remembered that Christ happily *associated* with prostitutes, to where, even if prostitution is wrong, it is (like all sins) very much *forgivable* by God, so that we must never judge nor exclude those who practice prostitution when we are *all* sinners in one way or another.

For Christ clearly showed, by his behavior and teachings, that prostitution in itself, even *if* sinful, is nonetheless *never* something that would keep some-one out of the Kingdom of God. For, as Christ himself explained to religious leaders who were questioning him as to why he associated with the same:

> Truly I tell you, the tax collectors and the prostitutes are going into the kingdom of God ahead of you. For John came to you in the way of righteousness and you did not believe him, but the tax collectors and the prostitutes believed him; and even after you saw it, you did not change your minds and believe him.
>
> Matthew 21:31-32

As a true follower of Christ, therefore, one should follow Jesus' example and never judge, condemn, nor ostracize those involved in prostitution – many of whom are amazing and very good-hearted people who have simply become stuck in the only industry that they feel they are able to survive in. As a *genuine* follower of Christ, therefore, one must follow Jesus' own example and be a friend, confidant, and life-line to those involved in prostitution. Anything else would be a much *greater* sin committed by those claiming to follow Christ than whatever a prostitute might do.

For we are no better than the prostitute risking life and limb out on the streets who oftentimes needs to get involved with people that only abuse and harass him or her, are we? Any answer other than a clear 'no', I believe, would be tainted with self-righteous hypocrisy and pride – two of the *greatest* sins against God Himself that Christ always spoke of – especially in comparison to the topic at hand. Furthermore, if you take on the recommended experiment, and look into the Gospels *for yourself*, you will realize that the sins Christ most *consistently* condemned had to do with sins of the heart and soul: such as arrogance, condemnations, judgementalism, envy, slander, self-righteousness, and oppression – rather than "sins of the flesh" so-to-speak.

Therefore, to condemn, exclude, or cast judgement on a prostitute rather than befriending him or her is a much, much *greater* sin than if one were to sleep with, or *be*, one. Anyone who states otherwise is merely playing religious legalism, and does not have the true teachings of Christ at heart. The same goes for the habitual drunkard or drug addict, the porn actor, the stripper...*whomever* it may be. As one blogger has stated about a church that genuinely strives to follow the teachings of Christ:

> Are we appalled at these stories of exotic dancers, child predators, drunks in church?

Imagine the stories you might hear right here
in your own church...no matter the darkness in your life, in this church, you are
not alone. You're surrounded by people who
struggle mightily with sin. You are welcomed
and loved here. Jesus loves you and yearns
for you to come to Him and grow in Him
and walk with Him in life...Jesus looked at
the party crowd, and he saw people who had
been completely rejected by those in power
both in government and especially in faith,
then the temple/synagogue, today, the church.
Jesus looked at the party crowd and saw a
people who knew themselves to be rejected
by the decent, upstanding members of society.
Jesus looked at the party crowd and saw a
group who had heard professional preachers
and theologians condemn them for so long that
they figured God had condemned them. God
certainly condemned some of their behaviors.
But they didn't know that God just as much
condemned the loveless attitudes and self-
serving actions of the preachers and theologians and churchmen who had condemned
them...Jesus has no time for us until we recognize our affinity with the base, reprobates of
our world. Until we realize we are them, Jesus
doesn't really have anything for us...Meeting
him, it is impossible to be unchanged...Did
they all immediately give up their greed, li-
centiousness, and sin? Does anyone ever stop
cold-turkey and turn their lives around on
a dime? It's a process...But once we come,
the work begins and goes on throughout our
lives...You and me in all our secret sins, all
our failings, all our dirtiness. Jesus says,
Come and bring the mess. He welcomes us and

> if we are receptive and cooperative, he goes to
> work in us. [20]

For, if statistics are correct, the *vast majority* of men[21] (as well as *at least* one-quarter, *if not* one-third of females)[22] watch porn on a regular basis. It would therefore be very hypocritical for "the religious", who themselves are *comfortably* included in said statistics, to shower fellow church goers (and church leaders) with honor and respect *as* 'church-goers', while at the same time condemning, ostracizing, avoiding, and being unwelcoming to those who are involved in any branch of the sex industry, those who might have an unhealthy addiction, or *anyone else* for that matter. For, what is *the difference* between watching a stripper in a night club to watching a porn actor in an x-rated movie in the privacy of one's own home? As Christ warned us all:

> Beware of the yeast of the Pharisees, that is,
> their hypocrisy.
> LUKE 12:1

---

[20] As in Blogspot, *Calling the Defiled.* ⟨URL: http://honesttalkwithgod.blogspot.co.uk/2012/08/calling-defiled-mark-714-23.html⟩.

[21] See also P. Goodson, D. McCormick and A. Evans, *Searching for sexually explicit material on the Internet: An exploratory study of college students' behavior and attitudes.* 30th edition. Archives of Sexual Behavior, 2001; as well as Jason S. Carroll et al., *Generation XXX: Pornography Acceptance and Use Among Emerging Adults.* Volume 23, 1st edition. Journal of Adolescent Research, January 2008.

[22] See also Ogi Ogas, *The Online World of Female Desire.* The Wall Street Journal, 2011.

... and in response to the religious leaders who had asked Christ why he associated with and was a true confidant and friend to so-called 'sinners', Christ responded:

> Those who are well have no need of a physician, but those who are sick; I have come to call not the righteous but sinners to repentance.
>
> LUKE 5:31-32

Furthermore, these same zealous leaders of religion drove a blind man out of their synagogue (one could easily say 'church' today) after Jesus had healed him of his blindness. The blind man had told them that he felt Jesus *must be* from God because no one could do what he did – to where they told him that he had been "born entirely in sin", so that he had no right to try to teach them about matters of faith.[23] On Christ's having heard about what had happened between the man that he had healed and the religious leaders, and that he had been driven out of the synagogue, it is said that:

> Jesus said, 'I came into this world for judgment so that those who do not see may see, and those who do see may become blind.' Some of the Pharisees near him heard this and said to him, 'Surely we are not blind, are we?' Jesus said to them, 'If you were blind, you would not have sin. But now that you say, "We see," your sin remains.'
>
> JOHN 9:39-41

-----

[23] John 9:13-34

Furthermore, as John rightly states:

> If we say that we have no sin, we deceive ourselves, and the truth is not in us. If we confess our sins, he who is faithful and just will forgive us our sins and cleanse us from all unrighteousness. If we say that we have not sinned, we make him a liar, and his word is not in us.
>
> I JOHN 1:8-10

Therefore, anyone who claims to follow Christ, but who would drive out, exclude, ostracize, or dehumanize a prostitute, strip dancer, porn actor, or what the world would gladly label a so-called "sexual deviant", is no better than the aboveforementioned religious leaders of Christ's day; and, according to Jesus Christ himself, such a person's sin of hypocrisy, arrogance, and self-righteousness – which in themselves are far worse than the 'sins' that such people are glad to condemn on others – their (the religious') sin remains.

For Christ came to give sight to the blind, not condemnation. Likewise, as Christ told these same religious leaders that he had come to call sinners – and not the 'righteous' – to repentance; it is clear that he was not calling these same religious figures 'righteous', as he himself made plain that, because of how they treated the ostracized, and condemned the weak, their sin *remained* – as we have seen above. Let us not be like these same religious leaders who Christ chastised; nor let us ever be like *many* in the world who, though always condemning Christ's followers, are themselves oftentimes just as arrogant, hypocritical, and self-righteous as these religious leaders were – only without the religion, but still with a sense of self-righteousness, but denying the One and Only God who *is* righteousness, and love, and mercy. For they condemn in the classrooms, in HR departments and corporate settings, in courts, in the media, in "reality t.v.", in governmental institutions – wherever they can put someone down in order to look 'righteous' before others. But, again, as Christ has said:

> Do not judge, so that you may not be judged.
> For with the judgment you make you will be
> judged, and the measure you give will be the
> measure you get.
> MATTHEW 7:1-2

Therefore, let us never be either like religious leaders who ostracize, nor like the world that slanders, defames, and excludes. For again, as Christ stated:

> All who exalt themselves will be humbled, and
> all who humble themselves will be exalted.
> MATTHEW 23:12

For this is a universal law, much like the law of gravity – it applies to *everyone* – whether believer, unbeliever, or anyone in-between. And it is God who does the exalting of the humble, and it is He who humbles the proud. As such, may this prayer be on every church attendee's and self-professed follower of Christ's lips:

> God, please send us those people that no one
> else wants.[24]

...and when they do come – *welcome* them with dignity, go on over and *speak to them* with a smile, and make them feel wanted, *valued*, and loved... as Christ *himself* did. For as he stated:

> ...I was a stranger and you welcomed me...
> MATTHEW 25:35

---

[24] As in Blogspot (as in n. 20 on page 413).

# Premarital sex seems *not* to be against God's laws

And now, as we come back to analyzing premarital sex and what scripture might (or might not) have to say about it:

As has been said, the phrase "sexual immorality" – as used in both MATTHEW 15:19 and MARK 7:21 – comes from the Greek word *porneia*, as derived from *porneuo* – to where it more often than not directly translates into the words *whoredom* or *prostitution*, as many biblical texts correctly translate it as.   In addition, *porneuo* comes from the Greek word *porne*, which literally refers to a female prostitute.[25]  Most importantly, the word *fornication*, as used in modern times, has wrongly been imposed a rather *contemporary* meaning – the word itself only having been in existence and used in recent centuries, to where by modern implication is commonly (but erroneously) *assumed* to mean premarital sex – even though the word never even *existed* before the 14th century when it was first used in the Middle English as derived from the Latin word *fornix* – meaning *vault*, an *arch,* and *brothel* – the derivative *fornix* referring specifically to a vaulted arch where prostitutes used to come together in Roman times to market their trade.[26]

Furthermore, the additional derivative *fornices* referred specifically to such arches, having been understood in said Roman times to mean *brothels* – thus

---

[25] Foundation (as in n. 1 on page 338), p.1559.
[26] See also T. F. Hoad, editor, *The Concise Oxford Dictionary of English Etymology*. Oxford University Press, 1993.

prostitutes selling their services "under the arches" so-to-speak. As such, from its original use centuries ago post the 14th century, the word *fornication* seems only to refer to sex strictly *involving* prostitution, and therefore having *nothing* at all to do with sexual activity or behavior between two consenting, unmarried adults (be they heterosexual *or* homosexual). In addition to this, no such word (*fornication*, that is) – nor any similar variant – ever even *existed* in the time of Christ – so that to *wrongly* attempt to force upon a translation of the Greek *porneia* as supposing to mean our *modernized* equivalent of *fornication* – with its own definition as referring to sex between unmarried people – is to simply put a word into Christ's mouth that he did *not* say – especially when what he most likely was referring to was sexual activity *involving* prostitution in the first instance as stated, and possibly to rape, incest with an immediate family member, and the worship of idols through sex-based ritualistic practices.[27] As has been said:

> Since neither the Torah nor rabbinical teachers contemporary with Jesus prohibited intercourse between unmarried partners as a moral offense, perhaps porneia referred primarily to sex with prostitutes, adultery, and other promiscuous relationships.[28]

Hence, these were the common things that cultures of the time would likely have thought of when hearing

---

[27] See also *from* Appendix C on page 477 regarding such pagan cult practices during Christ's time.

[28] As in James A. Brundage, *Law, Sex, and Christian Society in Medieval Europe*. University Of Chicago Press, 1987.

such a term, when taking both Old and New Testament writings that also use the phrase in both Hebraic and Greek versions of the same into account, as well as on considering cultural context and meaning at the time[29] – to where in reality the word *porneia* (as used by Christ) does *not* in fact seem to mean either premarital or any other form of "conventional" sex (again, either gay or straight sex) – and as such neither *porneia* nor *fornication* should erroneously be *assumed* to mean general sexual behavior between consenting and unmarried adults (which many lightly suppose it to mean in this day and age).  To do so is to not only inaccurately translate a phrase to fit our modern way of thinking about sex in general by modern man, but also to *presume* and impose upon Christ a modern definition which was not necessarily being referred to – neither explicitly nor implicitly. In other words, it would seem that Christ *never* explicitly said that premarital sex is wrong in and of itself. In fact, *nothing* of the sort is ever explicitly claimed by him in any manner whatsoever – contrary to what many major organized religions of today state as based on their *own* devised and man-made traditions and taboos.

Prominent biblical scholars and translators *clearly* make this differentiation as well – that the word *porneia* used herein refers to either "sexual immorality" in general, or prostitution – and therefore *not* particularly to either premarital nor gay sex – as seen in all the reliable and widely regarded biblical

---

[29] See also Thelos, *Divine Sex: Liberating Sex from Religious Tradition* (as in n. 1 on page 398).

translations of today[30] – either in footnotes referring to the same phrase, or in direct translations *not* as "fornication", but rather as either "sexual immorality" or "whoredom"...in other words, prostitution.   So when sister Eunice or aunt Tabatha shove this verse in your face and erroneously claim that the original translation meant "fornication" as interpreted into our skewed definition of premarital sex today, you can now show them this book along with a nice glass of whiskey to absorb the shock that they will surely experience from years of believing everything their priest, rabbi, imam, or self-proclaimed guru has fervently, fanatically, and erroneously claimed via religious tradition and the all-too-deceptive casual claims that originate from social taboo, political correctness, and the oft-times senseless deceptions of "moral majority rule".

Furthermore, even Paul *himself*, in I CORINTHIANS 5:1, used the same word – *porneia* – to refer to a case of *incest*; and Christ used it in reference to *adultery* and how divorce fits into it in MATTHEW

---

[30] Such Bible versions including:

- The New American Standard
- New Revised Standard Version
- Updated New American Standard Bible
- New International Version
- Hebrew Names Version
- Young's Literal Translation
- International Standard Version

5:32 and 19:9; while ACTS 15:20, 15:29, and 21:25 uses it in the context of what seems to be sexual rituals during the worship of idols – such rituals as having been common practice in the heavily pagan-influenced Roman times.[31] So it seems as though even Paul *himself* – when using the word *pornos* (which is derived from *porne* and meaning a *male* prostitute)[32] in I CORINTHIANS 6:9 and again in HEBREWS 13:4 – did *not* intend for this to mean "fornication" – or premarital sex.

In short, Christ himself seems to *never* have explicitly stated that premarital sex in and of itself was in any way against God – which would lead us to conclude that the use of the word *porneia* in MATTHEW 15:9 and MARK 7:21 was referring either *only* to prostitution; or *possibly* to prostitution, rape, incest involving an immediate family member, and sexual rituals in pagan idol worship when considering linguistic history as well as context of the cultural and normative use of the term at the time.

# Sexual desire is *meant to be embraced*

Another topic that people oftentimes take issue with relates to such things as pornography, visual appreciation, or simply fantasizing on the sexual beauty of another. They will, especially amongst most major religions, claim that involving oneself in such things amounts to sin – and in relation to Christianity, will

---

[31] See from Appendix C on page 477.

[32] Foundation (as in n. 1 on page 338), p. 1559.

– in my opinion – wrongly cite Christ when he was teaching on the Ten Commandments as he showed us that sin begins in the heart – though he himself never explicitly stated that either *fantasizing* or doing any of the above in and of themselves are in any way wrong – but rather that it is the overly-*excessive* and addictive use of *anything* – be it alcohol, drugs, work, religiosity and ritual,[33] porn, worry, fear, or whatever else that one can form a solid addiction to in the place of a healthy relationship with God, the self, and others – that is the contextual issue that was being referred to.[34]

Yet many who focus more on traditional aspects of organized religion will often look at it in a very conservative manner and will conclude that, on Christ's stating that to look at a woman to lust for her as being tantamount to *adultery* of the heart – again *notice* the word *adultery* – that such things as pornography, fantasizing, voyeurism, premarital sex, and the rest

---

[33] For instance, Christ taught us not to be repetitive when we pray – as this is ritualistic, and oftentimes is done to be seen by others, rather than as it ought to be – a *normal conversation* with God that can be done at any time, and wherever you may be. As he put it: "And whenever you pray, do not be like the hypocrites; for they love to stand and pray in the synagogues and at the street corners, so that they may be seen by others. Truly I tell you, they have received their reward. But whenever you pray, go into your room and shut the door and pray to your Father who is in secret; and your Father who sees in secret will reward you. When you are praying, do not heap up empty phrases as the Gentiles do; for they think that they will be heard because of their many words. Do not be like them, for your Father *knows* what you need before you ask him." [Matthew 6:5-8]

[34] See note 19 on page 409.

of it must be included in what he was talking about. This is found in the following:

> You have heard that it was said, "YOU SHALL NOT COMMIT ADULTERY"; but I say to you, that everyone who looks on a woman to lust[35] for her has committed adultery [*sex with one who is currently married*] with her already in his heart.
>
> Matthew 5:27-28

Yet many now believe Christ was *specifically* referring to the act of *coveting* with the intent to *pursue* the spouse of another for one's own possession or use. After all, Christ *did* make clear that what he was specifically speaking about was *adultery*, and not erotic thoughts or fantasies in and of themselves when taken into context with the fact that he was talking in reference to both the commandments *against* adultery as well as *coveting* what belongs to someone else by the original manuscripts' use of the Greek word *epithumeo* – which can both mean to *lust,* as well as *to covet*, as is further expounded upon herein.

In addition to this, some even question whether Christ was in fact referring to women in general – and feel that Christ was referring *not* to women in general, but to *married* women in particular in the above verses.  This is because the Greek word for *woman,* as was used in this text, can mean *both* 'woman' *as well as* 'wife' (or 'wives'). In fact, this word – *guné* – is used throughout scripture as 'wife' about 50% of the time.[36] Furthermore, Strong's defines the

---

[35] The Greek word for "lust" herein being epithumeo – which means to "earnestly desire" and "covet" something (or someone) belonging to someone else.

[36] See also Foundation (as in n. 1 on page 338).

word like so: "A woman, a wife, my lady".[37] If this is
in fact the case, than Matthew 5:28 can also be read
as follows:

> But I say to you that everyone who looks at
> another's *wife* with lust has already commit-
> ted adultery with her in his heart.
> MATTHEW 5:28

Furthermore, it makes perfect sense that Christ was
referring to the lusting after *another's* wife for two
main reasons.   First, the Sermon on the Mount,
where this scripture is taken from in the Gospel
of Matthew, seems to have been a commentary on
the Ten Commandments, and this scripture is in
fact in *context* to Christ's discussion on committing
adultery. As having previously been established that
adultery involves at least one person who is already
married, it makes much more sense that Christ was
essentially stating that it is not only wrong to commit
adultery by having sex with someone who is *already*
married, but it is also adultery to even *consider*
having sex with someone who is *already* married. If
this is the case, than Christ never said it is wrong
to be attracted to, nor to think, sexual fantasies
and thoughts about someone who is *not* married.
Secondly, if Christ *had* meant to include all women,
surely much more discussion (either between Christ
and others, or initially in the Old Testament itself)
explicitly regarding sexual thoughts would have taken
place.   And yet this cannot be seen anywhere in
said scriptures. Even Christ is recorded to have said

---

[37] See James Strong et al., *Strong's Exhaustive Concordance of the Bible with Greek and Hebrew Dictionaries*.
Royal Publishers, 1979.

this statement only once – that being in Matthew as cited above.  It would seem, therefore, that, if one could commit adultery simply by *thinking* or *fantasizing* sexually about someone – whether they were married or not – than the Bible would be *full* of such admonitions, and yet it is *completely silent* on this specific question.

In addition to this, on stating that "to lust after" – or *covet* – a woman as being akin to adultery of the heart, Christ was referring to those who *covet* an already married woman (again, in reference to MATTHEW 5:28) – especially when God hates divorce in that He is in the business of building relationships and not tearing them down.  This point is further strengthened by the fact that the translation of Christ's Aramaic speech used the Greek word *epithumeo*, which is translated as "to covet", "to set one's heart upon", or to "strongly desire" something – *epithumeo* having commonly been used *interchangeably* with both "to covet" and "to lust after".  Furthermore, the word was frequently utilized in both negative as well as positive contexts – to where the idea of *intent* to pursue (or follow through) with *action* being strongly present in its use – in other words, doing whatever is required to *achieve* or manifest the intent or desire.

As such, the word "lust" here would seem to mean that one "desire with intent at following through with", and not merely to "form a mental image" – as is commonly (but most likely erroneously) assumed.  Therefore, it can be seen that one having erotic thoughts does *not* mean that one is committing any wrongdoing – it is not what Christ meant *at all*. Furthermore, Christ used this very *same* word in other occasions – in a positive sense – where he was not talking about anything remotely to do with sex in any way whatsoever. Such occasions included the time when he stated, during the Last Supper, that "I have earnestly desired [*epithumeo*] to eat this Passover with you before I suffer...";[38] and on another occasion he stated that "...many prophets and righteous men desired [*epithumeo*] to see what you see, and did not see it...".[39]

Thus *epithumeo* was again used interchangeably by Christ in referring to both good and bad forms of "strong desire" – which again is *also* used in the Greek language to mean "covet" – as we see on Paul's likewise using *epithumeo* in reference against coveting a neighbor's property in ROMANS 7:7 and 13:9 – the act of *coveting* (to desire an object *specifically* belonging to, possessed by, or already owned by another) to the ultimate end at wishing to have *someone else's* possession as one's own being against one of the Ten Commandments not to covet another's personal belongings as found in DEUTERONOMY 5:21, which in turn states that "you shall not covet your neighbor's *wife*, and you shall not desire your neighbor's house... field... servant... ox... donkey... or anything that belongs to your neighbor."

Now, taking the fact that Christ stated that we are not to "lust after" – or alternatively *covet* – an already *married* woman lest we commit adultery – and that if we are angry with our brother without cause, that we are essentially committing murder[40]

---

[38] Luke 22:15

[39] Matthew 13:17

[40] The sixth Commandment stating that we must not commit murder, as stated in Deuteronomy 5:17.

in our hearts[41] – these reinforce the idea that the Sermon on the Mount which mentions the above (as well as other) issues was *indeed* a commentary or teaching as revolving around the Ten Commandments – in addition to the ultimate *two* of Christ's commandments which sums the aforementioned up in one sentence: that being, to love the Lord your God with all your heart, and to love your neighbor as yourself.[42] Taking all of these factors into consideration, it can be suggested that what Christ referred to in regards to "lusting" – or rather *coveting* – after an already married woman as committing *adultery* with her in one's heart was in reference to the commandment not to "covet your neighbor's wife" – to where one must not covet, or "lust after", the *wife* of another in wishing to take her as one's own – much as one must not be angry without cause against the innocent,[43] lest one commit murder in one's heart (again, against the commandment not to murder).   Thus Christ seems to be stating that the Ten Commandments apply even in one's deliberate *intention* to break them – such as the seventh commandment stating that one must not commit adultery (again, having an affair with one who is already married, or even conversely separating from one's lawful wife in divorce without just cause) – to where such "coveting" of another person's spouse without express permission is akin to breaking *both* the commandments against coveting as well as adultery in one's heart.

---

[41] See Matthew 5:21-22.

[42] Matthew 22:34-40

[43] As in Matthew 5:22.

In this respect, it is presumptuous and out of context to simply *assume* that Christ was stating we must not look at, appreciate, or maybe even think sexual thoughts regarding a woman (or man) who is *not* already married – and whom we do not wish to 'steal' from anyone else, nor break up a relationship by cheating with him or her if apart from their partner's knowledge or consent. In other words, to love our neighbor as ourselves extends to not having affairs with someone who *already* belongs to someone else, to where we would likewise not want anyone to cheat with our *own* spouses without our consent in like manner.

In conclusion, "lusting after", within the considered context of what Christ was speaking about – namely the Ten Commandments – is equal to coveting what *belongs to* another. Christ is addressing the act of *coveting*, not sexual fantasy in and of itself – *nor* of premarital sex between two unmarried people (again, whether gay or straight) for that matter. For sexual fantasies are thoughts that do not have intentions to *possess* or *go after* another's wife in and of themselves. In contrast, the intent at *attaining* another's wife (or if married, another woman at the detriment of breaking one's own marriage vows – and thus divorcing),[44] is the form of lust, or coveting, that was being spoken of in MATTHEW 5:28. Again, nothing to do with pornography, sexual fantasy, premarital sex, admiring the sexual beauty of another, or anything of the sort – and all to do with the *active* pursuit and *deliberate intent*

---

[44] When as previously stated: God is in the business of building relationships – between Him and ourselves, as well as between each other – and not on tearing them down.

of breaking a marriage vow – hence the *specific* use of the word "adultery" in combination with *epithumeo* (to covet another's possession). Sexual fantasy in and of itself seems to have had absolutely *nothing* to do with what Christ was talking about – pure and simple.

It should also be mentioned – for the sake of those who may be wondering – and most people do – that *neither* the Judeo-Christian Bible, *nor* Christ himself, *ever* list masturbation, oral sex, or anal sex (nor any other form of sexual act) as being forbidden at all[45] – they *never* condemn anyone for these natural joys, and they do *not* call any of these as sin in any way whatsoever... despite what you might have been misled to think from certain circles. For even Christ made clear that:

> There is nothing outside the man which can defile him if it goes into him; but the things which proceed *out* of the man are what defile the man.
>
> MARK 7:15

Thus if any of the aforementioned sexual vehicles towards human interaction and the expression of both love and desire were sinful at all, surely the scriptures would have *clearly* stated so in no uncertain terms. They *never* do.

Therefore, has been shown, *none* of these things are *ever* forbidden in the Judeo-Christian scriptures, *all* sexual positions and methods are natural and God-given, and our modern sexual hangups have originated *not* from scripture, but from mankind's

---

[45] See Jacob Milgrom, *Leviticus 17-22*. The Anchor Yale Bible Commentaries edition. Yale University Press, 2000.

own invented legalisms and traditions[46] which have nothing whatever to do with either the Jewish or Christian grass-roots origins of faith.[47]

Christ, through his words and actions, showed the world that he was *not* a sexual 'prude' of religious and preachy obsession (as many involved with religion often come across to their observers in this day and age), that he understood and accepted man's God-given desires, and that he was *much more concerned* about *genuine* sins of the heart that separate us from a relationship with God and from each other while making clear that, as stated beforehand, God is in the business of *building* relationships, and not tearing them down.

Christ's focus on sins mostly involved such things as arrogant pride, idolatry, the love for money to where the poor take a back-seat to one's selfish dedication to riches, greed, jealousy, all manifestations of social injustice, the neglect of the sick and desperate-hearted in our midst, religious-borne hypocrisy and self-righteousness, unprovoked violence, and all forms of deceptively-pious obsessions of religious-laden oppression. As such, revisit your views on sex not from *religion's* perspective, but rather from *Christ's* own words and actions through the Gospel *according to* Christ – and Christ *alone*.

And most importantly, don't let *them* make you stumble in your relationship to God because of your sexual lifestyle. This cannot be emphasized enough, as millions are *needlessly* being turned off to God

---

[46] See Raymond J. (as in n. 3 on page 399).

[47] See Thelos, *Divine Sex: Liberating Sex from Religious Tradition* (as in n. 1 on page 398); as well as Countryman (as in n. 2 on page 398).

on a daily basis because of the many man-made, invalidated, and *completely unscriptural* traditions and hang-ups, taboos, put-downs, religious lies and self-righteous anti-sex fanaticisms of mankind from virtually *all* forms of organized religions – and God has *absolutely nothing* to do with *any* of it – as Christ himself made clear. You don't *have* to be like them to *genuinely* love God and to have a personal relationship *with* Him. You *don't have to* have a sexless life in order to talk to Him as your Heavenly Father who cares for and loves you above all else. He is *always* with you – *fighting* for you – no matter *where* you are or what you are doing.

In fact, God does not want you to be like them *at all* – but rather to be *yourself* as He has made you...*just as you are.*   For He Himself loves you unconditionally – just as you are, and just as you are *meant* to be. Any improvements to be made He will let you know about – and will work from *within* you to accomplish His work *in* you, so long as you let go and let God.  That is the message of Christ.  That is the message for *all* faiths.  That is the message of genuine and *unconditional* love and acceptance – without preconditions or strings attached. And all of this *without* ever having to live in abstinence, celibacy, or sexual repression – that's *not* God's intent – *not* by the Gospel according to Christ.

# Appendix *C*

# Christ Allowed for Homosexuality

The claim made by the major organized systems of religion that homosexuality is a "chosen *behavioral lifestyle*" is oftentimes an illogical and unsubstantiated strategy to justify their own biases against their many homosexual neighbors (and oftentimes towards their very own children) in the forms of both overt as well as hidden homophobia and ill-intended injustices of many kinds that often include workplace bullying, expulsions from homes and communities, violence, and murder – these outright prejudices often manifesting themselves in schools, workplaces, places of worship, neighborhoods,[1] and whole communities. As a result, many innocent and well-intended people involved in said religions begin to believe that homosexuality is evil, and will take a black and white approach to the subject while inwardly not truly knowing whether it is right or wrong to hold to the opinions that they have adopted for such a long time. For, as has been said:

> If God is wiser that we, His judgement must differ from ours on *many* things, and not least on good and evil. What seems to us good may therefore not be good in His eyes, and what seems to us evil may not be evil. [2]

With this in mind, it must be stressed that intolerance against homosexuals *cannot* in any way ever be honestly nor legitimately justified by what *scripture* states – the very scriptures that make clear that we are *not* to follow man-made traditional opinion, status-quo, nor re-interpreted dogma; but rather the Spirit of the Living God alone, *His* wisdom – and *His* Word.

# Christ said that some are born gay

God intentionally predestined some to be homosexual. As PSALM 139 states:

---

[1] See also Sphero, *Escaping the Shithole: How and Why to Leave a Bad Neighborhood Once and for All* (as in n. 32 on page 378).

[2] As in Lewis, *The Problem of Pain* (as in n. 2 on page 106).

> For You formed my inward parts; You wove
> me in my mother's womb. I will give thanks
> to You, for I am fearfully and wonderfully
> made. Wonderful are your works; and my soul
> knows it very well. My bones were not hidden
> from you, when I was being made in secret,
> intricately woven in the depths of the earth.
> Your eyes beheld my unformed substance.
>
> PSALM 139:13-16

To state that homosexuality is a choice is to say that
God did not know what He was doing – or that He
made a mistake – when he formed the gay or lesbian
person in his or her mother's womb.  This is akin
to stating that heterosexuality, or the desire for the
opposite sex, is a choice.

So some will respond to this and state that, though
they will *always* have a desire for the opposite sex,
they have a *choice* as to whether they will act on
that desire – for instance, if they are already married.
But this does not nullify the fact that they *do* have
a desire for the opposite sex, even if they do not
*act* on it.  Therefore they will again respond to this
and state that, though their heterosexuality is not a
choice – they will proudly admit to having been born
as heterosexual – gay people on the other hand *did*
in fact choose to somehow *become* gay, and that this
choice is "unnatural".

But if gay people chose something *so* unnatural
for them, then why would they deprive themselves
of the joys of heterosexual sex?  Why would they
*then* agree to live a life of persecution, insults, and
ostracism in many social and cultural circles, and
suffer at the hands of man... for a choice?  So they
will turn around and state that, because homosexuals

are so lost, crooked, debauched, or somehow more prone to 'sexual' sin than they themselves are – as self-righteousness and arrogance begin to be revealed, the worst of *all* sins – as they continue and finally state that *all* gay people somehow one day made a conscious choice to *become* gay – just to be rebellious, different, to go against the grain, to flip the world off – you begin to realize that, at the very least, this person does not know their Bible as well as they may claim... and probably does not fully comprehend the vast works and purposes of God either.

For if that is the case – if in fact everyone was born as heterosexual *without exception* – than anyone choosing to *become* homosexual just for the sake of reasons external to whom they really are, is truly (and pitifully) denying themselves the *true* sexual pleasures that they were born with. Life's too short to deny oneself of whom one truly is... just for the sake of it. So we must conclude that either *everyone* – without exception – is *born* heterosexual, to where some have become martyrs who simply want to inflict needless social pain on themselves and be deprived of any "enjoyable" heterosexual sex life for the rest of their lives in this one single journey through our very short time on earth for *essentially* no good reason; or that some *are* in fact gay or lesbian from birth, to where those on the outside who question homosexual people's natural-born sexual preference are possibly just being closed-minded, comfortable with tradition and unquestioning of what has been forced upon them through their religion, legalistic in their thinking instead of looking at reality, bigoted against those different than they might be, or – as is probably the majority of the cases – genuinely *good* people who simply believe what they have been hearing from preachers, teachers, and the media in regards to what the Bible *supposedly* states about the subject.

God help some of the more *genuinely* closed-minded, legalistic, or bigoted people when one of *their* own children turns out to be gay. Or rather, God help the children *themselves* – too many of whom have already been sacrificed to the gods of social intolerance through suicides, murders, and violence-filled lives at the hands of *some* who to many turn out to be stubborn religious zombies, pharisee-like and self-righteous hate-mongers amongst us... these who coincidentally are usually also known to be the very *same* people who make even *fellow* heterosexuals suffer through their fervent and radical preaching against *any* form of natural heterosexual sex,[3] who turn out to be the workplace bullies[4] who have themselves

---

[3] See Appendix B on page 397 regarding why premarital sex is not against the Judeo-Christian Bible, but is rather a subject used by many of the same preachers to further repress the masses into traditionalist dogmas – as they make even the heterosexuals amongst them stumble on their relationship to God through their oftentimes very much unbiblical judgementalism without balance or remorse.

[4] Such as these often also being the very ones who think nothing of bullying and victimizing their believing co-workers as well – and neither corporate powers that be, nor the rest of the world, ever blinks twice at the daily hostile persecutions that go on in our offices today. But the treatment of these – as well as of our very own children – by such should become a high-profiled, much more publicly-denounced, and at times ultimately imprisonable offense due to the consequent heart attacks, strokes, mental breakdowns, and oft-times unbearable stresses directly

deliberately exchanged sexual desire for the worship of wealth and a pseudo-form of power only they seem to be aware of having, and who turn out to be the Hitlers and rapists on our streets who mistake sexual desire for the forced and violent dominion of anyone they can harass and exterminate – having never realized that sex is a natural vehicle from God for self-creativity, the expression of love for your partner, the tint of human friendship and unconditional acceptance towards that beautiful stranger, and the sign of life to those who have all but forgotten that *they still live*. Besides all this, even the animals of our world are *not all* born to be heterosexual,[5] as many studies have shown. Has not God created all... does God *ever* make mistakes?

Does it not seem more reasonable to conclude that homosexuality *is* in fact something that has naturally been given to some... from *birth*? Christ seems to have said just as much – that homosexuality *is* in fact a natural quality given to many from before they were even born – as found in Matthew 19. The full contextual text is as follows:

---

caused towards both the individual recipient as well as to his or her family by such corporate bullies and health-destroying murderers if we have any hope of creating a more civilized society for our children to live in. Political correctness has not worked, and more often than not victimizes the victim and rewards the perpetrator. We are in a modern age, and must begin to *behave* as such.

[5] See also note 68 on page 482 regarding the documented research into thousands of animal species, many of which are homosexual to the point of having a single same-sex partner for the entirety of their life-span.

> His disciples said to him, 'If such is the case of
> a man with his wife, it is better not to marry.'
> But he [*Christ*] said to them, 'Not everyone
> can accept this teaching, but only those to
> whom it has been given. For there are eunuchs
> who were born that way from their mother's
> womb; and there are eunuchs who were made
> eunuchs by men; and there are also eunuchs
> who made themselves eunuchs for the sake
> of the kingdom of heaven. He who is able to
> accept this, let him accept it.'
> MATTHEW 19:10-12

Christ did *not* say – nor insinuate in any manner
*whatsoever* – that this was in any way wrong, but
rather said that this fact should be *accepted* by those
– as he puts it – "to whom it has been given."[6] For
Christ *himself* stated that, although they were "made
male and female" – so that a man will leave his
parents on getting married, when speaking against
divorce in MATTHEW 19:3-9 – he is on the other hand
crystal clear in the *very next* set of verses when he
*then* adds that marriage is *not* meant for everyone,
and that there are some who were *meant* to be born
*not to marry* – despite how *some* (but certainly *not*
all) in fundamentalist circles of major religions will
wrongly refute these clear statements with their *own*
self-imposed concepts of what a so-called "nuclear
family" and "family values" should be defined as to the
spiritual hindrance and eventual stumbling of many
who hear them.

Furthermore, Christ *twice* repeats that only those
who can accept this statement – that it is "better
not to marry" – are "those to whom *it has been*

---

[6] See Matthew 19:11.

*given"*...these being the ones who should therefore "accept this". If being gay is natural and God-given, than why must we continue to condemn the innocent? More importantly, if Christ has *directly* told mankind that such diversity exists as having been part of God's plan for some of us, than how can we argue with God Himself? Is it because we have been *so* tainted by man's religious traditions (as well as by our own prejudices), that we will gladly go on about it, and by our own actions *refuse* to accept God-given common sense as well as what the Judeo-Christian Bible *really* says on the matter? May it never be!

As such, Christ clearly stated, in regards to not marrying, that there are some who are in his own words *"born eunuchs"* – the word "eunuch" *not* exclusively referring to castrated men as many people unfamiliar in Greek and Roman history will quickly state, but that in the majority of cases historically refers to those who have *no* sexual desire for the *opposite* sex, but who may be sexually active with the *same* sex...hence the word *eunuch* having been a term that *also* referred to homosexual people in earlier Greek and Roman times. The word "eunuch" referred not only to castrated people, but also to homosexuals,[7] to where Christ included *both* in

---

[7] More detailed studies and analysis of the word *eunuch* as having included homosexuals throughout ancient history – the very word Christ *himself* used in Matthew 19:12 to state that some people were *born* to be homosexual, and should therefore accept this as a fact of life – is given in resources such as Charles Humana, *The Keeper of the Bed: The Story of the Eunuch*. Arlington Books, 1973; David F. Greenberg, *The Construction of Homosexuality*. University of Chicago Press, 1988; Johannes Schneider; Gerhard

MATTHEW 19:12. Furthermore, it is a historical *fact* that what people *commonly* referred to as "eunuchs" in those times where whole-bodied individuals with absolutely no "parts" missing whatsoever. Christ's listeners had no doubt about what he was talking about, and understood by his comments that gay people are not meant to marry in the conventional sense of the word,[8] but that they should be *accepted* for who they are – and should likewise accept their homosexuality as it having been given to them by God from birth – as in verse 11 of the same. Christ *knew* who he was talking to — being fully aware that his audience realized *exactly* to whom the word *eunuch* could refer to – and *still* used it without any hesitation whatsoever.[9]

---

Kittel et al., editors, *Article on Eunouchos*. Theological Dictionary of the New Testament edition. Wm. B. Eerdmans Publishing Company, 1986; John J. McNeill, *The Church and the Homosexual*. Beacon Press, 1993; and Martti Nissinen, *Homoeroticism in the Biblical World*. Fortress Press, 1998. Furthermore, even ancient secular writers show through their works that the word *eunuch* clearly included homosexual people in and around the time of Christ. See also Clement Of Alexandria, *Paedagogus III [The Instructor]*. Kessinger Publishing, 2004; as well as Clement of Alexandria, *The Stromata III*. Kessinger Publishing, 2004.

[8] Though this does *not* preclude gay couples from entering into legally-binding agreements such as *civil partnerships* if they so wish. See Sphero, *The Gay Faith: Christ, Scripture, and Sexuality* (as in n. 1 on page 83).

[9] Hence the importance in taking both the listener's background knowledge as well as historical, linguistic, and cultural context of scripture into account [see note 18 on page 65 in regards to the importance of considering

Because Christ clearly states that some people were born this way "from their mother's womb" or "from birth", could this have been the precise time in which he made his official stance on homosexuality known to the world – namely that if God has created a person as gay or lesbian, that she *must* accept who she is and move on with her life? And if God creates someone as such, could that person actually be doing wrong to herself by *not accepting* the gift that He has given her – and this due solely to the often overbearing influence of skewed and closed-minded ways of thinking by the insincere and uninformed around her, by sub-cultural bigotry, and by deceptive traditional taboos from organized religion? Is it actually *incorrect* in God's eyes, therefore, that one betray the self that God has meant for one to be – *despite* what the religious might say, scream about,

---

context when reading scripture]. Likewise, the same can be said of Matthew 19:12 in reference to "eunuchs", where Christ *knew* to whom he was speaking to, realizing that his listeners did not have to hear an explanation of what the then common-day definitions of the word included... to where Biblical readers of modern times must honestly consider whether Christ was *indeed* referring to and directly affirming gay and lesbian people when he stated that "some are born eunuchs from their mother's womb", to where "those who can accept this should accept it". See also resources given in note 7 on page 440, and the main text in this appendix, for a fuller explanation of how the word "eunuch" was defined by Christ as filling three different categories, the first of which was in direct reference to gays and lesbians having been born as eunuchs from their mother's womb, to where they are meant not to marry in the *conventional* sense... even though the world must *accept* homosexuality as part of God's *intended* design.

protest against, and self-righteously condemn in order to attempt to have themselves proven right at the expense of making others different than they stumble on their way to God?

And they do make many millions stumble on having the relationship to God that they are willing to have – but feel trapped because they erroneously feel that they must somehow magically 'change' who God has made them to be – which is an impossibility – and this because they have been led to believe by those who profess to follow Christ but who are often – possibly unintending, but nevertheless – stumbling blocks to these who seek to have a personal relationship with God. But as Christ himself put it in regards to man-made doctrine and religious legalistic traditions that so easily cause mankind to stumble:

> But woe to you, scribes and Pharisees, hypocrites! For you lock people out of the kingdom of heaven. For you do not go in yourselves, and when others are going in, you stop them.
> Matthew 23:13

And by persecuting, maligning, and condemning those who God has chosen to form as homosexuals – they are doing these very things to Christ himself. To condemn a homosexual person who has come to Christ irrespective of what society, their pastor, or contemporary religion might say about them, one condemns a member of the body of Christ who deserves dignity, love, support, and acceptance – and thereby condemns Christ himself. For as Jesus clearly stated:

> Truly I tell you, just as you did it to one of the least of these who are members of my family, you did it to me.' [MATTHEW 25:40]

Furthermore, knowing the homophobic hostility that might have existed amongst certain circles – such as from within *some* of the Pharisees of organized religion and such – is this why he adds that "he who is able to accept this, let him accept it"?[10] Of course, many today will quickly say that it is a "lifestyle choice". But if that is the case, than why can't the same be said for heterosexuals? Surely there are few homosexuals who by choice have *decided* to live as heterosexuals... but that does not change who they are, does it? Nor does a heterosexual become gay simply because he may experiment with homosexuality, does he?

No, a tiger cannot, and *will not*, change his strips. Why *should* he be miserable being something other than what he has always been – and will continue to be – till the day he dies? To try to change him into a parrot is to become a stumbling block to his own self-esteem as a tiger, and to desecrate the God who created him as such. Yet the *legalistically* religious does not lift a finger or make a mere *effort* to consider even this, as he is obsessed at proving himself right at *whatever* cost for the sake of ego and pride – even to the point of *ignoring* the very words of Christ himself – choosing rather to misquote Paul and thereby misrepresent his mere three passages completely out of context in order to wrongly condemn homosexuality altogether, which is in itself an exercise in self-deception as we will see further on in this appendix – and all this while *deliberately* failing to *at the very least* take but a moment to reconsider what Christ *might* have meant in the first

---

[10] Matthew 19:12

place. No matter, for the God-fearing homosexual does not need *legalism* any longer, when God *Himself* is his vindicator.

Again, Christ explicitly stated that some were *meant* to be gay from birth, as once more seen here in Matthew 19:12 where he says:

> For there are eunuchs who were born that way from their mother's womb; and there are eunuchs who were made eunuchs by men; and there are also eunuchs who made themselves eunuchs for the sake of the kingdom of heaven. He who is able to accept this, let him accept it.
>
> MATTHEW 19:12

– to where he clearly defined and categorizes three *types* of "eunuchs":

1. those "born that way from their mother's womb" – to where those to whom Christ was speaking to would have known that he was referring to gay and lesbian people here, as having been *one* of the common definitions of what the word "eunuch" referred to in Greek and Roman times – again, people having *no* sexual desire for the opposite sex, but who had sexual attractions and physical relations with the *same* sex as previously mentioned; [11]

---

[11] See also note 7 on page 440; as well as Humana (as in n. 7 on page 440); Jeff Miner and John Tyler Connoley, *The Children are Free*. Jesus Metropolitan Community Church, 2002; Schneider (as in n. 7 on page 440); and Sphero, *The Gay Faith: Christ, Scripture, and Sexuality* (as in n. 1 on page 83) for a full examination of the same.

2. those "made eunuchs by men" – namely castrated men, as is commonly thought of today; and –

3. those who, by personal choice and free will, chose to *become* eunuchs "for the sake of the kingdom of Heaven" – in other words, those who have chosen to *remain* unmarried in order to focus on God's work without having to be distracted by responsibilities that come with having and supporting a family.

All of these categories of people to whom the term "eunuch" referred to at the time of Christ, as explicitly enumerated and *affirmatively* redefined by Christ himself – were meant *"not to marry"*; to where, having mentioned the second category (those made eunuchs by the hands of man... in other words, having been castrated), it becomes even clearer that the first category *did* in fact refer directly to those who are attracted to the same sex (i.e. gays and lesbians, as his listeners would have understood it to mean as per the inclusive definition of the word at the time), and are thus *not* meant to marry in the same manner that he previously described in verse 19:4 in regards to male and female marriage. As has been said:

> The first category - those eunuchs who have been so from birth - is the closest description we have in the Bible of what we understand today as a homosexual.[12]

As such, the promise in Isaiah in reference to eunuchs, this being:

---

[12] J. McNeill (as in n. 7 on page 441).

> For thus says the Lord: To the eunuchs who keep My Sabbaths, who choose the things that please Me and hold fast My covenant, I will give, in My house and within My walls, a monument and a name better than sons and daughters; I will give them an everlasting name that shall *not* be cut off.
>
> ISAIAH 56:4-5

– is a promise to all homosexual people, whomever they are, who choose to honor God in their lives. For Christ did not exclude the first category from this promise, and neither must we as sincere followers of Christ.

Yet a very small number of modern translations seem to intentionally mis-translate the word *eunuch* into the word 'celibate', though this is an outrightly insincere substitute which only seems to attempt to mislead the reader – being that there is no disputing the clear and *original* linguistic meaning. The word that was used in the original – as well as subsequent copies – of the Greek biblical manuscripts *has* in fact always been EUNOÛCHOS – as is easily found in reputable Bible translations of today that are faithful to the original *literal* language – which most are. Anyone who has *any* knowledge whatsoever of ancient Greek, and of the importance of being faithful to original language, and who tells you that the word means 'celibate', is simply being misleading.

For even Dr. Robert Gagnon, one of the most vocal Christian authors on the subject who *respectfully* speaks *against* homosexuality, has himself nonetheless publicly admitted in regards to the word *eunuch* as used by Christ in the above quote of MATTHEW 19:12, that:

> Probably "born eunuchs" in the ancient world *did* include people homosexually inclined, which incidentally puts to the lie the oft-repeated claim that the ancient world could not even conceive of persons that were congenitally influenced toward exclusive same-sex attractions.[13]

Likewise, for some to state that what Christ was referring to were people who are either "physically incapable" of marriage due to their having been born sexless, made sexless by others, or who made themselves sexless – or that it may also mean those "incapable" of marriage because they are impotent or handicapped in some way – is again a totally ludicrous claim due to the fact that neither the original language *ever* suggests this in any way whatsoever, and because everyone knows that neither a physical handicap, nor impotence, *ever* stopped anyone from getting married. Christ *never* said that an impotent or sexually "handicapped" person should not get married. And we all know that neither impotence, nor any physical handicap (even to the point of castration) will *ever* prevent someone from marrying if they wish to do so - and *have* done so – throughout the ages. [14]

In the same way that Christ clearly *acknowledged* those who were born eunuchs – knowing that his listeners would realize he was speaking of homosexual men and women[15] – and this without any condemna-

---

[13] As in Robert Gagnon, *Robert Gagnon's Answers to Emails on the Bible and Homosexuality*. January 2007 ⟨URL: http://www.robgagnon.net/AnswersToEMails.htm⟩.

[14] See also note 7 on page 440 for more on the historic use of the word eunuch.

[15] See also Nancy Wilson, *Our Tribe: Queer Folks, God, Jesus, and the Bible*. Alamo Square Distributors, 2000.

tion whatsoever, but rather out of a genuine procla-
mation of unconditional love – so he *legitimized* their
rightful existence and validity in the eyes of their
Heavenly Father, and furthermore let us all know
that the world should accept that people *are* different,
and that God loves gay and lesbian people enough
to explain that they also are His intended children
formed from their mother's womb to *be* homosexual
from birth[16] – to where they themselves must also
accept who they have been created to be as well – no
matter what the rest of the world, organized religion,
or family might say or protest against. After all, why
else would he have added that such teachings are
given *only* "to whom it has been given"?[17]

Could it be that Christ took the time to mention
homosexual people, acknowledging their existence as
a diverse and *legitimate* part of humanity, and stating
that "he who can accept this, let him accept it"[18]
because he *knew* that there would come a day in
the future where homosexuality would cease from
being a non-issue in society (as had for the most part
been the case in the Greek and Roman times when
Christ spoke these words),[19] and that mankind would
attempt to criminalize, ostracize, judge, persecute,
and at times even execute those very people who once
had been as socially accepted as everyone else? Could
he have been speaking more to *us* in modern times
than to his listeners that day – telling us once and for
all what Greek and Roman society had understood all

---

[16] As stated in Jeremiah 1:5,

Before I formed you in the womb I knew you...

[17] See Matthew 19:11
[18] See Matthew 19:12
[19] See note 20 on the following page.

along – that some *are* born gay and are nonetheless still God's intended children, and that the world should accept this as a fact of life?

# Christ taught us not to be prejudicial

Although *homophobia* was not as widespread amongst Roman and Greek cultures during the time of Christ as it is today throughout the world – as homosexuality was not "an issue" in those times, and was for the most part widely accepted as a normal part of life[20] – homophobia nonetheless still existed to a lesser degree.  As such, Christ explicitly *condemned* any form of anti-gay speech coming from those – whether religious or not – who went around hating, judging, and condemning gay people.   In fact, he was so adamant and intolerant towards anyone who insulted another due to one's innate and God-given sexuality, that he stated that the repercussions of displaying such hatred were dire indeed from God's perspective. In affect, Christ actively *defended* the homosexuals of his time, as well as gays and lesbians of today, by his clear stance *against* any form of homophobia-borne action, speech, or hate-crime.

---

[20] In fact, homosexuality was widely practiced in ancient Mesopotamia, and there is no evidence that this was ever frowned upon by either society or the early Christians in general.  See Vern L. Bullough, *Sexual Variance in Society and History*. University of Chicago Press, 1980; Gwendolyn Leick, *Sex and Eroticism in Mesopotamian Literature*. Routledge, 2003; and Raymond J. (as in n. 3 on page 399).

In MATTHEW 5:22, Christ clearly states that we must not insult someone by calling him a *raca*. For a long time, no one knew what this word meant, to where it now often shows up as an untranslated word in our modern Bible but which is usually noted as meaning "empty head", "good for nothing", or "you fool" – as scholars initially thought it might have been a derivative of the Hebrew *reqa*, which means the above.

But in 1934, an Egyptian papyrus dating back to 257 BC and written in Greek *contained* the word *rachas*, meaning *kinaidos* – or "faggot" as the closest parallel term in today's modern English slang. Many scholars now accept this to have been the true meaning of what Christ referred to as *raca* – thus making it clear that he was teaching against one being homophobic either through action or by one's spoken word.[21]

This makes a lot of sense if we consider the fact that *none* of Christ's followers who had *specifically* known and walked with him during his earthly ministry *ever* mention anything derogatory about homosexuals or the subject of homosexuality in their writings... ever! Even Phillip himself never raised an issue when he met and explained the Gospel to the Ethiopian eunuch in ACTS 8:26-40, and wholeheartedly considered him to have become a *genuine* and complete child of Christ without ever even lifting an eyelid regarding what his sexuality might or might not have been. Essentially, one's sexuality was never

---

[21] See also Warren Johansson, *Whosoever Shall Say to His Brother, Racha*. Volume 10, Cabirion, 1984; and Wayne Dynes, *Racha*. The Encyclopedia of Homosexuality edition. Garland, 1990.

an issue in any way by the early Christians – thanks in part to Christ's having made clear, once and for all, that this is *not* an issue for God, who Himself created homosexuals to be who they are. It must therefore never be an 'issue' for us as well as *genuine* followers of Christ.

# What about Sodom and Gomorrah?

Another of the most cited sections of scripture in the Judeo-Christian Bible that is *deliberately* misused by those arguing against homosexuality is the story of Sodom and Gomorrah in GENESIS 19.[22] But the truth is, Sodom and Gomorrah had absolutely *nothing whatsoever* to do with homosexuality, and everything to do with the citizens of these two cities' blood thirst for violence, inhospitality, and an outright arrogance and resulting neglect for the poor. The Bible itself says so in various places, both in the Old *and* New Testament – yes, specifically in reference to Sodom and Gomorrah – without mentioning homosexuality in one single reference. Essentially, attempting to provide an argument against homosexuality by using the story of Sodom and Gomorrah has turned out to be one of the most bold-faced and shamefully dirty lies that has been fed to the world in modern times.

The account of Sodom and Gomorrah revolves around the story of Lot, who had migrated to Sodom

---

[22] See also Philo Thelos, *God is not a Homophobe: An Unbiased Look at Homosexuality in the Bible*. Trafford Publishing, 2006.

and who was visited by two angels. The people of Sodom, believing Lot's guests to be spies, gathered outside his door and demanded that the angels be brought out of his property, some of whom then stated "...so we can have relations with them." Lot told them he would give them his two virgin daughters instead – something he would not have done if the mob had been *entirely* composed of gay people, obviously.[23]   The crowd was struck with blindness, and Sodom and Gomorrah were eventually destroyed. What those using this story in a weak attempt at arguing against homosexuality fail to mention are the following points:

1. All scriptures referring to this story that are strewn throughout the Bible in both the Old *and* New Testaments which specifically list the actual sins committed by Sodom and Gomorrah never mention *nor imply* homosexuality in any manner whatsoever. For example, EZEKIEL 16:49-50 states:

   NOW THIS WAS THE SIN OF YOUR SISTER SODOM: SHE AND HER DAUGHTERS WERE ARROGANT, OVERFED AND UNCONCERNED; THEY DID NOT HELP THE POOR AND NEEDY. THEY WERE HAUGHTY[24] AND DID DETESTABLE THINGS BEFORE ME.[25]

---

[23] Genesis 19:8

[24] In other words, full of pride and arrogance.

[25] "Detestable things" being in reference to the worship of idols and false gods – as is what is commonly referred to as detestable acts within the Old Testament almost exclusively; and as is inferred through the context of the story of these two cities.

Modern biblical scholars now agree that the Judeo-Christian Bible makes it very clear that the *specific* sins committed by these two cities were arrogance, an appetite for violence, not being hospitable to foreign guests, the worship of idols, and being *ambivalent* to the needs of the poor – as seen here, and as other references clearly show as we read on – again, *nothing* whatever to do with homosexuality.

2. ISAIAH 1:10-17 further affirms the above, especially in regards to the worship of idols, the *violent* ways of life and atmosphere in the two cities, and their neglect of the less-fortunate, in stating:

   HEAR THE WORD OF THE LORD, YOU RULERS OF SODOM; GIVE EAR TO THE INSTRUCTION OF OUR GOD, YOU PEOPLE OF GOMORRAH. WHAT ARE YOUR MULTIPLIED SACRIFICES TO ME? BRING YOUR WORTHLESS OFFERINGS NO LONGER. INCENSE IS AN ABOMINATION TO ME...I HATE YOUR NEW MOON FESTIVALS AND YOUR APPOINTED FEASTS...YOUR HANDS ARE COVERED WITH BLOOD... LEARN TO DO GOOD; SEEK JUSTICE, RESCUE THE OPPRESSED, DEFEND THE ORPHAN, PLEAD FOR THE WIDOW.[26]

3. Furthermore, the sin of arrogance is *especially* emphasized throughout more than *any* other sin in reference to the story of Sodom and Gomorrah, as again seen in ZEPHANIAH 2:9-10:

   SURELY MOAB WILL BE LIKE SODOM, AND THE SONS OF AMMON LIKE GOMORRAH...THIS THEY WILL HAVE IN RETURN FOR THEIR PRIDE, BECAUSE THEY HAVE

---

[26] Isaiah 1:10-17 [abridged]

TAUNTED AND BECOME ARROGANT AGAINST THE PEOPLE OF THE LORD OF HOSTS.[27]

4. Even Jesus affirms that the sin of Sodom was inhospitality and the deliberate rejection of God, as he states the same when he was sending out his disciples to preach the Good News of the arrival of the Kingdom of Heaven on earth; where he says:

BUT WHENEVER YOU ENTER A TOWN AND THEY DO NOT WELCOME YOU, GO OUT INTO ITS STREETS AND SAY, "EVEN THE DUST OF YOUR TOWN THAT CLINGS TO OUR FEET, WE WIPE OFF IN PROTEST AGAINST YOU. YET KNOW THIS: THE KINGDOM OF GOD HAS COME NEAR." I TELL YOU, ON THAT DAY IT WILL BE MORE TOLERABLE FOR SODOM THAN FOR THAT TOWN.[28]

5. Finally, JUDE 7 in the New Testament talks about how Sodom and Gomorrah were destroyed for their people having gone after *"strange flesh"* – biblical and linguistic scholars agreeing this being in reference to the flesh of *angels* that Jude mentions in the previous verse, and clearly not the flesh of man. This because the flesh of man is *not* considered to be "strange flesh" – or *different, other* flesh – as defined in the Greek[29] in contextual reference to the flesh of another human. Thus Jude is referring here to humans seeking to have sex with angels – as seen in the story of Lot which it directly refers to – and thus having nothing *whatsoever* to do with any

---

[27] Zephaniah 2:9-10

[28] Luke 10:10-12

[29] See Foundation (as in n. 1 on page 338) p. 1532.

form of sexual behavior between humans at all – homosexual or otherwise.

There is therefore absolutely *no* mention – neither in these verses, nor anywhere else in the Judeo-Christian Bible either directly or implied – of homosexuality having *ever* been a reason for the destruction of the two cities of Sodom and Gomorrah in any way, shape, or form – plain and simple. In affect, Sodom and Gomorrah's destruction, according to the Bible, had *nothing* at all to do with homosexuality – and everything to do with arrogant *pride*, a blood-thirst for *violence*, *inhospitality* to foreigners, the *neglect* of the genuinely needy, and a deliberate rejection of God.

As such, those who eagerly use the story of Sodom and Gomorrah to their homophobic ends are simply changing scripture to suit their *own* biases – and deceive many in the process.[30] Unfortunately, many who listen to such unsupported claims take these bold-faced lies at face value, believing that this is what the Judeo-Christian Bible truly states without bothering to look such assertions up for themselves – many of whom become unintending stumbling blocks to gay people who *genuinely* seek to come to Christ – or simply just turn them off altogether as they know they cannot change who they are and have always been. Can a heterosexual change into a homosexual? Of course not. And so the homosexual believer is put into a dilemma, where they finally feel that the only way they can deal with it is to quit the faith, and all because of the very Christians who, once eager to win

---

[30] See also Daniel A. Helminiak, *What the Bible Really Says About Homosexuality*. Alamo Square Distribution, 2000.

them over, soon make them stumble away from the faith through unnecessary guilt and overwhelming shame and hopelessness. That is not the Gospel of Christ. And it is God that such militant attackers of homosexuality will have to answer to some day. For as Christ has said:

> If any of you put a stumbling block before one of these little ones who believe in me, it would be better for you if a great millstone were fastened around your neck and you were drowned in the depth of the sea. Woe to the world because of stumbling blocks! Occasions for stumbling are bound to come, but woe to the one by whom the stumbling block comes!
> MATTHEW 18:6-7

Of course, most Christians who sincerely live in a gray area in relation to the issue of homosexuality are not intending stumbling blocks – but those who know full well what the Bible *genuinely* states (and does *not* state) about the issue and continue to judge, condemn, ostracize, and attempt to change homosexual believers in order to appease their own personal biases are indeed intentional stumbling blocks to the same. God help them.

But in regards to Sodom and Gomorrah: by simply considering *just how* the fateful story of these two cities has been widely used to brainwash billions into assuming that the Judeo-Christian Bible is against homosexuality should be enough to make it plain to see that some have simply lied to the world, and that neither Christ, the Bible, nor any individuals written about within it were ever against homosexuality at all. Don't worry, we'll get to Leviticus and Paul further on in this Appendix.

The common lie being put forth on a global scale that homosexuality is "wrong" or against God is a modern-day deception and divisive stumbling block (much like the erroneous arguments against pre-marital sex for heterosexuals)[31] frequently repeated by otherwise honest and well-intending people, and oftentimes *intentionally* told by those with ulterior motives designed to deceive the world towards their own man-made religious dogmas and away from God and the true faith of the Gospel of Christ – a faith that was *never* intended to become an organized form of religion in the first place, but which has always been – from its inception – a way of life that is centered on faith, hope, and love for God, for one's neighbor, and for oneself... though the greatest of these *is* love – as Paul himself rightly stated.[32] This, the faith that shall *never* be marred by pseudo-saints and television heroes – and that the Gates of Hell shall *never* prevail against, as said by Christ in MATTHEW 16:18.

In short, Sodom and Gomorrah had nothing to do with homosexuality, and the Old Testament does *not* prohibit one from being gay or lesbian... despite what you might have already heard.

---

[31] See Appendix B on page 397 regarding what the Bible has to say about premarital sex as clearly distinguished from adultery.

[32] As Paul puts it:

> ... and now faith, hope, and love abide, these three; and the greatest of these is love.   [I Corinthians 13:13]

# What of Leviticus?

But let us *also* consider the 613 Old Testament laws
that comprised the Torah's *Holiness Code* as distinguished and separate from the Ten Commandments[33]
– the latter of which by the way having absolutely
nothing whatsoever to say about homosexuality. Said
laws – which outlaw such things as the mixing of
certain types of garments, the mixing of different
seeds, and the forbidding of having oxen working
alongside donkeys – *also* included the forbidding of
what *some* might argue to have specifically referred
to as either same-sex intercourse[34] (most likely to
do with sexual rites – as having at the time been
performed during rituals of idol worship by pagans
living amongst the Hebrews when reading the same
in context, as will be further explained herein)[35] –
or alternatively to the act of a man having sex with
another man who was *already married* to a woman
when taken in context with proper Hebrew language
interpretation in addition to said scripture's context
to time, place, and culture.

Specific sexual guidelines to do with *heterosexual*
sex were also given in the aforementioned Holiness
Code of the Old Testament – some of which do not
apply in this day and age as most people would
agree,[36] even though those against homosexuality

---

[33] See Exodus 20:1-17.

[34] See Leviticus 18:22 and 20:13.

[35] See note 45 on page 464.

[36] Such as the prohibition against having sex with a
woman while she is menstruating (including sharing the
bed with her – regardless of whether sex is involved during
this time) – as in Leviticus 18:19 and 20:18 – and advice

will be happy to quote from the aforementioned rule regarding what they see as referring to homosexuality while at the same time disregarding all of the other Holiness Code laws – in addition to other rules to do with such things as the mixing of man's and woman's clothing,[37] taking the same woman back after having divorced and re-married,[38] the outlawing of women defending their husbands in violent quarrels by grabbing hold of the enemy's genitals, possessing different weights of measure[39]... and so the list goes on. Yet the breaking of *any* of these seemingly minor legalistic rules was described in the Old Testament as being "ritualistically unclean" (and *not* as "abominations" – as has *often* been mistranslated); and many of these regulations, as aforementioned, reflected on pagan temple ritualistic practices involving idol worship as having been commonly performed by the Hebrew people's pagan and idol-worshiping neighbors[40] – the critical importance of taking scripture into proper context to time, place, and to whom the text in question refers or is being written to.[41] As has clearly been put:

---

not to touch a woman when she discharges from her period for seven days (Leviticus 15:19 & 24). See also Appendix B on page 397; as well as the next section in this appendix – both detailing how Christianity as a faith – as opposed to as the organized form of religion that it is today – was always very liberal in regards to sexual differences and varieties of sexual acts in general (both gay and straight forms).

[37] Deuteronomy 22:5
[38] Deuteronomy 24:1-4
[39] Deuteronomy 25:11-16
[40] Leviticus 18:22, and similarly in 20:13.
[41] See also note 18 on page 65.

The Scriptures recorded Israel's distinctive faith and culture, and no where is this more true than in the books that dealt with the law, including Leviticus...Following the exile...as the people moved out into foreign lands among other nations...keeping a strong identity mattered for the sake of their survival as a nation...While there's no condemnation of homosexual acts in the Torah outside the Holiness Code; Deuteronomy forbids Israel from giving it's children – male and female – to serve as cult prostitutes (23:18-19). In all probability there were both male and female cult prostitutes which would explain the prohibition of homosexual acts in Leviticus 18–20, and therefore were a male to lie with a man as with a woman the lines of distinction between the practices of the Gentile nations and the nation of Israel would be blurred. The issue wasn't about homo-erotic behavior in and of itself in this regard but about abstaining from anything that could appear to mirror Canaanite rituals dedicated to gods other than the God of Israel.[42]

Clearly, the early Jewish-Christians understood these passages in LEVITICUS to mean what they are: a separation of the early Jewish people from social norms existing within pagan cultures surrounding them, and not the casting of judgment or taking a stance – one way or the other – on the morality of homosexuality itself. Context, time of writing, and to whom a passage is being written to is everything – if such things are not considered on examining scripture, one winds up with 21st Century homophobes within religious

---

[42] As in Anita Cadonau-Huseby, *Leviticus: Pagans, Purity, and Property*. WordPress, 2008.

institutions who become a stumbling block to God for *millions* of people.

Furthermore, in regards to the word "abomination" as used in the referred-to LEVITICUS passages, a favorite citation as made by those who today claim that the Bible states that "homosexuality is an *abomination*" due to the aforementioned – this is a loaded and very much *unbiblical* phrase as having only been used in modern times and utilized to ferment bias for sincere and unaware Christian listeners in the hopes that they will come *against* their homosexual neighbors, even though the Bible *never* uses such a term to describe homosexuality at all. Some English Biblical editions translate the word used (that being *toevah*) to mean "abomination", which is a total misinterpretation from the original Hebrew used in both Leviticus and Deuteronomy. In fact, the correct Hebraic interpretation of *toevah* literally translates to "ritualistically unclean". This is because the "Holiness Code" (the six-hundred and thirteen aforementioned rules found in the Jewish Torah which include the above Old Testament books) was written to set the Jewish people *apart* from the pagan cultures and their respective rituals – deeming said pagan practices as *unclean* – at a particular time in history, and this in order that the Hebrew people would hold to strict guidelines as to their *own* Hebraic practices.

As such, the Hebraic word *Toevah* does not in fact mean "abomination", but rather "ritualistic uncleanliness"... as is *also* the case in the forbiddence to eat pork as likewise specifically instructed *for the Hebrew people alone* at the time – though Christ declared *all* foods clean [see MARK 7:19]. In contrast, the Hebrew word *zimah*, which is also translated as "abomination", and which means "intrinsic evil" or "evil by nature", could have been used in the aforementioned passages in Leviticus *including* the one as deemed to be referring to homosexuality, and yet it *never* was. As such, it is clear that, even when these passages in the Old Testament mention male-on-male intercourse, they in fact do *not* call it an "abomination", but rather an act that is "ritualistically unclean", and this *specifically* for the Hebrews at that particular time in history... despite what you may have already been told by some in Christian media, in *some* churches, and the like. Even so, LEVITICUS 18:22 and 20:13 – the *only* Old Testament passages that could legitimately be claimed to be speaking of homosexuality directly – seem to refer *not* to homosexual acts in and of themselves, but rather to either homosexual practices during the worship of idols (which was common at the time in pagan practices), or alternatively to a male having sex with another male who is *already* married, as we will soon see.

These rules that became redundant in their applicability to everyday life millennia ago are mentioned herein because many people in modern times will gladly and without any genuine in-depth examination use the *one* singular rule from the aforementioned "Holiness Code" that at first glance could easily be taken to be in reference to homosexuality – within the long list of the above six-hundred and thirteen others, none of which ever mentioning or inferring anything to do with homosexuality *at all* – which states that "...thou shalt not lie with mankind, as with womankind: it is ritualistically unclean"[43] – to argue against homosexuality... even though, again, all the other rules that have been mentioned were *also* considered to be "ritualistically unclean" – *including* rules governing heterosexuality, such as the forbidding of a husband's having sex with his wife if she is menstruating, and to keep away from her for seven days thereafter.[44]

Yet focusing on the aforementioned rule while ignoring the rest is to take the statement *completely* out of context to all other surrounding rules that were *all* clearly meant – as a unified set of decrees within the Hebraic Holiness Code – to set the Hebrews *apart* from said idolatry-worshiping practices of those living amongst them[45] – these practices having been rampantly widespread amongst the people the Hebrews shared their social environment with at the time in which these edicts were imposed. To state that the rule that *might* refer to homosexuality is applicable and should be followed today, while ignoring the remaining 612 rules, is to pick and choose in a manner that will support one's personal bias against homosex-

---

[43] As in Leviticus 18:22. Some translations have in modern times been brave enough to erroneously translate "ritualistically unclean" into "abomination" instead – this error in translation by otherwise competent scholars being an abomination in and of itself. See main text above for the distinction and explanation as to why the translation of the Hebrew into the word "abomination" is not linguistically faithful to the Hebraic translation when in fact the Hebrew *toevah* literally translations into "ritualistically unclean".

[44] See Leviticus 15:19-24.

[45] See Milgrom (as in n. 45 on page 429). See also note 40 on page 460.

uality – which is hypocritical, deceptive, and a grave and deliberate intention to make sincere homosexual believers – as well as *potential* believers – stumble on their way to Christ, who himself liberated us from following these laws so that we would be saved by God's unwarranted grace towards us alone. Why not follow *every* rule in the Holiness Code if a single one demands observation by some in today's circles of demanding and weighty religious legalism?

But aside from all of this, there is in addition legitimate doubt as to whether the LEVITICUS verses even *intend* to refer to "homosexuality" in and of itself as the primary subject being talked about – and this primarily due to the literal Hebraic (as well as Hebrew to Greek) translations of "as with womankind", which might also be translated as either *wife* or as "woman's [*marriage*] bed", to where some believe this verse simply states that two men must not sleep together (sexually) if one of them is married to a woman – which would of course constitute adultery by its very definition[46] – as sleeping with someone who is *already* married is by definition considered adultery, irrespective of whether the participants are of the same or opposite sexes.

As such, this reasoning suggests that what the LEVITICUS verses actually do is forbid male-on-male adultery *only if* one of the men is married to a woman. Why else would the term "wife" or "woman" appear here – why not just state that a male should not lie with a male, and stop their? For this reason, many now feel this verse has absolutely nothing to do with

---

[46] See also Appendix B on page 397 regarding the definition of *adultery*.

any moral judgement on homosexuality whatsoever. Nevertheless, whatever the true meaning, this verse was written as part of the six-hundred-and-thirteen other laws making up the Torah's "Holiness Code" for a specific people at a specific time, and does not in the least seem to intend on making any moral judgments about homosexuality in and of itself when it – as well as heterosexual sex – is not being done during pagan rituals of idol worship or in the context of adultery.

Again, to choose to take *one* rule to be applicable today – one of the over six hundred odd in the Holiness Code that has *as a whole* been made null and void thousands of years ago by God's own choosing – and yet not keep all of the *rest* of said decrees, is to commit religious hypocrisy, and to choose pious legalism and the traditions of man over and above the commandments of God. For, as Christ himself *clearly* said to the religious leaders of his day:

> Isaiah prophesied rightly about you hyp-ocrites, as it is written,'THIS PEOPLE HONORS ME WITH THEIR LIPS, BUT THEIR HEARTS ARE FAR FROM ME; IN VAIN DO THEY WORSHIP ME, TEACH-ING HUMAN PRECEPTS AS DOCTRINES.' You abandon the commandment of God and hold to human tradition... You have a fine way of rejecting the commandment of God in order to keep your tradition!... thus making void the word of God through your tradition that you have handed on. And you do many things like this.
>
> MARK 7:6-9 & 13

For even Paul *himself* explicitly stated that we are *no longer bound* by the Holiness Code – or "the law" –

because he who comes to God and lives in Him lives *by* faith, and faith alone...not by ancient Hebraic religious rule and regulation. In fact, when he says this, he is actually quoting from the *very same* chapter of LEVITICUS in the Old Testament that *also* includes the aforementioned rule which at first glance seems to refer to homosexuality...and Paul states that such rules are *not* applicable any longer! Paul carefully explains – while quoting from *the very same* chapter of LEVITICUS (particularly 18:5) that mentions the passage in question – this the chapter that also states that the Hebrew people would live by the law – that we are *no longer bound* by the law [the Holiness Code], *nor* do we live by it any longer; but that we live by faith, and faith alone – as he states:

> For all who rely on the works of the law are under a curse; for it is written, "CURSED IS EVERYONE WHO DOES NOT OBSERVE AND OBEY ALL THE THINGS WRITTEN IN THE BOOK OF THE LAW" [*i.e.* LEVITICUS]. Now it is evident that no one is justified before God by the law, for "THE ONE WHO IS RIGHTEOUS WILL LIVE BY FAITH." But the law does not rest on faith; on the contrary, "WHOEVER DOES THE WORKS OF THE LAW WILL LIVE BY THEM." Christ redeemed us from the curse of the law by becoming a curse for us – for it is written, "CURSED IS EVERYONE WHO HANGS ON A TREE" – in order that in Christ Jesus the blessing of Abraham might come to the Gentiles [*all non-Jewish people*], so that we might receive the promise of the Spirit *through faith*. [GALATIANS 3:10-14]

So please do not let someone try to state that homosexuality is wrong because the Old Testament says so...they are either well-intended, sincere, but very misinformed about what the Bible itself actually says; or if they truly *know* scripture, are being very careless indeed with God's word for their *own* biased ends – and likely don't care *who* they run over or become a stumbling block to.

But as a friend once explained in regards to her own inhospitable exclusion from religion, when she finally first realized after two decades that of the *many* religious voices she had heard during her teenage years against her being lesbian, that *none* of these voices were ever from God – she states that one day she simply heard Him say – in whatever manner He may talk to us all – "*I* never said those things to you – *they* did". Likewise, if you *are* homosexual, don't let those who are more than happy to repeatedly quote one sentence in the Holiness Code, while not being willing to therefore follow *all* of the other edicts themselves because they *know* very well that these laws are *not* applicable to anyone in this day and age – make you stumble on your path to God. Their words are *not* God's words...*He* never said those things to you, *They* did.

Furthermore, Christ *himself* described these rules as null and void, unnecessary, legalistic, and having come from the "traditions of man"[47] – or traditions of *organized* religion – and that we are not bound by them any longer – to where we are now free to come to God *personally* and *directly* as He *Himself* draws us[48] without following or adhering to religious, traditional, and legalistic regulations whatsoever.[49]

---

[47] As in Mark 7:6-9 & 13.
[48] See Chapter 10 on page 187.
[49] See also note 19 on page 409

# And what of Paul's statements?

The Bible verses from the New Testament – a mere three in total – that are often misused by many in a very weak attempt at arguing against homosexuality, are all written *exclusively* by Paul alone, and *not* by any of Christ's apostles – nor by anyone else that had *physically* walked *with* Christ during his ministry for that matter – these verses being Romans 1:27, I Corinthians 6:9, and I Timothy 1:10.

Again, these three verses all having been written *solely* by Paul, someone who had never walked with Christ during his earthly ministry – but who turned to Christ years *after* his resurrection. It is interesting to note that you never find any of Christ's apostles such as Peter, John, James – nor any *other* early Christians for that matter – speaking against homosexuality in any way... *ever*.   Not to say that Paul did so, as you may conclude on reading this section – but this is nonetheless a noteworthy fact to mention.   For if homosexuality *had* been an issue to the earliest Christians, would it not have been mentioned by *other* writers of the New Testament – *especially* by those who actually lived, breathed, and walked with Christ all the way through to his crucifixion and resurrection?

For if homosexuality *had* been an issue either for Christ or for the early Christians, surely there would have been clear and *decisive* statements made to this affect... which of course is not the case, or else much of today's modernized forms of fundamentalism would be using more than a mere *three* passages as exclusively written by Paul to attempt to argue against homosexuality in the first place. Apparently they cannot find any more than these in the New Testament, and neither can I... plain and simple.

And although a very small number of modernized, *post*-1900 Bible translations attempt to *erroneously* place the word "homosexual" within two of these three verses for reasons soon to be explained in detail, there were only less than a handful of words that existed at the time of Paul's writings that were available to him that could be translated into today's English word "homosexual" or "homosexuality". Such words included the Greek *arrenomanes* and *erastes*. And yet neither Paul, nor any other New Testament writers, ever used *any* one of these – *ever*.

The same goes for the original Hebrew scriptures of the Old Testament, by the way. No such words were *ever* used. In short, translations that are faithful to either the original Hebrew or Greek manuscripts of *both* Testaments *never* use the words "homosexual" or "homosexuality" – because these words don't even *exist* in the Judeo-Christian Bible in *any* way whatsoever – save for the word *eunuch* as also referable to homosexuality, as explained from the beginning of this appendix as having been used by Christ in MATTHEW 19:12 to publicly *affirm* that homosexuals are in fact *born* gay, and must therefore *not* be condemned for their natural-born sexual preference.

For even prominent biblical scholars, many of whom are not particularly "pro-gay", have nonetheless now publicly *admitted* that the use of words such as "homosexual", "sodomite", and such are but complete *mistranslations* of these verses[50] – again, as only found in a mere *handful* of modern versions. One cannot, therefore, *legitimately* state that scripture somehow blanketly "denounces" homosexuality – it is simply not true. And one cannot use Paul as a weapon against homosexuality when even his very *own* choice of words never included well-known phrases available to him in his time that would clearly refer to the same, as will be further examined herein.

In addition, the Greek terms Paul deliberately *chose* to use in I CORINTHIANS 6:9, and again in I TIMOTHY 1:10 – the two other passages by Paul that many again erroneously misuse as "clobber passages" to argue against homosexuality in modern times – were *malakoi* and *arsenokoitai* – again, these having nothing to do with homosexuality in and of itself as a moral issue. These words have at times been *incorrectly* (one might even say recklessly, or haphazardly) been interpreted to mean "effeminate", in the case of the term *malakoi*; and "homosexual" or "sodomite", in the case of *arsenokoit* (these English terms having not even *existed* until the 17th Century) in a small number of modern English Bible translations since 1946 (which will be discussed in more depth herein) within these Paulinian verses that short-list certain sins that were especially relevant in Greek and Roman societies at the time of Paul's writing – these including the worship of idols, rape, incest, murder, theft, coveting, fraud, and kidnapping.

---

[50] See also Dr. Gordon D. Fee, *The New International Commentary on the New Testament, The First Epistle To The Corinthians*. Eerdmans, 1987; as well as note 18 on page 65.

Yet let me digress for a moment here before looking further into the true meaning of the two Greek
words used by Paul from the above verses and state
that – due to the wholly ambiguous meanings of these
two specific verses as relating to the issue at hand,
Christianity in the form of a modern-day *organized*
form of religion – as opposed to as a sincere personal
faith that comes from within and that it was always
meant to be *from the beginning* – has in current
times *become* one of the greatest stumbling blocks to
millions of innocent gay and lesbian people who yearn
to turn to Christ in their personal faith – in spirit
and in truth. And that is why this topic is included
herein – as the Gospel in accordance to the teachings
of Christ *never* condemns homosexuality in any way
whatsoever. Again, as Christ told "the religious" of
*his* time:

> But woe to you, scribes and Pharisees, hyp-
> ocrites! For you lock people out of the Kingdom
> of Heaven. For you do not go in yourselves,
> and when others are going in, you stop them.
> MATTHEW 23:13

Modern Christianity *as* an organized form of religion
is in many instances behaving in exactly the same
way that the scribes and Pharisees who Christ was
speaking to did when he made this statement. As
such, it is simply nothing more than a hijacking of the
Gospel of Christ by some to have very liberally chosen
to reinterpret textual context having nothing to do
with homosexuality, and to attempt to forcefully imply
negative spiritual and moral connotations against gay
and lesbian people of today. And as a result, many
uninformed people who cannot be bothered to actually

*investigate* for themselves what Paul meant when writing his passages, have oftentimes now become *unintended* stumbling blocks and spiritual maligners of the works of the Holy Spirit on gays and lesbians of today (created by God as who they are). And spiritual – as well as oftentimes *physical* – blood is on the hands of the more knowledgeable and *intending* modern-day religious leaders for their deliberate and very unfair incitements against homosexual people[51] – and this not just in their actions against them, but also in their crafty and slick manipulations against *heterosexual* people as well on giving them burdens hard to bear[52] in the form of guilt trips and biblical misinformation regarding such things as premarital sex[53] – and they will have to give an account to God for their unashamed prejudices regarding homophobia (*and* heterophobia, if you will) when it's all said and done.

Anyhow, as we go back to examining what the words *malakoi* and *arsenokoit* refer to in the other two aforementioned Paulinian verses – let us first take *malakoi*, which is *only* found in I CORINTHIANS 6:9 within the small group of *three* New Testament "clobber passages" – the word *sometimes* being completely mistranslated as "effeminate" in *some* English Bibles. This Greek word actually means "soft", such as in reference to "soft clothing" as used consistently in

---

[51] See also Rod Brannum-Harris, *The Pharisees Amongst Us: How the anti-gay campaign unmasks the religious perpetrators of the campaign to be modern-day Pharisees*. BookSurge Publishing, 2006.

[52] See note 13 on page 130.

[53] See also Appendix B on page 397; which thoroughly examines the issue of premarital sex.

Greek texts, and nothing more. The word is *never* used in original manuscripts of the Greek New Testament – *not anywhere* – to mean homosexuality at all... not *ever*.

Many now agree that what Paul was describing in the list of sins in I CORINTHIANS 6:9 when using the word "soft" – or *malakoi* – was an attitude of "lazy and low morals" – in essence an *ambivalent attitude* towards true evils done against humanity – and *not* homosexuality in any manner whatsoever – ambivalent morals being one of the undesirable characteristics that he was describing in a person when also including other sins such as theft, coveting, jealousy, fraud, and such within the aforementioned list of sins that he was writing against.[54]

I suppose one might therefore say – along these lines of reasoning – that a religious person who either supports or acquiesces to *homophobia* against gay people – or to *heterophobia* against our straight youth with misleading and oppressive talks against premarital sex[55] and the brainwashing-induced and unscriptural burden as forced upon by such things as so-called "chastity rings" – and this with the resultant undue pressure to marry, to where listeners are more likely to marry the *wrong* person due to sexual repression and desperation, especially when they already have *more than enough* to worry about in what they face as young Christians in today's ever-growing anti-Christian society without having to *additionally* deal with such unscriptural nonsense – is

---

[54] See also John Boswell, *Christianity, Social Tolerance, and Homosexuality*. University of Chicago Press, 1980.

[55] See also Appendix B on page 397, which deals with this topic in detail.

him- or herself being very *malakoi* indeed, and would
be well advised to repent from these ways before they
*themselves* become active stumbling blocks (either in
action or through their own *inaction*) towards anyone
– regardless of sexuality – who seeks to come to God
and maintain a personal faith in spirit and in truth
within the *real* world in which we live in.

Christianity *cannot afford* to continue to be wrongly
*perceived* as a sexual downer – which in reality it
is not and was never intended to be – that turns
many people off who come across its path when it
is at times so *flagrantly* misrepresented by radical
followers. Certainly *most* Christians are not like this,
but the very few who are are those that the media
simply *loves* to focus on in order to attempt to give
Christianity as a faith a bad name.

Nevertheless, the outside observer will see this on
television and on Internet sites and blanketly *assume*
that *all* Christians are simply a bunch of anti-sex
prudes – which, although completely and utterly false,
only creates more and more of a challenge for good,
sensible, intelligent, genuine, and balanced Christian
people to try and prove the media wrong. Much like
the incomprehensible and heinous terrorist acts done
by few Muslims. Because the media is focused on
the radicals, the outside observer will again wrongly
assume that *all* Muslims throughout the world are
like this, which again is untrue. Likewise, as is
oftentimes the case in Christianity, they *themselves*
constitute most of the victims of atrocious acts as
committed by their very own fellow but radicalized
sharers of their religion.

But as we delve even deeper into Paul's statements, we can see that the word *arsenokoit*, used *only*

in two verses of the entire Bible[56] – and these again *both* written by Paul in *two* of the three New Testament "clobber passages" mentioned above – has been clearly mistranslated in *very few* versions in modern times simply as "homosexual", which as stated before is a descriptive noun that many scholars now agree in reality had to do *not* with homosexuality as a sexual behavior or of same-sex attraction, but rather with an injustice done *against* a homosexual – hence its literal translation from the Greek to the English language being "trader of homosexual slavery"[57] ... and *not* simply "homosexual" nor "homosexuality" in and of itself as whom one has been born to become.

---

[56] I Corinthians 6:9, as well as I timothy 1:10.

[57] Or literally translated to "homosexual slave trader" – same meaning – hence reflecting on the challenges facing the early Christians regarding the kidnapping and enslavement of homosexuals for purposes of pagan ritualistic enjoyment or private use by those who could afford to buy a sexual slave of their choosing. Could Paul have also been concerned about the personal safety of younger homosexual Christians in the early churches, to where he uses the word arsenokoit instead of other words that would more directly mean "homosexuals"? As stated, it was common in the Greek and Roman cultures at the time for some to possess slaves exclusively for sexual exploitation, and nothing more – to where some feel Paul was specifically referring to such practices of human exploitation – which we unfortunately still see today from time to time. See Martin et al., *Meanings and Consequences. Biblical Ethics and Homosexuality*. Louisville: Westminster Press, 1996; Cantarella, *Bisexuality in the Ancient World*. Yale Press, 1992; Williams, *Roman Homosexuality : Ideologies of Masculinity in Classical Antiquity*. Oxford UP, 1999; Dover, *Greek Homosexuality*. Harvard University Press, 1989; as well as 67.

Furthermore, this very same word – *arsenokoit* – has been recorded as having been used seventy-three times throughout history in ancient non-religious (in other words, *secular*) Greek texts (and again, only *twice* by Paul in the aforementioned verses)[58] – *none* of which refer to homosexuality as a way of life in their context, but rather to the aforementioned definitions regarding sexual slavery and rape *alone*. Could Paul had had gay friends or acquaintances who had been enslaved for purposes of homosexual rape, to where he was actually *defending* homosexual victims of such crimes by condemning kidnappers and enslavers of those and others who's stories he had known about?

When interpreting scripture – as in real life – context is everything. Why do so many ignore this? Maybe in their zeal to jump to predetermined – if not biased – conclusions, they simply *ignore* context altogether – and this at the expense of the suicidal gay teenager down the road who has had enough rejection by his community, or the dead homosexual person beaten by thugs who in turn have the gall to wrongly cite scripture in their court cases after having been charged with murder in order to attempt to somehow *justify* what they have done. How will it be when *they* try doing the same in God's presence one day? Good luck to you buddy.

As such, Paul in fact *never* stated that being gay is wrong in and of itself, and could have very well been pro-actively *defending* homosexual people through these verses by, as a good Christian who loved his neighbor, condemning the acts of kidnapping and

---

[58] See full listing in TLG, *The Thesaurus Linguae Graecae*. ⟨URL: http://www.tlg.uci.edu⟩.

forced-upon enslavement of homosexuals for purposes of taking advantage of their natural sexuality with the intent at making them into sex slaves – whether for purposes of pagan idol worship within temple prostitution, or for unconsenting and forced-upon pederasty – to where Paul's statements could turn out to have been nothing more than clear-cut condemnations that actively opposed anti-gay and *homophobic* acts and crimes against homosexuals, especially as these crimes against gay people often took place in order to either supply pagan shrines with enslaved prostitutes to be exploited by both male and female participants, or alternatively to supply wealthier men with private sex slaves when they somehow could not, or would not, enter into consenting homosexual relationships.[59]

In affect, Paul never chose to use any terms whatsoever that *directly* and *clearly* refer to either gay people or to homosexuality anywhere in his writings, even though said terms were available for him to use – and this despite what we currently see in a few modern translations today in said two of the three Paulinian verses. For instance, both *arrenomanes* and *erastes* were used by Greek society at the time of the New Testament writings to refer to homosexuality, although these words are *never* found in the Bible at all.[60] If early Christian writers such as Paul – and *especially* the writers of the Gospels – genuinely *had* any inclinations against homosexuality, surely they would have made this crystal clear, and would have in addition used the *proper* contemporary terms to name

---

[59] See also note 67 on page 481.
[60] See also Dover (as in n. 57 on page 476).

it in their texts... they never did.[61]  All the authors
of the New Testament books were master writers and
did not beat around the bush when putting forth their
points of view. They were *not* stupid men in the least —
certainly not as we commonly see in modernity today.
If homosexuality had been an issue in any manner,
they would have been raving idiots not to have stated
this directly and unequivocally. Again, nothing of the
sort is found within *any* original manuscript from any
biblical record whatsoever. In short, homosexuality is
*never* condemned in scripture when actually looking
at the linguistics in the oft and erroneously used
"clobber passages".

Likewise, ROMANS 1:26-27 is the last of the remaining three Paulinian "clobber passages" in our discussion that is frequently and very much erroneously
*misused* by many to claim that Paul was against
homosexuals when he describes ritualistic practices
performed during idol worship by what many now
believe to have been the Cybelean/Attic Mystery Cult
– as well as other similar pagan cults[62] – which was
especially popular in Rome during Paul's time, and
which had already been around for a few hundred
years.  When taking this passage into context as
to what (as well as to *whom*) Paul was writing[63] –
namely that he is explaining that, although God's
existence is evident in His creation, to where his
intended audience (the church in Rome) were on a
daily basis observing many within their community

---

[61] See also note 18 on page 65 regarding the importance
of heeding attention to both context and background
knowledge.

[62] See also Appendix A on page 357.

[63] See also note 18 on page 65.

who openly and boastfully *refused* to acknowledge God as the Creator of all – much like many in the New Age and Spirituality movements of today likewise do[64] – and instead wholeheartedly worshiped the creation – namely beasts and human/animal-representative idols via violent ritualistic rape – it is in these verses where one can clearly see that Paul was speaking of the cult's violent sexual ritualistic practices performed by *both* men and women members of the Cybelean Cult alongside temple prostitutes which involved permanent bodily mutilations and disfigurements of all kinds... and *not* to homosexuality in and of itself. Even modern-day biblical scholars, such as the editors of the NRSV Study Bible, have stated in regards to this passage and the context surrounding it – the entirety of which being ROMANS 1:22-32, that:

> These verses clearly refer to Gentiles, as seen from the standpoint of Jewish horror of idolatry....[65]

As such, many now agree with the aforementioned premise that Paul was referring to sexual practices (both heterosexual as well as homosexual in nature) *specifically involving* pagan idol worship ceremonies and rituals, as seen here in the Roman Cybelean Cult at the time of Paul's writing – to where such references made by Paul have absolutely *nothing* to do with homosexuality from a moral standpoint when taken into context with the topic he was writing

---

[64] See Appendix A on page 357.

[65] As in the NRSV; Harold W. Attridge et al., editors, *The HarperCollins Study Bible, Revised Edition: New Revised Standard Version*. Harper Collins Publishers, 2006.

*specifically* about in regards to the participants and operations of this and similar pagan cults.[66]   In addition, some suggest that Paul may have been referring *exclusively* to either involuntary prostitution or the kidnapping and keeping of sex slaves via Greek pederasty[67] when forcibly coerced by the perpetrator as opposed to where a consensual relationship was involved – and not to homosexuality in and of itself *when* it does not involve the ritualistic worship of idols, violent rape, or forced-upon sexual slavery.

The aforementioned Cybelean/Attic Mystery Cult believed in two deities (Attis and Cybele) who *functionally* exchanged sexual roles within Roman mythology – to where the participants would re-enact their sexually-neutral deities' roles in order to *become* more like them – hard-core women worshipers often literally cutting off their breasts to resemble men, and men cutting off *both* their testicles *as well as* their penis in order to be more like women – and allowing willing participants to rape them to the rapist's

---

[66] See also Appendix A on page 357.

[67] This involving the forced rape, kidnapping, and enslavement of young males that would sometimes take place under Greek pederasty common at the time in Greek society – though this was not always forced nor involved unwilling slaves but for certain violent exceptions that some feel Paul might have been referring to – and which again, Paul's referring to the same in these passages would have had nothing whatever to do with any moral judgment on homosexuality in and of itself.  See Dover (as in n. 57 on page 476); William Armstrong Percy III, *Pederasty and Pedagogy in Archaic Greece*. University of Illinois Press, 1998; Robin Scroggs, *The New Testament and Homosexuality: Contextual Background for Contemporary Debate*. Fortress Press, 1983.

heart's content – while other temple prostitutes, both young males and females who were often kidnapped and forced into such temple rituals, would be used as sex slaves over and over again without their free-will or consent – though volunteers (namely *galli* priests and priestesses) were known to willingly give themselves over unreservedly to the religion as well.

Yes, this was what Paul was speaking of all along in Romans 1:18-32, when read in its *entire* context, and *not* in regards to natural homosexual acts done by consenting individuals (as we also see in nature)[68] – to

---

[68] For some of us to state that being gay is "unnatural" is to be both unaware of the science of nature, and by that naiveté, to unintentionally make ourselves into liars. For it has been proven without a shadow of a doubt in this day and age – as has been studiously observed for centuries – that many animal species, such as the male swan for instance, often develop faithful, long-term homosexual relationships that last for years, if not decades. Furthermore, there have been over one-hundred mammalian species studied where homosexuality is frequently found within their kind, including sheep – which is interesting when taken into account the fact that Christ often used sheep as illustrations to tell his parables. Likewise, at least ninety-four types of bird species are now known to engage in homosexual sex. In addition, it has been proven that up to fifteen percent of geese pairs are homosexual, and that their relationship is oftentimes monogamous – lasting for up to a decade and a half or more. Such geese have even been shown to display characteristics of grief when their same-sex partner dies. Furthermore, even lions, foxes, deer, zebras, African elephants, bears, squirrels, chipmunks, and vampire bats have been known to engage in homosexual acts. And the bottle-nose dolphin, the killer whale, the harbor seal, the Australian sea lion, and the West Indian manatee have all been shown to be

where what he referred to had to do with the exchange in sexual behavioral norms between men and women as relating to extreme psychological and physical role reversals during pagan worship rituals where *genuine* life-threatening violence and *permanent* body mutilation was involved, and not to normative and natural uses of homosexuality. Believe me, *nothing* we see today – not even within the casual browsing of hard-core porn sites in cyberspace – comes even *close* to what Paul was talking about as experienced in cults such as the Cybelean Cult... which moved sex way *beyond* pleasure and into *religious obligation* and *enslavement* – not, mind you, "pretend" enslavement or sadomasochism, but real, *genuine* enslavement – consequently taking the fun away from sex for the participants, where sex turned instead into painful and very much unpleasant *religious* duty. *That* was what Paul was referring to... nothing more, nothing less. Literary and historical context *is* everything.[69]

---

exceedingly active in homosexual activity amongst their kind. See the very revealing book Joan Roughgarden, *Evolution's Rainbow: Diversity, Gender, and Sexuality in Nature and People*. University of California Press, 2009; which deals in great and specific detail with the scientific studies revolving around this intriguing topic.

[69] See also Firmicus Maternus, *The Error of Pagan Religions*. Newman Press, 1970; Will Roscoe, *Priests of the Goddess: Gender Transgression in Ancient Religion*. The University of Chicago, 1996; Hippolytus; Alexander Roberts and James Donaldson, editors, *Refutation of All Heresies: Book V.2*. Scribners, 1903; as well as the excellent scholarly research by Jeramy Townsley, *Paul, the Goddess Religions and Queers: Romans 1:23-28*. ⟨URL: http://www.jeramyt.org/papers/paulcybl.html#_edn4⟩.

It is also interesting to note that it was not *until* 1946 that the word "homosexual" even *appears* in the aforementioned Paulinian "clobber passages" – and this being after German psychologists in the late 19th century first began using the word, to where it was eventually translated into the English language by the early 1900's, and to finally be *inappropriately* utilized within the aforementioned Paulinian passages – these verses having again been *exclusively* written by Paul alone – the word having been included in only a very small number of modern English Bible translations from 1946 until today.[70] The first of these three versions was the Revised Standard Version (RSV) in its 1946 edition, although translators of the same version later decided a more appropriate translation should be "sexual perverts" – a huge difference from the word "homosexual" – and therefore changed it again in the 1971 edition.

The New International Version (NIV) first used the word "homosexuals" in 1973, and a United Kingdom English translation (the NEB) used the word a few years later. A small number of versions that in the last decade have attempted to translate the Bible into the most *contemporary* forms of English (including street slang interspersed with bracketed additions that are no more than editorial commentaries) have recently attempted to do the same – though this being very limited in number to where any reputable translation, such as those that are focused on the literal translations from the Greek into a reader's native tongue, *never* include the words *homosexual* nor *homosexuality*...and *neither* do they

---

[70] See also Boswell (as in n. 54 on page 474).

include *sodomite* – the latter being yet another relatively *contemporary* word if one looks at it from a two-millennial standpoint (first used around the early 1600's); the word *sodomite* being just as erroneous to use as "homosexual" – especially since Paul, *again,* in reality chose to use words such as *arsenokoites* instead of words specifically referring to homosexuality that had been available to him – again, *arsenokoites* having never been previously used, and which began to be utilized by later ancient Greek texts to mean "traders in homosexual slavery", or alternatively, "traders of *sexual* slaves"[71] – the latter of which plainly not even hinting at anything to do with homosexuality at all. Assuming that Paul was referring to homosexuality in general as a lifestyle is at best an assumptive leap to a haphazard conclusion of what he was talking about if one is sincerely being faithful to linguistic analysis.

To put it plainly, Paul *never even used* the word "homosexual" or "homosexuality" – nor any other Greek, Aramaic, or Hebrew word available to him that would somehow even *infer* homosexuality in any direct manner – anywhere in his writings, plain and simple. Anyone who claims otherwise is simply not willing to heed deserved attention to linguistic analysis in regards to ancient Greek, nor to the known and well-recorded history of pagan cults and their practices.

Paul's verses had nothing at all to do with any moral passing of judgment on homosexuality in one way or another – but rather referred to exceptionally forceful and victimizing roles within certain circles at the time involving both homosexual and heterosexual

---

[71] See also note 57 on page 476.

pagan ritualistic practices. To state that Paul was giving a blanket condemnation on homosexuality is simply not being true to scripture – nor to historical context – and is essentially illogical, non-contextual, and dangerously deceptive. Yes, dangerously deceptive because of the thousands of gays and lesbians that have had to suffer at the hands of those claiming to be doing "God's work" – and this far too many times to the point of violence, ostracism, persecution, and death. After all, are we imitators of Christ, or imitators of global religions of hate? Is it that we *seek* to be like them? Are we being accurate witnesses of the Gospel of Christ, or are we tainting and maligning it with our own personal biases, prejudices, and ignorance? What would Christ say?

Yes, some people *are* born gay by God's intended purpose and design...and He does *not* make mistakes, so that sincere Christians must not try to 'change' them, but to rather accept them for who God has created them to be. Christ said so himself, as we have seen in MATTHEW 19:11-12 and as explained from the beginning of this appendix. As such, people who state that homosexuality is "curable" or "treatable", and who in addition try to force or manipulate their own homosexual children to attend courses in order to "cure" them of their sexual preference, are inadvertently persecuting Christ *himself* by being stumbling blocks to those who are meant by God to be who they are – sometimes even to the point of ultimately turning them completely off to their personal faith in Christ as a result of such well-intended ignorance. Such actions are akin to what a cult might do [see Chapter 14 on page 307]. Furthermore, they do the very same thing to straight young Christians by often imposing skewed "contracts" towards celibacy until marriage [see also Appendix B on page 397], instead of focusing on preaching the Gospel, visiting the sick and prisoner, helping the poor, and being a support to the desperate-hearted. As has rightly been said:

> Homosexual orientation has been increasingly recognized in our time as a given of human sexuality. While most people feel some sexual attraction to members of both the same and the opposite sex and, in the majority of these, attraction to the opposite sex dominates, there is a sizable minority for whom sexual attraction to persons of the same sex is a decisive shaping factor of their sexual lives. It appears that this orientation is normally inalterable and that there is no strong internal reason for the homosexual person to wish to alter it. To deny an entire class of human beings the right peaceably and without harming others to pursue the kind of sexuality that corresponds to their nature is a *perversion* of the gospel. [72]

Many in modern Christianity *must* accept this, and move on... lest they continue to be one of the *biggest* stumbling blocks towards innocent spiritual seekers of truth who want to have a personal relationship with Christ. For, as said by Jesus himself,

> Whatever you did to the least of these, you did it unto me... whatever you did *not* do to the least of these, you did *not* do unto me.
>
> MATTHEW 25:40-45

---

[72] Countryman (as in n. 2 on page 398).

Paul never condemns gays or lesbians – though even if he had, do we follow Paul, or Christ? Are we to be imitators of Paul, or imitators of Christ? Furthermore, the New Testament does *not* condemn gays and lesbians. In significant addition – not even the early Christians, nor the apostles of Christ, *ever* condemned gays and lesbians – there is no evidence whatsoever that they *ever* did.

In fact, it was not until the 4th Century AD, when the Greco-Roman Platonic philosophy began to *casually* push its way into the church, that Christianity as an *organized* form of religion – which was *never* what it was intended to ever become in the first place – began to adopt restricted views on sex in general, which over the centuries developed to where we are today.[73]  Neither the early Christians, nor Jesus, nor the Old *or* New Testament... not even Paul *himself*... had such stringent viewpoints towards sex that many Christians now erroneously have due solely to tradition and to what they hear every day in their churches. And this to the detriment of the rest of the world who has been widely misled into believing that Christianity is a "puritanical" faith. It is not, and has *never* been... not true Christianity at least.[74]

So why does much of modern Christianity do so *now*? Why does it do what is *completely* contrary to the calling of Christ and of the early churches? Does it not have *more important things* to do in this day and age – such as feeding the poor, taking care of the sick and dying, healing the broken, preaching the Gospel, and loving the outcast in action? Can it not start to re-

---

[73] See Appendix B on page 397.

[74] See Raymond J. (as in n. 3 on page 399).

prioritize its obligations on earth, and *be* the reflection of Christ that it was *meant* to be from the beginning? The time is short. Be faithful to what you have been called for. And leave meaningless man-made dogma behind.

# Today's Christian must follow Christ's example and accept homosexuals for who they are

To the believer – our dogma is the power of the blood of Christ, the love of an unambiguous Father and Friend, and the meaning of *Truth* in a world where deceptions of every kind have oftentimes stolen the rightful place of justice and mercy... and *not* religiosity, man-made tradition, nor the condemnation of the innocent. For as Christ unequivocally said:

> But if you had known what this means, "I desire mercy, and not a sacrifice", you would *not* have condemned the innocent. [MT 12:7]

Organized religion must stop deceiving the masses into thinking that Judaism and Christianity is anti-gay as based on their scriptures, as this is a lie without any solid foundation to cause confusion, turmoil, repression, and in extreme cases even violence towards innocent homosexual men and women throughout the globe – many of whom are in complete and truthful love with God their Father, but who have been rough-housed, bullied, and continuously prevented from having a fulfilling relationship with their Creator by the very ones who claim to *know* God... and from being who they were *meant* to be by God's own will and deliberate design.

Yet the unconditional love of Christ will *never* forsake nor condemn these, his very own outcasts and persecuted children of modernity, religion, and strife – whatever the "religious" and the world might say... or do.

> We reject [homosexuals], treat them as pariahs, and push them outside our church communities, and thereby we negate the consequences of their baptism and ours. We make them doubt that they are the children of God, and this must be nearly the ultimate blasphemy. We blame them for something that is becoming increasingly clear they can do little about.
>
> DESMOND TUTU
> ANGLICAN ARCHBISHOP OF SOUTH AFRICA.[75]

---

[75] As quoted in Marilyn B. Alexander, *We Were Baptized Too: Claiming God's Grace for Lesbians and Gays*. John Knox Press, 1996.

# *Appendix D*

## The Love Letter

### *Father's Love Letter:*
### *An Intimate Message From God to You.*

My Child,

You may not know me, but I know everything about you.

PSALM 139:1

I know when you sit down and when you rise up.

PSALM 139:2

491

I am familiar with all your ways.
PSALM 139:3

Even the very hairs on your head are numbered.
MATTHEW 10:29-31

For you were made in my image.
GENESIS 1:27

In me you live and move and have your being.
ACTS 17:28

For you are my offspring.
ACTS 17:28

I knew you even before you were conceived.
JEREMIAH 1:4-5

I chose you when I planned creation.
EPHESIANS 1:11-12

You were not a mistake, for all your days are written
in my book
PSALM 139:15-16

I determined the exact time of your birth and where
you would live.
ACTS 17:26

You are fearfully and wonderfully made.
PSALM 139:14

I knit you together in your mother's womb.
PSALM 139:13

And brought you forth on the day you were born.
PSALM 71:6

I have been misrepresented by those who don't know
me.
JOHN 8:41-44

I am not distant and angry, but am the complete
expression of love.
1 JOHN 4:16

And it is my desire to lavish my love on you.
1 JOHN 3:1

Simply because you are my child and I am your
Father.
1 JOHN 3:1

I offer you more than your earthly father ever could.
MATTHEW 7:11

For I am the perfect father.
MATTHEW 5:48

Every good gift that you receive comes from my hand.
JAMES 1:17

For I am your provider and I meet all your needs.
MATTHEW 6:31-33

My plan for your future has always been filled with
hope.
JEREMIAH 29:11

Because I love you with an everlasting love.
JEREMIAH 31:3

My thoughts toward you are countless as the sand on
the seashore.
PSALMS 139:17-18

And I rejoice over you with singing.
ZEPHANIAH 3:17

I will never stop doing good to you.
JEREMIAH 32:40

For you are my treasured possession.
EXODUS 19:5

I desire to establish you with all my heart and all my
soul.
JEREMIAH 32:41

And I want to show you great and marvelous things.
JEREMIAH 33:3

If you seek me with all your heart, you will find me.
DEUTERONOMY 4:29

Delight in me and I will give you the desires of your
heart.
PSALM 37:4

For it is I who gave you those desires.
PHILIPPIANS 2:13

I am able to do more for you than you could possibly
imagine.
EPHESIANS 3:20

For I am your greatest encourager.
II THESSALONIANS 2:16-17

I am also the Father who comforts you in all your troubles.
II CORINTHIANS 1:3-4

When you are brokenhearted, I am close to you.
PSALM 34:18

As a shepherd carries a lamb, I have carried you close to my heart.
ISAIAH 40:11

One day I will wipe away every tear from your eyes.
REVELATION 21:3-4

And I'll take away all the pain you have suffered on this earth.
REVELATION 21:3-4

I am your Father, and I love you even as I love my son, Jesus.
JOHN 17:23

For in Jesus, my love for you is revealed.
JOHN 17:26

He is the exact representation of my being.
HEBREWS 1:3

He came to demonstrate that I am for you, not against you.
ROMANS 8:31

And to tell you that I am not counting your sins.
II CORINTHIANS 5:18-19

Jesus died so that you and I could be reconciled.
II CORINTHIANS 5:18-19

His death was the ultimate expression of my love for
you.
I JOHN 4:10

I gave up everything I loved that I might gain your
love.
ROMANS 8:31-32

If you receive the gift of my son Jesus, you receive me.
I JOHN 2:23

And nothing will ever separate you from my love
again.
ROMANS 8:38-39

Come home and I'll throw the biggest party heaven
has ever seen.
LUKE 15:7

I have always been Father, and will always be Father.
EPHESIANS 3:14-15

My question is... Will you be my child?
JOHN 1:12-13

I am waiting for you.
LUKE 15:11-32

Love, Your Dad Almighty God

# Resources

# Bibliography

**Adams, Mike**, *How to spot a sociopath - 10 red flags that could save you from being swept under the influence of a charismatic nut job.* Natural News, 2013.

**Akira, Hirakawa**, *History of Indian Buddhism: From Sakyamuni to Early Mahayana.* Motilal Banarsidass, 2007.

**Aland, Kurt et al., editors**, *Synopsis of the Four Gospels: Completely Revised on the Basis of the Greek Text of the Nestle-Aland, 26th Edition, and Greek New Testament, 3rd Edition, English Edition.* United Bible Societies, p. 1985.

**Aland, Kurt et al.**, *The Text of the New Testament: An Introduction to the Critical Editions and to the Theory and Practice of Modern Textual Criticism.* 2nd edition. Wm. B. Eerdmans Publishing Co., 1995.

501

**Alexander, Marilyn B.**, *We Were Baptized Too: Claiming God's Grace for Lesbians and Gays*. John Knox Press, 1996.

**Alexandria, Clement Of**, *Paedagogus III [The Instructor]*. Kessinger Publishing, 2004.

**Alexandria, Clement of**, *The Stromata III*. Kessinger Publishing, 2004.

**Allen, Rance**, *The Live Experience*. Tyscot Records, 2004.

**Allen, Rance**, *Front Row Live: The Rance Allen Group*. Tyscot Records, 2007.

**Armstrong Percy III, William**, *Pederasty and Pedagogy in Archaic Greece*. University of Illinois Press, 1998.

**Assisi, Saint Francis of**, *Prayer of Saint Francis of Assisi*. La Clochette, 1912.

**Band, Rez**, *Between Heaven 'N Hell album*. Sparrow Records, 2008.

**Band], Rez Band [a.k.a. Resurrection**, *REZ: Compact Favorites album*. Sparrow Records, 2008.

**Barnes, Albert**, *Notes on the New Testaments*. 1837.

**Barrett, David P. and Comfort, Philip W.**, *The Text of the Earliest New Testament Greek Manuscripts*. Tyndale House Publishers, 2001.

**Barrow, John D.**, *Impossibility: The Limits of Science and the Science of Limits* . Oxford University Press, 1999.

**Beattie, Melody**, *Codependent No More: How to Stop Controlling Others and Start Caring for Yourself* . Hazelden, 1986.

**Beattie, Melody**, *The Language of Letting Go*. Hazelden, 1990.

**Behe, Michael J.**, *Darwin's Black Box: The Biochemical Challenge to Evolution*. 2nd edition. Free Press, 2006.

**Behe, Michael J.**, *The Edge of Evolution: The Search for the Limits of Darwinism*. Free Press, 2007.

**Berenbaum, Michael**, *A Mosaic of Victims: Non-Jews Persecuted and Murdered by the Nazis*. I.B. Tauris, December 1990.

**Blogspot**, *Calling the Defiled*. ⟨URL: http://honesttalkwithgod.blogspot.co.uk/2012/08/calling-defiled-mark-714-23.html⟩.

**Blomberg, Craig L.**, *The Historical Reliability of the Gospels*. 2nd edition. IVP Academic, 2007.

**Borel, Emile and Scott, Douglas**, *Probability and Certainty*. Walker & Company, 1963.

**Boswell, John**, *Christianity, Social Tolerance, and Homosexuality*. University of Chicago Press, 1980.

**Braeunig, Robert A.**, *Did We Land on the Moon? A Debunking of the Moon Hoax Theory*. Rocket & Space Technology, 2012.

**Brannum-Harris, Rod**, *The Pharisees Amongst Us: How the anti-gay campaign unmasks the religious perpetrators of the campaign to be modern-day Pharisees*. BookSurge Publishing, 2006.

**Bruce, F. F.**, *New Testament History*. Doubleday, 1983.

**Bruce, F. F.**, *The Books and the Parchments: How We Got Our English Bible*. Fleming H Revell Co., 1984.

**Bruce, F.F.**, *The Canon of Scripture*. IVP Academic, 1988.

**Bruce, Frederick Fyvie**, *The New Testament Documents: Are They Reliable?* Wilder Publications, 2009.

**Brundage, James A.**, *Law, Sex, and Christian Society in Medieval Europe*. University Of Chicago Press, 1987.

**Buck, Charles**, *Buck's Dictionary*. 1838.

**Bullough, Vern L.**, *Sexual Variance in Society and History*. University of Chicago Press, 1980.

**Cadonau-Huseby, Anita**, *Leviticus: Pagans, Purity, and Property*. WordPress, 2008.

**Cantarella**, *Bisexuality in the Ancient World*. Yale Press, 1992.

**Carroll, Jason S. et al.**, *Generation XXX: Pornography Acceptance and Use Among Emerging Adults*. Volume 23, 1st edition. Journal of Adolescent Research, January 2008.

**Channel, National Geographic**, *The Second Coming*. National Geographic, 2010.

**Countryman, L. William**, *Dirt, Greed, and Sex: Sexual Ethics in the New Testament and Their Implications for Today*. Fortress Press, 2007.

**CultWatch**, ⟨URL: http://www. cultwatch.com⟩.

**CultWatch**, *Attack of the Super Apostles!* ⟨URL: http://www.cultwatch.com/ superapostles.html⟩.

**Damour, Tom**, *Do You Still Have Your First Love?* . Volume 9, 3rd edition. Virtual Christian Magazine, March 2007.

**Dover**, *Greek Homosexuality*. Harvard University Press, 1989.

**Driscoll, Mark and Breshears, Gerry**, *Doctrine: What Christians Should Believe*. Crossway, 2011.

**Dumoulin, Heinrich**, *Zen Buddhism: A History, India & China*. World Wisdom, 2005.

**Durant, Will**, *Caesar and Christ - A History of Roman Civilization and of Christianity from their Beginnings to A.D. 323 (Story of Civilization)*. Simon & Schuster, 1944.

**Dynes, Wayne**, *Racha*. The Encyclopedia of Homosexuality edition. Garland, 1990.

**Ehrman, Bart D.**, *The New Testament and Other Early Christian Writings*. Oxford University Press, 1998.

**Fee, Dr. Gordon D.**, *The New International Commentary on the New Testament, The First Epistle To The Corinthians*. Eerdmans, 1987.

**Foundation, Lockman, editor**, *Greek Dictionary of the New American Standard Exhaustive Concordance*. Zondervan, 2000.

**Francoeur, Robert T. et al.**, *The Religious Suppression of Eros; in The Erotic Impulse*. Tarcher, 1992.

**Gagnon, Robert**, *Robert Gagnon's Answers to Emails on the Bible and Homosexuality*. January 2007 ⟨URL: http://www.robgagnon.net/ AnswersToEMails.htm⟩.

**Gaither, Bill and Gaither, Gloria**, *Because He Lives*. Warner/Chappell Music, 1971.

**Geisler, Norman L.**, *Baker Encyclopedia of Christian Apologetics*. Baker Books, 2000.

**Geisler, Norman L. and Turek, Frank**, *I Don't Have Enough Faith to Be an Atheist*. Crossway, 2004.

**Georgescu-Roegen, Nicholas**, *The Entropy Law and the Economic Process*. iUniverse Publication, 1999.

**Giorgio, Gail**, *Footprints in the Sand - The Life Story of Mary Stevenson*. Gold Leaf Press, 1995.

**Gladwell, Malcolm**, *The Tipping Point: How Little Things Can Make a Big Difference*. Back Bay Books, 2002.

**Gombrich, Richard F.**, *How Buddhism Began: The Conditioned Genesis of the Early Teachings*. Routledge, 2005.

**Goodson, P., McCormick, D. and Evans, A.**, *Searching for sexually explicit material on the Internet: An exploratory study of college students' behavior and attitudes*. 30th edition. Archives of Sexual Behavior, 2001.

**Graham, Billy**, *Hour of Power - Crystal Cathedral: Robert Schuller*. May 31, 1997 broadcast.

**Graham, Franklin**, *Billy Graham in Quotes*. Thomas Nelson, 2011.

**Green, Keith**, *For Him Who Has Ears to Hear Album*. Sparrow Records, 1977.

**Greenberg, David F.**, *The Construction of Homosexuality*. University of Chicago Press, 1988.

**Grosse, Henry Thomas**, *Thomas De Thomas*. Henry Grosse Publications, 1996.

**Gutt, Ernst-August**, *Relevance Theory and Translation: Toward a New Realism in Bible Translation*. International Meeting of the Society of Biblical Literature, 2004.

**Helminiak, Daniel A.**, *What the Bible Really Says About Homosexuality*. Alamo Square Distribution, 2000.

**Hemfelt, Robert, Minirth, Frank and Meier, Paul**, *Love is a Choice: Breaking the Cycle of Addictive Relationships*. Monarch Publications, 1990.

**Hippolytus; Roberts, Alexander and Donaldson, James, editors**, *Refutation of All Heresies: Book V.2*. Scribners, 1903.

**Hitchcock, Mark and Walvoord, John F.**, *Armageddon, Oil, and Terror*. Tyndale Momentum, 2007.

**Hoad, T. F., editor**, *The Concise Oxford Dictionary of English Etymology*. Oxford University Press, 1993.

**House, H. Wayne**, *The Jesus Who Never Lived: Exposing False Christs and Finding the Real Jesus.* Harvest House Publishers, 2008.

**HowCultsWork**, ⟨URL: http:// howcultswork.com⟩.

**Hoyle, Fred**, *Mathematics of Evolution.* Acorn Enterprises Llc., 1999.

**Humana, Charles**, *The Keeper of the Bed: The Story of the Eunuch.* Arlington Books, 1973.

**Hunt, Dave**, *Yoga and the Body of Christ: What Position Should Christians Hold?* The Berean Call, 2006.

**Hunt, Dave et al.**, *The Lie of The Serpent: The New Age and the End Times.* Adullam Films, 2008.

**J. McNeill, John**, *The Church and the Homosexual.* Beacon Press, 1993.

**Johansson, Warren**, *Whosoever Shall Say to His Brother, Racha.* Volume 10, Cabirion, 1984.

**Jones, Peter R.**, *One or Two: Seeing a World of Difference.* Main Entry Editions, 2010.

**JPUSA**, *Jesus People USA.* ⟨URL: http:// jpusa.org⟩.

**Keller, Timothy**, *King's Cross: The Story of the World in the Life of Jesus.* Dutton Adult, 2011.

**Kenyon, Sir Frederic et al.**, *Our Bible and the Ancient Manuscripts.* Harper and Row, 1962.

**Kruszelnicki, Karl**, *Great Mythconceptions: The Science Behind the Myths*. Andrews McMeel Publishing, 2006.

**Leafe, G. Harry**, *Muddy Water*. Scriptel.

**Leafe, G. Harry**, *The Heart of Man*. Scriptel.

**Leick, Gwendolyn**, *Sex and Eroticism in Mesopotamian Literature*. Routledge, 2003.

**Lewis, C.S.**, *God in the Dock: Essays on Theology and Ethics*. Wm. B. Eerdmans Publishing Co., 1972.

**Lewis, C.S.**, *The Four Loves*. Houghton Mifflin Harcourt, 1991.

**Lewis, C.S.**, *Mere Christianity*. Touchstone Books, 1996.

**Lewis, C.S.**, *The Problem of Pain*. HarperOne, 2001.

**Lindsey, Hal**, *Satan Is Alive and Well on Planet Earth*. Zondervan, 1972.

**Love, Robert**, *Fear of Yoga*. Columbia Journalism Review, November 2006.

**Magdalene, Father Gabriel of St. Mary**, *Divine Intimacy: Meditations on the Interior Life for Every Day of the Liturgical Year*. Tan Books, 1996.

**Maharaj, Rabi R.**, *The Death of a Guru*. Harvest House Publishers, 1984.

**Manning, Brennan**, *Brennan Manning, Abba's Child: The Cry of the Heart for Intimate Belonging*. NavPress, 2002.

**Manning, Brennan**, *A Glimpse of Jesus: The Stranger to Self-Hatred*. HarperOne, 2003.

**Manning, Brennan**, *Brennan Manning, The Wisdom of Tenderness: What Happens When God's Fierce Mercy Transforms Our Lives*. HarperOne, 2004.

**Manning, Brennan**, *The Ragamuffin Gospel: Good News for the Bedraggled, Beat-Up, and Burnt Out*. Multnomah Books, 2005.

**Martin et al.**, *Meanings and Consequences. Biblical Ethics and Homosexuality*. Louisville: Westminster Press, 1996.

**Maternus, Firmicus**, *The Error of Pagan Religions*. Newman Press, 1970.

**Matrisciana, Caryl**, *Out of India: A True Story about the New Age Movement*. Lighthouse Trails Publishing, 2008.

**Matrisciana, Caryl**, *Yoga Uncoiled From East to West*. Caryl Productions, 2009.

**Metzger, Bruce**, *The Text of the New Testament: Its Transmission, Corruption, and Restoration*. 4th edition. Oxford University Press, 2005.

**Metzger, Bruce M.**, *The Canon of the New Testament: Its Origin, Development, and Significance*. Oxford University Press, April 1997.

**Meyer, Joyce**, *Enjoying Everyday Life broadcasts*. Joyce Meyer Ministries (URL: http://www.joycemeyer.org).

**Meyer, Joyce**, *Battlefield of the Mind: Winning the Battle in Your Mind*. Hodder & Stoughton, 2007.

**Meyer, Joyce**, *I Dare You: Embrace Life with Passion*. FaithWords, 2007.

**Meyer, Joyce**, *Woman to Woman: Candid Conversations From Me to You.* Faith-Words, 2008.

**Michaelsen, Johanna**, *The Beautiful Side of Evil.* Harvest House Publishers, p. 1982.

**Milgrom, Jacob**, *Leviticus 17-22.* The Anchor Yale Bible Commentaries edition. Yale University Press, 2000.

**Miller, Elliot**, *The Yoga Boom: A Call for Christian Discernment – Part I: Yoga in its original Eastern Context .* 31th edition. Christian Research Journal, 2008, 2.

**Miner, Jeff and Connoley, John Tyler**, *The Children are Free.* Jesus Metropolitan Community Church, 2002.

**Moo, Douglas J.**, *The Letter of James (Pillar New Testament Commentary).* Wm. B. Eerdmans Publishing Co., 2000.

**Moreland, J. P. et al.**, *Love Your God with All Your Mind: The Role of Reason in the Life of the Soul.* NavPress, 1997.

**NASB; Scofield, C.I., editor**, *The New Scofield Study Bible: New American Standard Bible.* World Bible Publishers, 1988.

**NASB; LockmanFoundation, editor**, *Updated New American Standard Bible.* Zondervan Publishing House, 1999.

**Nissinen, Martti**, *Homoeroticism in the Biblical World.* Fortress Press, 1998.

**NIV; Thompson, Frank Charles D.D. Ph.D., editor**, *Thompson Chain-Reference Bible: New International*

*Version*. Zondervan Bible Publishers, 1983.

**Nix, William E. et al.,** *A General Introduction to the Bible*. Moody Publishers, 1986.

**NRSV; Throckmorton, Jr. Burton H., editor**, *Gospel Parallels: A Comparison of the Synoptic Gospels, New Revised Standard Version*. 5th edition. Thomas Nelson, 1992.

**NRSV; Attridge, Harold W. et al., editors**, *The HarperCollins Study Bible, Revised Edition: New Revised Standard Version*. Harper Collins Publishers, 2006.

**Ogas, Ogi**, *The Online World of Female Desire*. The Wall Street Journal, 2011.

**Petra**, *Not of This World album*. Star Song Music, 1983.

**Petra**, *Beat the System album*. 1985.

**Petra**, *Back to the Rock Live*. Provident, 2011.

**Petra, Classic**, *Back to the Rock album*. Sony Music Distribution, 2011.

**Plato, Jan von**, *Creating Modern Probability: Its Mathematics, Physics and Philosophy in Historical Perspective (Cambridge Studies in Probability, Induction and Decision Theory)*. Cambridge University Press, 1998.

**Price, Randall**, *The Coming Last Day's Temple*. 1999.

**Quick, O.C.**, *Doctrines of the Creed*. Scribners, 1938.

**Raymond J., Jr. Lawrence**, *The Poisoning of Eros: Sexual Values in Conflict*. A. Moore Press, 1989.

Robertson, A. T., *A Harmony of the Gospels*. Reprint edition edition. HarperOne, 1932.

Roscoe, Will, *Priests of the Goddess: Gender Transgression in Ancient Religion*. The University of Chicago, 1996.

Roughgarden, Joan, *Evolution's Rainbow: Diversity, Gender, and Sexuality in Nature and People*. University of California Press, 2009.

Sayers, Dorothy L., *Are Women Human? Penetrating, Sensible, and Witty Essays on the Role of Women in Society*. Wm. B. Eerdmans Publishing Co., 1970.

Schlachter, Christina Tangora, *Newsless: How the American Media is Destroying Democracy*. CIPP, 2009.

Schneider, Johannes; Kittel, Gerhard et al., editors, *Article on Eunouchos*. Theological Dictionary of the New Testament edition. Wm. B. Eerdmans Publishing Company, 1986.

Schuler, Charli, *Apollo 11 Experiment Still Going Strong after 35 Years*. California Institute of Technology.

Scofield, Cyrus I., *Scofield Reference Bible*. Oxford University Press, 1917.

Scroggs, Robin, *The New Testament and Homosexuality: Contextual Background for Contemporary Debate*. Fortress Press, 1983.

Simmons, Jim, *The Last Generation: Prophecy, Current World Events, and the End Times*. Focal Point Publications, 2008.

**Singleton, Mark**, *Yoga Body: The Origins of Modern Posture Practice*. Oxford University Press, 2010.

**Slick, Matt**, *Baptism and John 3:5*. Christian Apologetics & Research Ministry CARM (URL: http://carm.org/baptism-and-john-35).

**Spencer, Robert et al.**, *What the West Needs to Know*. DVD edition. Quixotic Media, 2007.

**Spetner, Lee M.**, *Not by Chance*. Judaica Press, 1997.

**Sphero, M.W.**, *Escaping the Shithole: How and Why to Leave a Bad Neighborhood Once and for All*. Herms Press, 2009.

**Sphero, M.W.**, *The Gay Faith: Christ, Scripture, and Sexuality*. Herms Press, 2011.

**Spurgeon, C. H.**, *The Education of Sons of God*. Sermon by Spurgeon as delivered at the Metropolitan Tabernacle, London, June 1880.

**Stoner, Peter**, *Science Speaks. Online Edition*. November 2005 (URL: http://www.sciencespeaks.net).

**Stoner, Peter and Newman, Robert C.**, *Science Speaks: Scientific Proof of the Accuracy of Prophecy and the Bible*. Moody Press, 1969.

**Strobel, Lee**, *The Case for Christ*. Zondervan, 1998.

**Strong, James et al.**, *Strong's Exhaustive Concordance of the Bible with Greek and Hebrew Dictionaries*. Royal Publishers, 1979.

**Stryper**, *Soldiers Under Command album*. Hollywood Records, 1985.

**Sultan, Wafa**, *A God Who Hates*. St. Martin's Griffin, 2011.

**Tannahill, Reay**, *Sex in History*. Scarborough House, 1992.

**Thelos, Philo**, *Divine Sex: Liberating Sex from Religious Tradition*. Trafford Publishing, 2006.

**Thelos, Philo**, *God is not a Homophobe: An Unbiased Look at Homosexuality in the Bible*. Trafford Publishing, 2006.

**Thomas, B.J.**, *Happy Man album*. Myrrh Records, 1978.

**Thomas, B.J.**, *You Gave Me Love [When Nobody Gave Me A Prayer] album*. Myrrh Records, 2010.

**Tkach, Joseph**, *Do All Religions Lead to God?* ⟨URL: http://www.gci.org/gospel/pluralism⟩.

**TLG**, *The Thesaurus Linguae Graecae*. ⟨URL: http://www.tlg.uci.edu⟩.

**Townend, Stuart and Getty, Keith**, *In Christ Alone*. Thankyou Music, 2001.

**Townsley, Jeramy**, *Paul, the Goddess Religions and Queers: Romans 1:23-28*. ⟨URL: http://www.jeramyt.org/papers/paulcybl.html#_edn4⟩.

**Trio, Bill Gaither**, *He Touched Me*. Gaither Music Company, 1963.

**various**, *Gods of the New Age*. Jeremiah Films, 1984.

**Walvoord, John F.**, *The Holy Spirit*. Zondervan, 1991.

**Walvoord, John F.**, *Every Prophecy of the Bible: Clear Explanations for Uncertain Times*. David C. Cook, 2011.

**Watch, Jihad**, ⟨URL: http://www.jihadwatch.org⟩.

**Webster**, *Webster's New Universal Unabridged Dictionary*. Barnes & Noble Books, 2003.

**Weidle, Armin**, *Bowing to Yoga? The truth about the roots and fruits of yoga*. Xulon Press, 2010.

**Whitfield, Charles L.**, *Co-Dependence - Healing the Human Condition*. Health Communications Inc., 1991.

**Williams**, *Roman Homosexuality : Ideologies of Masculinity in Classical Antiquity*. Oxford UP, 1999.

**Wilson, Nancy**, *Our Tribe: Queer Folks, God, Jesus, and the Bible*. Alamo Square Distributors, 2000.